THE BOOK OF ELI

THE BOOK OF ELI

Reverend Doctor
Mark Germine

Copyright © 2011 by Reverend Doctor Mark Germine.

Library of Congress Control Number:		2011914486
ISBN:	Hardcover	978-1-4653-3954-6
	Softcover	978-1-4653-3953-9
	Ebook	978-1-4653-3955-3

All rights reserved. No part of this book may be reproduced or transmitted in any form or by any means, electronic or mechanical, including photocopying, recording, or by any information storage and retrieval system, without permission in writing from the copyright owner.

This book was printed in the United States of America.

To order additional copies of this book, contact:
Xlibris Corporation
1-888-795-4274
www.Xlibris.com
Orders@Xlibris.com
101585

Contents

The Book Of Eli 10
Introduction... 19
Chapter One Toward A Synthesis Of The Disciplines 29
Chapter Two Background Regarding Eli 37
Chapter Three Usury And The Current Crisis 41
Chapter Four The Engine Of Usury 53
Chapter Five The Consequences Of Usury 60
Chapter Six The Ends Of Usury 67
Chapter Seven The Call Of Eli 70
Chapter Eight The "I" And The "Not I" 73
Chapter Nine The New Faith And The New Science....................... 84
Chapter Ten The Rejection Of Materialism 102
Chapter Eleven The Meaning Of The Hidden Time 111
Chapter Twelve Experiences Of The Hidden Time........................ 119
Chapter Thirteen The Theory Of Mind 127
Chapter Fourteen The Plague 134
Chapter Fifteen The Creation And The Fall 140
Chapter Sixteen The End And The New Beginning 150
Chapter Seventeen The Unseen 154
Chapter Eighteen The New Science 159
Chapter Nineteen Science And Faith... 174
Chapter Twenty The Great Lie 176
Chapter Twenty-One Foundations Of The New Science 180
Chapter Twenty-Two Forsake Usury... 190

Chapter Twenty-Three The Future Of Usury 198
Chapter Twenty-Four The New Judgment And Atonement 203
Chapter Twenty-Five Justice And The Hidden Time 220
Conclusion 227
Glossary 229
Index 253
References 291

Dedication

*To future generations of readers
If you are reading this book, its purpose will have been achieved.*

We experience our difference from and conflict in a world of objects—and even mother can then become an object. This is the separation between self and world, the split between existence and essence. Mythologically, it is a time when each child re-enacts the "fall" of Adam.

—Rollo May (1989, 284)

*You say I took the name in vain
I don't even know the name
But if I did, well really, what's it to you?
There's a blaze of light in every word
It doesn't matter which you heard
The holy or the broken Hallelujah*

—Leonard Cohen

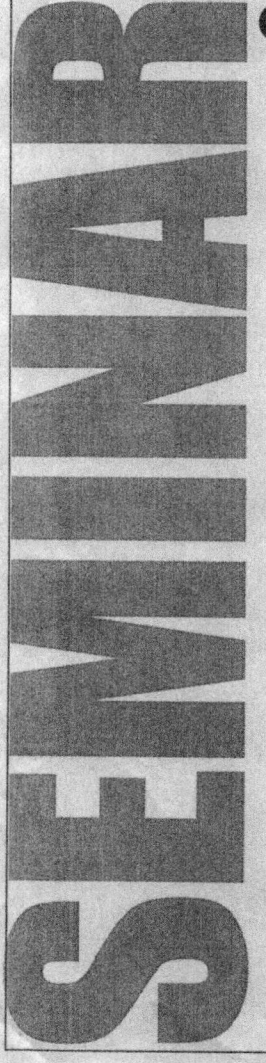

CENTER FOR PROCESS STUDIES

Proudly Presents:

Mark Germine

Clinical Psychiatrist and Chair of the Department of Psychiatry at Patton Hospital. He trained at Yale University where his specialty was anxiety disorders. His background includes research in the physical sciences, in neuroscience, and in psychiatry. He has written scores of professional papers and two books entitled, *Beyond Personal Consciousness* and *The Science of God.*

"Can the Existence of God be Proven Experimentally?"

Thursday, Oct. 30, 1997
4:10pm to 6:00pm
Claremont School of Theology
Butler Building
Davis Community Center
call (909) 621-5330
for more information
Free and open to the public

THE BOOK OF ELI

Chapter I

1. God has spoken to me, without words, to my heart. He has told me that I am to teach a new faith.
2. My father gave me the name Eli. My legal name is not important. My person is not part of the teaching.
3. Throughout the ages, the same wisdom has been taught.
4. Now the language has changed, and truth is given in the language of science.
5. Hear about the hidden time. Some think the hidden time is yet to come. The Kingdom of God does not come by observation. It is hidden in the inner dimension.
6. The hidden time is an eternity that runs through every moment. It is all-time.
7. The hidden time is a thread, and moments are the beads on the thread.

Chapter II

1. Those of little understanding say the world will soon end. It is the current age that is coming to an end. The end of this age is the beginning of the next.
2. Focus on the beginning, not the end. Forget about earthquakes, comets, asteroids, and the like. The process proceeds in the inner dimension.
3. All the truths of God are discoverable through science.
4. The inner dimension and the hidden time have already been discovered.
5. There is no truth without faith. We are faithful to verities. Nothing is proven except to the heart of one who believes.
6. Science has given us a great lie. It is this lie that ends the current age of faith in God.
7. The great lie that science has given us is that reality is material.

Chapter III

1. God has permitted the great lie for a short time only. That time is now coming to an end.
2. Believers in the lie! You have been raised on the milk of your concrete beliefs. Now it is time for you to be weaned to partake of the solid food of a new science.
3. The great lie is like a sword that has been thrust into the heart of humankind.
4. God is the one subject of reality. Take away the one subject and there is nothing real.
5. The truths of the one subject have already been discovered, but have not been accepted because they spell the death of the faith in the lie.
6. Humankind must no longer permit the lie to be taught to its children.
7. The new science will be established in our schools and through research and scholarship.

Chapter IV

1. The great lie can only be defeated by the new science. The sooner the new science is established by the institutions of the world, the sooner the suffering caused by the lie will end.
2. The new science is established by degrees.
3. The first degree is the truth of the one subject, which follows from the existence and the oneness of the universe, and from the ancient belief that God is all-knowing.
4. It is far easier to move a mountain than to move science by this one degree.
5. We have the power to move the mountain, if we have the faith that the mountain can be moved.
6. It is now that our faith is tested. The future of humankind hangs in the balance.
7. SEARCH GOD.

Chapter V

1. There is no greater crime than a crime against humanity.
2. There is no greater crime against humanity than usury.
3. The greatest violence, and the greatest threat to humanity, is the growth of money.
4. In the new faith, there is only one commandment. It is this commandment, and this commandment alone, that must be followed to end the times of suffering, which are soon to come.
5. FORSAKE USURY.
6. Those who have assets must withdraw them from the markets of loans. Do not accept notes of loan on speculation. Buy those things that provide food, water, clothing, shelter, and medical care for humankind.
7. The time will soon come when you will gain no profits from the markets of loans, and your wealth will be taken by the very few.

Chapter VI

1. Now hear of the new judgment.
2. You are judged many times more by what you do in groups than for what you do as individuals.
3. If one thousand of you participate in the murder of one child, then one thousand of you are a thousand times guilty.
4. You are judged many times more by what you give assent to others doing than what you do yourself.
5. If one million of you give assent to the one thousand who participate in the murder of a child, then one million of you are a million times guilty.
6. You are judged more by what you do passively than by what you do actively.
7. If one billion of you watch and do not intercede as one million of you assent to the one thousand who participate in the murder of a child, then one billion of you are a billion times guilty.

Chapter VII

1. Justice is paramount. The new judgment is the justice of the hidden time.
2. No crime is a means to an end. No crime can be rationalized.
3. The murder of a child has no justification, even if the bombs have missed their mark.
4. The starvation of a child has no justification, even if the crops have failed, or the population is too large.
5. Act correctly. Incorrect action cannot be justified by incorrect action. An incorrect action taken to cover an incorrect action is doubly incorrect.
6. Cleave to the common good. We are all responsible for bringing about the time of great suffering, for its continuing, and for its ending.
7. There is nothing hidden in the hidden time. Know that this, the hidden time, is your everlasting, and live.

Introduction

Ego is the biggest enemy of humans.

—Rig Veda (1700-1100 BCE)

This is not an ordinary book. *The Book of Eli,* which we will call *Eli,* reproduced in the preceding pages to this introduction, is a book of prophecy, written by the anonymous author Eli. There is also an oral tradition of Eli, which I have on good authority, and which has helped guide me in the writing of this book. As a book of interpretation, this book, also called *The Book of Eli,* seeks to offer an interpretation of the revealed work, but is just one out of a number of possible interpretations of *Eli.* In this interpretation, there is the possibility of a false interpretation, as the author has taken the words, which can have more than one meaning, and has developed ideas as to how *Eli* is best interpreted. Some of these interpretations relate to the times as they began in 1999 when *Eli* was written, and how the prophecies have unfolded up until the spring of 2011. Our interpretations are understandings of the original text as it was written and published in 1999.

First, we ask, who is Eli? Of this we can say little, for reasons to be discussed later. The name Eli, however, has a history and a meaning, which arose in Judaism. However, the author does not seek to confine the interpretations in this book to Judaism, Christianity, or any other religion, and will more broadly address the spiritual traditions of the major world traditions. The *new faith* is not the continuation of any single religion.

This book aims to lay down the foundations for a new religion, associated with a new science, which will be totally compatible and interrelated, intended for the age that is now ending and the age that is to come. However, we will give ourselves some license to elaborate on points that are not strictly scientific, but belong to the Hebrew tradition, as well as other traditions, seeking to preserve the wisdom and spiritual truths of these sources.

We are calling *Eli* a sacred or revealed text, written by the prophet Eli. How do we know that Eli is a true prophet and not a false prophet? In Matthew (7:15-2), it is written, in the King James translation:

15. "Beware of false prophets, which come to you in sheep's clothing, but inwardly they are ravening wolves."
16. "Ye shall know them by their fruits. Do mean gather grapes of thorns, or figs of thistles?"
17. "Even so every good tree bringest forth good fruit; but a corrupt tree bringest forth evil fruits."
18. "A good tree cannot bring forth evil fruit, neither can a corrupt tree bringest forth good fruit."
19. "Every tree that bringest not forth good fruit is hewn down, and cast into the fire."
20. "Therefore by their fruits, ye shall know them."

The only *fruit* that we have before us is *Eli*. What will be its fruits? This is very hard to say. This book may, perhaps, be a part of that reckoning. However, by examining *Eli* carefully, we have a good idea of what that fruit is intended to be. Prophecy may or may not involve prediction. *Eli* has made quite a few predictions, and with respect to the economy and the times, these predictions seem to be coming true. On this basis, we had better examine *Eli* more carefully and draw out the implications of its full content. We will also try to elaborate on the general nature of understanding granted to Eli by the God of Abraham. The God of Abraham gave Eli to know, when inquiry was made as to why the God of Judaism and the Abrahamic tradition should come to him instead of Jesus or Mary that Jesus and Mary were just people, not gods of goddesses. Let the reader be the judge of whether the understanding of *Eli* is correct, and whether our interpretations of that understanding are correct.

Perhaps it is best not to frame *Eli* in terms of the Western tradition and prophecy. It is the Atman, Self, the self-same in all there is, that is source of the illusory ego. Eli is really no different from anyone else. Prophecy is granted to the Soul, the Self, the Atman, not to the ego-consciousness. We come from eternity, the unmanifest, or, as it is called in *Eli*, the hidden time—and to there we return. In the Indian tradition, God can come down to earth, so for the Hindu, Krishna was God. The same is not true for the Abrahamic tradition, and the idea that a human being can be God is not to be found in either tradition, or in the other great traditions of the sacred wisdom. In the words of Krishna (Bhagavad Gita 2: 28):

> All beings, O Arjuna, are unmanifest
> Before birth and after death.
> They are manifest between birth and death only.
> What is there to grieve about?

Prophecy is just a small window into the unmanifest. It is nothing special. What is special are the things of the ego, of which the unmanifest has no part.

There will be many, of course, who will reject *Eli*. Perhaps *Eli* will remain obscure and bear no fruits whatsoever. The understanding chooses the road of compassion for humankind and the love of God. Its exhortations will be challenged for a variety of reasons. First and foremost, as our world is currently dominated by the practice of usury, and as usury now has tremendous power, it has taken over virtually the entirety of civilization. If *Eli*, abjuring usury, ever gains any recognition, it might be considered dangerous to some interests. Eli's only interest is the welfare of humankind, he is not a ravening wolf, and seeks no gain, or even any acceptance of the doctrine of *Eli* within his own lifetime.

Another reason to reject *Eli* is its rejection of materialism and its introduction of God back into science. This will be perceived as dangerous in a different kind of way, and certainly rejected by mainstream science for a considerable time, just as the church rejected Galileo, but now in reverse. Materialism is a dogma that is deeply entrenched in science. However, it gives us no explanatory principle for mind, experience, and consciousness. It makes these things concrete, and the abstract cannot be expressed in materialistic terms. What is the weight of an idea? It weighs nothing. Are we then to say that ideas do not exist? Where is the soul or Self, what is it made of, does it have a material substance? It does not. Are we then to say that it does not exist? Materialistic science is on a slippery slope, and it is bound to fall.

There is one reason, however, that will be most compelling for those who chose to reject Eli, and that it makes some dire predictions, which people will react to with disbelief and denial, projecting that denial on to *Eli* by concluding he is a false prophet. Chapter 5 predicts the collapse of the world economy, which now seems inevitable. When the international financial sector defaults, all or those who have money in the bank or who hold various types of investments will lose them, as their wealth will be taken by the "very few." The people of Eli, if there be such, must create a separate economy, as the gears of production and distribution of goods will come to a halt, and there will be great suffering. At this point, it seems most likely that the people of Eli will initially by black Americans, as we will later discuss. There are also a number of abominations that rule the current international global sector, prime among which is usury, the loaning of money at interest. *E*li instructs us that usury if forbidden. The content of chapter 5 of *Eli* gives specific instructions that are meant for preparation and action that will be necessary as this dire prediction eventuates, as is explicit in verse 5:7.

Humans of the genus *Homo* emerged on earth about 2.3 to 2.5 million years ago. Humans are thought to have evolved from *Australopithecus*, one of the great apes. The cranial capacity or volume of the brain increased in the evolution of *Homo habilis* to about 600 cc from the 450 cc of *Australopithecus*. The cranial capacity of *Homo habilis* was doubled to about 1200 cc in the evolution of *Homo heidelbergensis* about 600,000 years ago, and this is within the range of modern humans. Evolution from this point was by the growth of the Species Mind, and this growth of the Species Mind, or collective consciousness, is reiterated with every becoming of our minds, as we will describe later. It was not so much a matter of physical change as it was a matter of the progressive manifestation of the Mind of God in the Species Mind. The increase in brain size had this as a final cause within the hidden time to develop the capacity for the psyche to accommodate the further evolution of the Species Mind. This process is still progressing, such that further evolution will occur, not according to natural selection, but from the progressive actualization of the Mind of God in the Species Mind. In this sense, the Species Mind is still in its infancy, with verbal language emerging about 50,000 years ago.

The higher order dictates that humans should exist on this planet for a very long time, and not die in its infancy. The Species Mind develops much like the individual mind in humans. The infant is born into the hidden time, the field of subjectivity. It is thrust into objectivity when it learns to distinguish self and world. There actually is no such distinction in the hidden time, so the problem had never arisen when humans lived in the hidden time, the field of subjectivity.

This thrusting of the Species Mind into objectivity was a traumatic process. Our ancestors, much like the Aborigines of Australia, lived in the hidden time, or dreamtime, and this development of the objective attitude occurred well after the development of language. The development of the objective attitude caused the separation of humans from its roots in the animal kingdom, possibly with the shift from hunting and gathering to agriculture, perhaps seventeen thousand years ago. This was a traumatic event for the Species Mind, and as such, it caused it to split into two parts, the Self and the alter ego, commonly termed just "ego." This was a dissociative event in the psychological understanding of the response of the Species Mind to that trauma.

The nature of the true ego and the false or alter ego has been summarized from the Vedanta (Maharaja, not dated or paginated):

> Real ego exists in the spiritual world. All experience is found there, but it is full of beauty and charm . . . What we find here is only a shadow, a black imitation.

> But reality means full-fledged theism—Krishna consciousness—where the infinite embraces the whole finite . . . The false ego—"I am," and "It is mine," which constitute the basic principle of material existence (temporary existence)—includes ten sense organs for material activities (temporary activities) (Bhagavad Gita 7.4.) The false ego in the sum total form of *mahat-tattva* (the sum total of the material creation) is generated from the marginal potency of the Supreme Spirit—God, and due to this false ego of lording it over the material creation, ingredients are generated for the false enjoyment of the living being (Srimad Bhagavatam 2.5.25.) . . . Materialistic ego, or the sense of identification with matter, is grossly self-centered and hence . . . devoid of real knowledge.

The division of real and false or alter ego is to be found only in the Eastern tradition. This literature fundamentally supports the author's intuition that the ego itself is real, part of the Eternal Soul, and that the ego that is false is an alter ego. As such, it is much the same as the alter ego that is found in multiple personality disorder, and it may be possible to treat it in the same way (Germine 2004). Religion meets science, and this is a recurring theme of this book. The new world religion takes all the world's religious wisdom into account and, although stemming from the Abrahamic tradition, is inclusive of all world religions without preference. This book takes the wisdom of all major legitimate world religions and, in effect, translates it into the language of science, such that science and religion augment rather than contradict each other.

It remains that humans, as creatures, have a dissociated Species Mind through the dissociation of alter ego from Self. It is an alter ego in the sense that, when ego separated from self, its status changed such that it was dissociated into a fragmented identity. This alter ego has existed from ancient times, and was recognized as our greatest danger in the *Rig Veda*, some 1700-1100 BCE, as quoted in the opening of this introduction.

The pernicious doctrine that entered into Christianity was that Jesus was the Son of God, and later became God, elevated to "the right hand of the Father." The Hebrew Abrahamic tradition never intimated that the Messiah would be God, or the son of God, so the Jewish people, by and large, reject this doctrine, as do the Moslems, who considered the doctrine blasphemous, as is written in the *Qur'an*. The *Gospel of Barnabus* existed in the canonical Bible in the churches of Alexandrea until 325 CE, at which time the Nicene Council rejected it and ordered that all versions of the gospels written in Hebrew be burned and that anyone possessing such a gospel be put to death. It is very difficult to know whether the *Gospel of Barnabus*, which was referred to in the literature as early as 100 CE, is the authentic version. However, in such that exists on the Internet, Jesus denies being the son of God. *Barnabus* accuses Paul of taking portions out of the *Gospel of Barnabus* and, of being deceived by Satan, in his interjection of Greco-Roman mythology into the *Bible*. The first recorded mention of Mary and the Immaculate Conception that now survives dates around 300 CE. Christianity, as we know it, reflects the politics of the church more than it does the actual teachings of Jesus, who was a prophet of great wisdom, quite clearly, and this can be read in the quotations in the Bible that seem to be the true words of Jesus. Recently I attended a baptism and was quite offended when all those present were asked to say "I do" in their profession of faith in the dogma of the Apostles Creed, including the belief in "Jesus Christ His [God's] only son."

Such is the forcefulness with which this false doctrine has been and is being thrust upon Christianity at the behest of Paul and the church. But what does the doctrine entail? It is, fundamentally, standing the Abrahamic tradition on its head by nailing God to a cross. In 2004 I wrote a review of the Passions of Christ, lauded by Evangelical Christians, and was amazed at the carnage and bloody horror of the movie. I wrote,

> In the Passion we see Jesus portrayed as the embodiment of the apotheosis of the ego. Apotheosis of the ego is its assumption of the status of God, and is inferred by the presence of the demonic shadow of the ego-persona in the garden, which was inserted by the filmmakers in the place of the biblical angel. In a subtle way, what Mel Gibson is delivering to us is a

kind of "Passion of the Antichrist," a Christ whose ego has been identified as God. He is therefore haunted and tormented by his own demonic shadow, which is externalized as the numinous images of the demon and demonic infant.

Paul seems to have borrowed from the wisdom of the original *Gospel of Barnabus*, by all accounts, and perverted the teachings for some 1,700 years by deification of Jesus. Now we are to believe that, essentially, God was crucified by men as a bloodletting atonement for our sins, so that, having been "washed in the blood" of God, we have been expiated of all our sins, the direct opposite of the doctrine of atonement in the Hebrew faith. As I have quoted above, this doctrine has made Christianity into the "doctrine of the Antichrist." Who else would have God bloodied and beaten and nailed to a cross, and then use his blood as a sacrifice?

This was quite an unfortunate development, because the dissociated alter ego was deified at the expense of the Self, God within us, and has come to rule the world. We are now faced with the ultimate consequences of having given ascendancy to the alter ego and darkening the image of the one true God. This allowed us to do all manner of evil, as the evil one, the ravenous wolf dressed in sheep's clothing, the great deceiver of humankind, has brought us, through the glorification of the worst of sins, usury, to the brink of annihilation. The God of Abraham has been merciful and has permitted this for a time, but that time is now over. The sentinel events that ended it were the demolitions orchestrated by the usurers themselves on 9/11, in order to preserve their dying order by plunging the world into warfare against the externalization of our own shadow selves, the dark side that has been engendered by the worship of the Antichrist, on to an external enemy, the "terrorists," who they falsely convinced the public were the ones who committed the heinous atrocities of 9/11.

The fornication of children by the clergy of the Roman Catholic Church was not the product of a few bad apples. It is the ritual sacrifice demanded by the Antichrist, who is not a single person, but an archetype in the Species Mind. The alter ego, the great deceiver, has conquered the earth, as was prophesized. The return of Jesus is yet another archetypal process of the Species Mind. The advent of the Messiah was supposed to be the beginning of an age of peace and prosperity. However, by the actions of one man, Paul, it has been frustrated and perverted.

There is a phenomenon in evolution called neoteny, whereby, instead of moving forward, we move backward into a former stage of development. It is now time to turn back consciousness to an earlier phase in development of the Species Mind, back to our lives in the hidden time. This is the meaning of the very last verse of *Eli*. The infant no longer needs to go through the trauma of being thrust into objectivity. Reality is subjective, as it is written in *Eli*. If we take away the one subject, God, nothing is real. This is introduced as a possible element of the new science, which will not be based on any pontifications, but on the possibilities inherent in the true method of science. It is not science that is evil. Science is the creation of God for the purpose of understanding, and we are still very far from understanding. In the hidden time, the objectification of self in the form of the dissociation of the alter ego can never occur, and our collective memory of the trauma is healed in the body of humankind. This book will be condemned in our time, but will be projected into the future, which is to come after the deluge we now face. As it was in the movie, which, coincidently, came years later under the same name, *Eli* will survive, as this book will survive.

However, regardless of how this book is received, it is incumbent upon us to realize the new judgment, which falls on us all as we plunder the earth. The new atonement is not the same as it was for the ancient Hebrews. The atonement is our collective action in preventing certain possible futures, such as full-scale nuclear war. If there is a worldwide and total nuclear disarmament, these possible futures go into extinction. The process proceeds in the hidden time, and there is nothing hidden that will not be revealed.

When the horror of 9/11 is recognized as it truly was, we take collective responsibility, and this is our atonement before the God of Abraham. It is now time for the infant Species Mind to stand on its feet. This is the hidden message of *Eli*. The times of the suffering will come out of the hidden time and manifest on earth. Within the hidden time, there are options. Species suicide is not among them.

Chapter One

Toward A Synthesis Of The Disciplines

It has been two million years since *Homo* (humans) emerged on to the face of the earth. The final cause of our enormous brain capacities will eventuate in the Species Mind. All the species and subspecies of *Homo* have gone extinct, with the exception of *Homo sapiens*. There has been a series of glaciations and several bottlenecks of near-extinction of *Homo* during this time. It is thought that about seventy thousand years ago the Tobo supereruption in Sumatra spewed an enormous amount of ash and fumes that enveloped the earth, leading to a volcanic winter that lasted sixty to one hundred years, and nearly drove *Homo* into extinction. The same will happen if there is a nuclear war, but we do not know what the parameters involved in nuclear winter are, and what scale of nuclear warfare would bring it about.

The hidden time is a concept that appears over and over in the Old Testament, as the word *olam*, which it is generally translated as eternal, forever, or some other English term connoting timelessness. It is an important concept in view of its relationship to God, as, for example, *El Olam* is the primordial God that exists for all time and is beyond time. So before the universe was, *El Olam* was.

Imaginary time was popularized by physicist Stephen Hawking (1988) in his book *A Brief History of Time*. Fundamentally, quantum physics has found a need for mathematically imaginary time, which is as real as anything else in physics. In the Big Bang that is thought to have occurred at the beginning of time real time emerged out of imaginary time, and thus imaginary time is the primary time and real time is secondary. However, it is thought that perhaps just a small portion of the unmanifest emerged, like the tip of an iceberg. Hawkings (1988) found it necessary to introduce it as an axis of time that could be used that is at a right angle to real time, such that all imaginary time intersects real time at every mathematic point along the real-time axis.

There has been some problem with the concept of imaginary time because it seems to violate causality. Causality in simple space-time is derived from light cones, which determine the causal limits of any event. It has been said that the "real" time is causal and deterministic, while the imaginary time is acausal and nondeterministic, and that faster than light propagation can occur in the imaginary time. Particles called tachyons are said to move faster than light and go backward in imaginary time.

The propagation of light defines the parameters of time in relativity such that one event may occur prior to a second event from one observer's frame of reference and previous to the first event for another. This is why space-time must be a continuum with relative terms regarding the frame of reference. Therefore, the law of causality, that a cause must proceed its effect, becomes ambiguous, even in the standard space-time theory.

A feature of imaginary time as described by Hawking (1988) was that it forms a closed loop such that an effect can precede its cause, and there is no beginning or end to imaginary time. In this sense, time can reiterate in cycles of imaginary time without any passage of real time at its pointlike intersection. Although imaginary time is necessary, according to Hawking and others, to perform certain calculations in the quantization of particles and fields, opinion on it varies widely, as it is not an observable. Its manifestation, however, is observable, and chief among them is final causation, long banished from science. Movement in imaginary time is the same as movement in real space, since it is the real time that is mathematically imaginary with respect to real space. So real and imaginary become interchangeable terms that depend on the formulation.

Beyond all the complex mathematics and theory the fact remains that time as we know it does not pass in imaginary time, and thus, imaginary time is eternal with respect to real time. It is the hidden time because we cannot see it, but some physicists believe it is the most fundamental physical quantity. The imaginary time seems to correlate nicely with the hidden time, leading to a convergence of the physical and spiritual concepts befitting the ideas expressed in *Eli*. We will return to this theme later in this book.

Philosophy has struggled with the terms of reality for centuries, and idealism seems to have the upper hand in *Eli*. Plotinus, a Greek idealist, in the First Tractate (2), of the Enneads (250 years CE), wrote,

> This first enquiry obliges us to consider at the outset the nature of the Soul—that is whether a distinction is to be made between Soul and Essential Soul ... if Soul and Essential Soul are one and the same, then the Soul will be an Ideal-Form unreceptive of all those activities which it imparts to another Kind but possessing within itself that native Act of its own which Reason manifests.

Our education, in general, gives us no way of comprehending what is expressed in ideal terms, but only that which is expressed in materialism terms. The ancient Greeks, as well as the Eastern idealist philosophers, were in many ways much further advanced than we are. Soul is the separate soul, each of us having our own. Essential Soul is the same as Self, or Atman, as the much-earlier philosophy in India that is recorded in the Vedanta described it.

Alfred North Whitehead, in his major work, *Process and Reality* (1929) described a different sort of philosophical orientation related in many ways to the Greek idealists. Elements of his "process relational theory of organism," include, most notably, panexperientialism and panentheism. Panexperientialism holds that the only reality is experience, thus avoiding the pitfalls of materialism, pure idealism, and dualism. For Whitehead, experience covers the range of reality from the smallest to the grandest level. Panentheism differs from pantheism, the idea that everything is God. Panentheism holds that God is inside everything, within everything, again, through all levels of description.

Whitehead is difficult to understand, as he created his own terminology, so do not be discouraged if you don't fully understand our attempt here to give a synopsis of our understanding of the human mind using these terms. We will do our best.

Whitehead (1929) described the equivalent of what Plotinus did in his idea Ideal Forms (one of the concepts of Plato), which he called Eternal Objects. It is thus that Whitehead said that the soul is no more original than a stone, being an Eternal Object. However, other process philosophers following in the same tradition tended to consider the Soul or Self to be an actual entity, a unit of experience of the same nature as God. In Whitehead's view, all phenomena manifest from the physical to mental in a discontinuous fashion of perishing and being recreated every moment through the feeling or prehension of all its prior occasions of actuality or existence.

Actually, what Plotinus is saying arises anew in neuropsychology, supported by scientific evidence in the corpus of neurology (Brown 2011). We will present a kind of synthesis of Brown, Whitehead, Eli, and others. The human mind, functioning though the brain, has a single "dominant occasion," which Brown (2011) calls the core of self, or just self, which we might consider Essential Soul. Through a hierarchy of expression self (soul) goes through a process of "mitosis," (Brown 2011) forming a society of "occasions" that differentiate, and are ultimately derived from the one soul, or one subject in *Eli*, which is God. The dissociated alter ego is one such occasion. Thus, the extraordinary capacities of the human mind science attributes to the isolated material substance of the brain are actually derived from the Knower of all things. These derivatives of the one subject include the first derivative, the individual human soul, which, in the hidden time, holds within it the entire universe. The dominant occasion, Self, produces further derivatives, or occasions, by "mitosis," a term of Brown borrowed from the biological term for cell division.

These occasions form a society or system of relations they begin in the unconscious hidden time and each of these occasions, derived from Self or Soul, holds within it some aspect or object of perception of that exists in the hidden time. Thus the Soul, in the hidden time, holds within itself all the objects of experience that we perceive of as existing in the external world. What is internal in the hidden time is external in ordinary, manifest time. The objects of perception thus exist within the Soul, as well is in the external world. They are exactly the same objects viewed from the perspective of these two species of time.

The derivative occasions of Self, those of its Kind (Plotinus), are imbued with the Eternal Objects or Ideal Forms of the Mind of God, and are thus receptive to the objects of perception which we view as existing externally. Internal relations of feeling then are shared between the dominant occasion of Self and its derivative occasions, each of which feels or experiences the relations of all the other occasions internally. These relations exist within what we would otherwise view as a mathematical point in our manifest reality, which is the intersection of the dimensions of the hidden or imaginary time and manifest space-time. Each of these points is extended in the dimensions of the hidden time, forming the "extensive continuum" (Whitehead 1929) of internal relations which is the actual field in which the mind operates.

The occasions that comprise the organic unity on the individual mind also feel all those occasions as exist in the universe. Within this organic unity the individual mind is in no way separate from the One Mind. The product of the organic unity is than an occasion of the Soul which we call Now, feeling and incorporating every former Now within the hidden time. Thus the Now is Eternal within the hidden time, the world that exists just beneath our ego consciousness. With the progression from Nows Past to Now Present, we form a world line or thread, on which each Now is like a bead on the thread, thus the verse in

Eli (1:7): "The hidden time is a thread, and moments are the beads on the thread."

The integrated occasion of experience or Now is then a perception of the external world within the internal world or extensive continuum, as it manifests discontinuously. In the Now perceptions in the hidden time are integrated with prehensions or feelings from the sensory field of the indivisible human organism and become the objects of the senses and the external object world. This process involves the passage of the Now into the past as an immortal actuality within the hidden time. The extinction of the Now that we view as the passage of time is then simply the progressive manifestation of recursive Nows, like the adding of beads unto the thread of the world line.

The Soul, as derivative from the One Soul, God, holds God within it, such that there is a single actuality of the universe that continually reenacts the entire history of the universe in every instant of what we perceive as ordinary time. In physics this is the role of the imaginary time in the sum over all histories.

We can understand the mind far more readily in the terms of the new science, where God is an essential element, than in the primitive terms of materialism. Thus the words in *Eli* (4:7): SEARCH GOD. Materialism has fundamentally gotten nowhere in their construction of the theory of mind and its relation to the brain because mind is not material, it is of the nature of experience through feeling. Feeling is the most fundamental element if we consider the fact that this is the mode of experience in the mind/brain of all the animal kingdom, of which we are a member, while thought is a thin veneer of alter-ego consciousness where feelings are replaced by symbols in language—verbal, mathematical, or otherwise. The objects of our world are imbued with the feeling derived from their internal existence in Mind, and these feelings have only recently in the history of humans been withdrawn from the objects of its experience, as the alter ego has become the locus of perception, which is objectified and comes to supplant the functions of Self or Soul, which alone holds the internal universe.

Brown (2011), on the basis of the neurological evidence in science, conveys some of the same meaning in his "microgenesis," a reiteration of prior actual states of mind in development and evolution in each mental state. In this case the process of mitosis differentiates into the objects of perception and our view of the "external" world. This takes away the division of internal and external worlds, such that the object as it exists "out there" is the very same object that exists "in here." Brown, however, makes the mistake of reifying the extensive continuum, which we have placed in the hidden or imaginary time, into a sheet of mentation that extends into the object world, making each of us, in effect, creators of our own universe.

This may be excused, but Brown's (2011) concept of natural selection as the means by which the brain achieves congruence between its internal object world and the images of the senses is a serious and damaging error with respect to the sanctity of the human Species Mind, which progresses by final causation in the hidden time.

Natural selection, as currently formulated, involves some kind of competition and adaptation of entities vying for existence, and is, even when applied to evolution, a specious concept that lacks evidentiary support in its role as the motive principle that guides the evolutionary process, as we will discuss later. The idea that natural selection is actually the creator of worlds is absolutely ridiculous, but the people behind intelligent design movement are equally ridiculous when they appeal to some kind of supernaturalism. Nature has plenty of room to accommodate the role of God, who is not outside of nature, as nature and all that is actual are within God. God is absolute, preexisting, and not in the realm of conditionality. There is nothing that transcends God. Science is absolutely correct in its rejection of the supernatural, because there is no supernatural; it is the dead remnant of the prescientific world. The language of science with which *Eli* posits is the language of the new religion requires that we dispense of this notion of the supernatural. There is no need for it.

The reason why we can dispense of the supernatural is that the schism between God and nature is a false dichotomy, and here *Eli* seems to part ways with process theology, which has concocted an interrelationship of God and nature as being separate. In doing so, the nature of God is changed such that there is a mutual transcendence of God and the world. In *Eli* there is nothing that transcends God, and no negotiations of the sort implied by the notion that God somehow needs the world in his "consequent nature." God is eternal, so there can be no consequent nature, since a consequence is within the field of efficient causation (the present being caused by the past). God, as eternal in the hidden time, is not affected by the passage of time. In former times, God was united with nature, and the earliest forms of human religion involved the worship of nature. Nature and wisdom are subsumed under the female side of God's many manifestations and are ways we use to conceive of the God in the realm of manifestation, as is described in the *Zohar*.

Idealism and theism suit the manifest nature of mind, nature within God, far better than our materialistic machinations. In the writings of Plotinus in 250 CE, there lies the germ of a fully developed theory on mind, which has a direct correspondence with a philosophy fashioned more about 780 years later, and a neuropsychology that is current and fully based on science. This is quite remarkable, and we could go on and on with examples, but the principle is what is important. Idealism, experientialism, and process theory, with a bit of systems theory thrown in by the author, can produce an explanatory model that integrates science, philosophy, and theology. Science is all about explanation, and in this example, materialism has utterly failed to give us a satisfactory explanation.

Chapter Two

Background Regarding Eli

As with so much of the translation of the Hebrew texts, the meaning of the name Eli is complex, and not altogether clear. Some translations render Eli as meaning Almighty or as signifying high, uplifted, ascend, or ascension, and identify it with the high priest, often in the context of Eli, the high priest and teacher of Samuel.

Eli was written in its entirety in 1999. It is a short book of seven chapters of seven verses, which was originally published in 1999 in English and in translation to several languages on the now-defunct website bookofeli.com. There is also, as we have mentioned, an oral tradition of Eli, which we have on good authority. This book seeks to expand and expound on *Eli*, which is a revealed book, written early in 1999 by an anonymous author, and published on the Internet on the website bookofeli.com in the same year, eight years prior to the creation of the screenplay of the same name. The current book uses the same name as it presents the real and pre-existing sacred book, followed by a treatise of what the book may mean which contains some additional information regarding the revelation of Eli.

In *Eli*, there is but one new commandment, and that is that we FORSAKE USURY. Usury is the loaning of money with interest, irrespective of what that interest is, and similar practices where money makes money without the actual production of new wealth.

We will start with a critical examination of usury and some of the other contents of the sacred text by way of introduction, and attempt here to explain why, as it states in *Eli*, the practice of usury has now become the greatest danger now facing humankind. Many of the prophecies included in the sacred text have already occurred, and could not have been foreseen in 1999. The consequences of usury are just beginning. It has caused a worldwide economic crisis, and the world-changing events predicted by *Eli* have become progressively manifested. Our current economic crisis and many of the events predicted in *Eli* will continue to unfold, and the *Book* is intended to help humankind avoid the extreme suffering and disruption of world civilization that will ensue if the practice of usury is not abandoned. It is our sincere hope that *Eli* and this book will become available to readers to allow them to judge for themselves what we must now do as the "times of suffering" deepen, which is God's purpose for this revelation to humankind.

Eli seeks the unity of religion and science, holding that they contain the same truths in the final analysis, and that God wills that certain mysteries involving God and science be known in the age to come. The calling of *Eli* is to initiate the creation of a new kind of religion, not formerly known to humankind, which embraces science as it is properly defined. This religion involves the study or a new kind of science, which accepts the existence of God, not as a dogma, but as the principle of the presence and action of God in the field of nature. This new science in characterized by a meaning and purpose that are the final cause, in the realization of the will of God.

In all times we have held a conceit that our ways of thinking and our view of the world and of the universe had reached some kind of finality, and in these times that finality is demonstrably false, as we will attempt to demonstrate, or begin to demonstrate, in this book. The concepts of final cause and idealism or experientialism have been falsely rejected by the field of science with the rise of Darwinism and the materialist dogma. This has been due to a lack of understanding of the full scope of science, which includes those things we have not yet been discovered or described. Science is not completed. It is, in fact, very early in its development, and the time has come when God has willed that the mysteries be revealed, transforming science to its proper role in enriching culture and serving as a positive force (Krishnamurti) in the ongoing evolution of humanity.

Therefore, we seek to create a scientific discipline, which does not abjure faith in God, but supports it. This is a challenge to science in that God is not an observable, but is Mind itself, which is the One Mind, Universal Mind, or Universal Consciousness, the Spirit and Hidden Energy (energy as it manifests in the hidden or imaginary dimensions of time) that animates all things, that reifies the actual amidst the field of the potential, and that is the basis for all relations. We have adopted an illusory concept of relations as the interactions of dead matter, and rejected the felt sense of the Unity of all things.

The foundation of mind is feeling, not thought. Thought is the system of symbolic representation through which we take our felt sense of our oneness with nature and replace it with an inner dialogue that we have within the alter-ego consciousness. Symbolic language (speech) emerged about fifty thousand years BCE and allowed us to differentiate from the animal kingdom, and was most likely the most important development in our history in terms of our success as a species and our domination of the planet. The fundamental basis of the human psyche, however, is not in thought, but in feeling, which we have traditionally assigned to the heart.

The heart longs to be reunited with its Beloved, for the mind to be once again enlightened by the light that comes from the heart or the soul. Symbolic thought has gone awry in replacing the soul with a symbol, with the word "I," the ego. The word ("I") is not the thing (Self, Atman), the map is not the territory (Watts), but the symbolism of "I" and of your personal name wields tremendous power, transforming the true nature into the alter ego, which has no light of its own, but which rather obscures the light, and casts us into darkness.

This is a temporary situation, and it is the proper function of religion to reunite us with the Beloved, with God, through the felt sense of the love of God and the love for God. In this function, in our time, it has failed miserably to do so. God has become a symbol, fundamentally a proxy for the alter ego, and the living God has been denied and forgotten. The reason for this unfortunate development is not symbolic language, it is usury, the worst of all sins, because it is money that we then come to love, and the increase thereof. The beloved God is replaced by the love of money, and despite the fact that this theme is the core of the teachings of Jesus, Christians have fallen into this world of darkness that usury has created.

According to our treatment of the spiritual or ideal realm, the realm of eternity is the hidden time of the *Bible*. We examine the hidden time equivalent to the timeless and space-less imaginary time dimensions of modern physics, and find favorable evidence that this is the case. The absolute infinity of the Mind of God can only exist in the imaginary time, if we are to believe that the hidden time is a two-dimensional loop that can reiterate in cycles indefinitely within the point of intersection with the real time.

We are really not separate creatures, but part of the One, God. Our individual souls are plurality within a unity, which we call humankind, for which Eli has great compassion. Eli judges no one, his purpose is to help those who are struggling to understand religion in the age of science, at a time when the superstitions and mythologies of former religions are not adequate to provide a spiritual basis for humans over the next millennium, and to perhaps help avoid some of the suffering of the tribulation which has fallen upon humankind. Usury was forbidden in former times as a great sin. In fact, usury may be the unforgivable sin spoken of by Jesus as the sin against the Holy Spirit in the Gospels. He turned over the tables of the money changers rather than offering them forgiveness, because of God's wrath regarding usury. It seems that all other sins were forgiven, but usury was not.

Other prophets will follow, as has been predicted by Eli, some far greater than Eli, as, in times to come, the gift of prophecy will be bestowed on an increasing number of people. *Eli* is just a prelude to a new golden age of prophecy on earth. We will begin our discussion with the economic themes that run through the sacred *Eli*.

Chapter Three

Usury And The Current Crisis

The American gross domestic product, a measure of the standard of living of Americans, is about $14.7 trillion, and the national debt is now about $14.2 trillion. The national debt has been projected to reach $23.3 trillion by 2019. At the time of this writing (June 11, 2011) the US public debt was estimated to be equivalent to over $46 thousand dollars per US citizen, and over $129 thousand dollars per American taxpayer. An estimated $4 trillion dollars of this debt is owed to foreign countries, primarily Japan, China, the United Kingdom, oil exporters, Caribbean Banking Centers, Brazil, Hong Kong, Russia, Luxembourg, and Taiwan. About two-thirds of the debt is considered to be owned by the American people. The remaining third is owned by the American government, much of which has been borrowed from government entitlement programs. This money has literally been stolen from the American people, and the only reason why there has not been a total collapse of the American economy is a direct result of this theft. We did not "save" America in this process; we lost it to the international financial sector, the entity that we are actually indebted to. This sector includes banks—the very same banks that we bailed out of crisis with taxpayer dollars—insurance companies, real estate, and investment funds. The sector finances mortgages and loans, the value of which increases when the central system of US government banks, the Federal Reserve or Fed, lowers interests on loans, the rate of which is called the prime interest rate. The Federal Reserve is not a branch of government, like the US Treasury Department. Among other things, it is responsible for printing up American currency.

Up until the early sixties, our money represented value, primarily in silver and gold, and in the metal used to make our coins. The last article of money that was worth its value was the penny, which was made of copper prior to 1981 and less-expensive metals afterward. The dollar is now just a piece of paper, a form of debt held with the promise that the future will be able to give us a dollar's worth of goods at some time in the future. This promise of cashing in this debt is far from a sure bet. The dollar could be worth far less at such time as we decide to spend it, and likely will be as this will be the only means we have to pay the debt, by devaluing the dollar.

Holding paper money is not usury, but neither is it necessarily a secure way for us to carry wealth into the future, as when the International Financial Sector (IFS) collapses, it is bound to become worthless. We have no choice at this time but to participate in the practice of usury, and the money we deposit in the bank, or place in our insurance policies, is loaned at interest by creditors and mortgage companies. Thus, usury has the features of the "mark of the beast" of *Revelation*, in that one cannot buy or sell without it. However, when the IFS defaults, the thieving hands of the "very few," the superrich who have made their money by stealing it from all of us in the form of usury, will take the money and run.

It would be extremely foolish to place our bets on the honesty and integrity of these people. They will steal the hard-earned Social Security that working people, the true sources of wealth, have invested in through deductions from their wages, as well as the wealth we have placed in entitlement programs. These actions have been planned, and the execution of these plans has been set up by our government and our presidents, from Ronald Reagan through Barack Obama. We have all been deluded that wealth will continue to grow indefinitely, and Mr. Obama has embraced this delusion in the form of his endorsement of the economic policies of Reagan and Clinton. The latter president's battle cry was to "grow the economy," and he did so by creating a run for the usurers to profit on an unsustainable growth that has become the albatross that we now must carry around our necks of "debt" that has been placed on each and every American citizen.

Americans never agreed to carry such debt, so in a very real sense, our government has stolen the wealth we have entrusted to them and, in doing so, has endangered its constitutional right to govern on behalf of the American citizenry as a privilege granted by the American citizenry. Their abuse of this privilege will play itself out in civil unrest. This has been foreseen. A shadow government was enabled to replace our legitimate government by the events of 9/11, which were, in fact, the actions of this shadow government itself.

They will have no mercy on those Americans that will take to the streets when the IFS defaults. They will suspend habeas corpus and incarcerate a segment of our citizenry without due process, under the assumption of an internal enemy that we must engage in warfare. The military, under command of the shadow government, will take to the streets, and Americans will see the same kind of warfare it has engaged in around the world within their own nation. When the IFS defaults, so will the banks and insurance companies. There will be blood on the streets of our nation. It is possible that all these things could be prevented, but it is unlikely. These are the fruits of usury, and if we were to shift to a sustainable, steady state economy (Cobb at the same time as we gradually dismantle the machinery of usury and build an economy where usury is not allowed, they will be prevented. But there is very little time left, and it is much more likely that, when usury goes down, it will take the world with it.

Ordinary Americans are now seeing the devaluing of its currency or money in the price of consumer goods such as food and gasoline. The petroleum industry, by its power over the value of the currency, becomes critical to the economy, as the price and value of petroleum goes into all our consumer goods. It must continue to flourish if the current American economy is to hold up the value of its currency. In a sense, you might say that the dollar is no longer held up by silver, gold, nickel, or copper, but by barrels of petroleum. Despite claims of US reserves, the strategic source of American petroleum lies in the Middle East, and is being produced at such a rate that it will be gone by the end of the century, at which point we will have expended, for all practical purposes, all the world's petroleum resources, which, or course, are not renewable.

With the Middle East faced with a total draining of their petroleum resources, and thus there means of future survival, a small e-mail group called al-Qaida formed a franchise, a loose affiliation of Muslim fundamentalists, already divided into sects with different belief systems, under the supposed leadership of Osama bin Laden.

The bin Ladens were an extremely wealthy family in Saudi Arabia with close ties to the Bushes. The economy, at the time of the 9/11 "attacks," was itching to find an enemy to justify its petroleum wars, and it needed a "false flag." A demolition was staged to correspond to the crashing of two passenger planes into the twin towers, and the idea that Osama bin Laden and the al-Qaida franchise was the cause of the death of over three thousand people was sold to the American public. The only way the Twin Towers could have come down as a result of the passenger plane "attacks" would be if God suspended the laws of physics for a sufficient time for steel-framed structures, lauded for their engineering and construction, with interlocking beams of support firmly welded into a horizontal and vertical matrix much like the mesh of a window screen, to come down free-fall against the mighty resistance of tons of welded steel beams. Even given the fact that the beams were systematically severed by explosives, it is remarkable that the weight of the building fell very nearly at the acceleration of an object falling through thin air, given the immense amount of kinetic energy expended during the fall by the pulverization of concrete and other construction materials.

As an asbestos expert, the author was informally consulted regarding the apparent formation of mineral wool from asbestos used in the construction of the Twin Towers, which was found on the ground after the building fell. I was asked whether asbestos turns into mineral wool when it melts, apparently under the presumption that the jet fuel from the planes had melted the asbestos. I had done experiments with the melting of asbestos, and was also familiar with the technology of mineral wool production. My professional opinion, based on observation, was that asbestos would melt just like any other mineral substance into a nonfibrous glass, and could form rock wool only if it were melted very quickly and the spun out with explosive force. My opinion is probably nowhere on the record, but it was given with integrity and had no relation to the idea that the buildings had been destroyed by explosives. I can only guess that mineral wool with remnants of asbestos was found, such as to justify the conjecture that resulted in the need for my expertise, since ordinary mineral wool would be an expected component in the construction of the buildings.

The suspension of the laws of physics would be a miracle, but the demolition of the Twin Towers and other events were no miracle. This was the signal event that the times of suffering foretold by *Eli* had begun and brought about a new order within our nation and the world. The question is not whether the Twin Towers, and Building 7, were demolished. They most certainly were.

The question is who actually set up the demolition, how they did it, and why there is no record of their activities, i.e., there is no "paper trail." The demolitions, as documented in numerous places, were exquisitely engineered, and required advanced technologies and expertise in the manufacture of explosives and their use in the severing of steel beams. It would have required the efforts of numerous people, some with advanced understanding of obscure information obtained from high-level academic sources in the United States. The only sector within society that could stage such events in this manner is organized crime.

The author has direct knowledge of the presence of organized crime in American government, acquired during his tenure as Chief of Staff at Patton Hospital in Southern California, the largest forensic psychiatric facility in the world. There he came to know a man, who will go unnamed, of immense power and wealth, involved in high-level administrative activities in the State of California, making important administrative decisions and directing state personnel, involved in a range of government activities, with political connections going all the way up to the executive branch of the federal government, including the president. Yet his name appeared nowhere in the vast sea of papers regarding meetings at which he was present, decisions he had made, or in any documents that I had access to regarding the operation of state government and the many other agencies of government in which he was involved. His name was also not on the Internet, which is a great feat, even for the most humble among us, and he had no paper trail.

I met this man at an administrative meeting of the Governing Body, a group of high-level state government officials, in 1999. For some reason, he took me into his confidence. On state time, he took me to his Beverley Hills mansion and took me to lunch in his chauffeured Rolls-Royce. He even had me do surgery by removing a large mole from the side of his dying wife, in the comfort of their own home, on state time, and with no payment. It seemed that all the connections that he told me he had were real, and on one occasion, I was present as he stated he was speaking on his cell phone to George W. Bush. It was almost as if this man was boosting about his secret government functions. The odd thing was, as I overheard him talking, he was giving Bush orders!

Knowing some of the mob hang outs in New York, I found that he had frequented them, which he told me about with delight. I knew quite a bit about the mobs in New York City, as I had lived close to the City up until 1990, and my father had owned and operated a restaurant in Manhattan, New York City. The Italian-American side of my family was, to my knowledge, never involved in organized crime, but I had an in-law of a friend of the family who was, and who I knew. So I had information from a variety of sources.

The man being spoken of described to me in some detail how he had been involved with the former mayor of New York, Rudy Giuliani, and had enlisted the various organized crime organizations to clean up New York. It did not appear that he was lying, since he spoke with some authority about the organized crime syndicates, and their involvement in state and federal government. He told me that he had orchestrated the mob bosses in the actions taken to clean up New York for a time, with the full knowledge of Mr. Giuliani. This being unknown, one has to wonder whether a similar process preceded the events of 9/11. The mobsters can be quite persuasive, in a variety of ways, which are mostly illegal, and were well suited to the task at hand, which they completed with enormous success. They work for favors—contracts that brought money into their coffers, and special favors, such as admission of one of the boss's daughters to Harvard University. If true, it demonstrates the scope of the clandestine network controlling our government and institutions.

There was no record of this mob activity in New York City or of the purported use of the organized crime system to clean up New York on the Internet. The organizations of the mob leave no paper trail and have a hierarchy in which the lower-order mobsters, "made men" (and perhaps women), did not know the structure of the syndicate of gangsters, who the bosses are above their own lower-order connections. They are mostly psychopaths, some of whom would kill someone without blinking an eye. The syndicates have a code of silence, and breaking this code is enforced by in some instances by homicide of the "canary" and even members of his family. They also have networks throughout the government, banks, businesses, corporations, and academic institutions. A physician colleague of mine, who had worked for the CIA, described to me quite frankly of the CIA's involvement in enabling millions of dollars of transactions in the illegal cocaine trade. We don't see these things on the television, or even on the Internet.

As time went on, I learned that I was being recruited, for some odd reason, by the American organized crime syndicate. This involved a network of people representing the power elite in a secret shadow government. The network became obvious as I was brought into confidence, and came to know that it was no accident that I had run into one of the syndicate's operatives. There were many, many others—some of whom this man conversed in my presence on his cell phone. He obviously made an error in judgment by trying to bring me into the fold, but I continued to play the game in order to inquire more deeply into the syndicate's operations. It involved clandestine operations of all kinds. It was heavily into the drug trade, gambling interests, police organizations, the movie industry, and the agencies of state and federal government. Although meeting one of its operatives, who had become extremely wealthy, yet had no legitimate employment, was not an accident, as there are a large number of people involved. However, it was quite curious that this individual was feeding me information that was highly secretive in an indiscriminant manner.

When I disobeyed orders from this individual to squelch the investigation by the medical staff of a death, which had occurred as a result of staff actions, I fell out of ranks. As Chief of Staff, I had asked for an inquiry into the circumstances of the death, but nothing was done, and the Executive Director, who is now deceased, made sure of this.

At that time, I directly disobeyed my orders from the syndicate and reported the incident to the special investigator. Shortly thereafter, while at another job I had part-time, I was called by an associate on the medical staff and told that I should drop what I was doing, cancel my patients, and meet him and two others of the medical staff at the Hilton in San Bernardino, California. I did so, and orders from the subject individual were conveyed to me that I had to resign as Chief of Staff immediately, or "something ominous" would happen to me. This was clearly a "terrorist threat," as it is currently defined, so I came to know the strong arm of the syndicate. I took it as a threat on my life and called an emergency meeting of the medical staff the next day. No one wanted to be involved, and my circle of associates and friends scattered from my midst.

I was told that I could never again have a position of authority on the medical staff by the chief of long-term services, who was highly involved with this syndicate operative, at his behest. I did not resign as requested, but it was alleged that I was a paranoid schizophrenic by a member of the medical staff who had an axe to grind. This was taken seriously, and I was put on a kind of trial in which it was claimed that my professional opinion regarding the death was said to be delusional, even though everyone, including the coroner, knew that it was true. The situation was quite bizarre and Kafkaesque, but in order to hold my job, I had to negotiate my position.

I continued to be highly regarded in the psychiatry department, and was convinced to run for Chair, a position I had held previously. I agreed to do so after some arm pulling, and this may have been the worst decision I have ever made. In an unprecedented manner, my election was nullified twice on the basis of technicalities. This had never happened before in the long history of the hospital. I finally won a third election, and entered a position of authority as Chair, something which I was warned I could never do by the syndicate shadow boss.

Thereafter, there was a concerted campaign to question my clinical judgment. I had formerly been regarded by many as the best psychiatrist among the scores that worked in the complex, with no previous complaints, and the complaints were solicited from staff by administration. These staff members were under my direction when they tried to second-guess my clinical decisions on the basis of their very limited knowledge. There were a total of eleven complaints that I had made the wrong judgment, such that I had to leave the meetings of the medical executive committee as investigations were conducted regarding the complaints. However, on each one there was a favorable outcome, and I had not flawed in my clinical judgment.

Shortly thereafter, I was arrested as a terrorist, and during the period of my incarceration, I was replaced. I was never charged with any crime, but had few options but to challenge administration, which became involved as a result of the false complaints they themselves had solicited, and risk my licensure in the process or to resign. I chose the latter, and soon got a job as a psychiatrist elsewhere.

Such is the awesome power of the syndicate. It was uniquely to plan, orchestrate, and execute the 9/11 atrocities without leaving a paper trail, and with no informants, as they had apparently done with Giuliani and the cleanup of New York City, and I am fairly certain, based on what I know, that it was involved along with the good mayor who became Time magazine's person of the years as he stood over the carnage and wreckage of the Twin

Towers, an American hero for "victims" of the terrible atrocity. He apparently knew the buildings were going to fall, as has been videotaped, before they fell, and at a time, there was no reason to believe that they would fall except foreknowledge. His involvement with the syndicate has remained a total secret but for my placement of it on an Internet blog, where it remains obscure.

I am recounting these things so that the citizens of our nation should know. I am not in the business of conspiracy theories or sedition, or of sensationalism for the purpose of selling this book. All the reports you will find on the Internet are speculative and not given much credence. My reports are what I have observed. Perhaps I may reach the wrong conclusions, but my conclusions are generally accurate. Our shadow government and the organized crime syndicate have no legitimacy under the Constitution. They need to be removed from government process. I am only saying this, at great risk, because, should I remain silent, I become guilty under the new judgment of *Eli*.

The American organized crime syndicate, part of our terrorist shadow government, does not work for free; they are in business to make money at the behest of the power elite, who have commissioned them in order to create a false flag for warfare, which was necessary for their governance and for the overturning of the American democracy and creation of a police state, ruled by the "very few," the power elite, who are now the masters of the American government. The day before 9/11 Secretary of Defense Donald Rumsfeld held a press conference aired on national television to announce that $2.3 trillion was missing from the Pentagon budget. Some sources said that the actual amount missing was $4 trillion. Unfortunately, many of the sources of information and people who knew about the missing money were destroyed or killed the next day by the so-called plane crash into the Pentagon. One women, who survived, but was in the area of the crash, said she never saw a plane, but did hear an explosion. With all the cameras positioned around the Pentagon, they have been unable to produce one image of the plane. No witnesses saw a plane. There were no remnants of a plane at the scene.

It would be overly speculative to suggest that this money that was missing from the Pentagon paid for the resources and mob blood money in the 9/11 atrocities. However, we are still left with a great many more questions than answers. I watched the events on CNN on that morning from the time that coverage began. The commentator stated, before the buildings came down, that Osama bin Laden had warned he would have a passenger plane hit Manhattan three weeks prior to the incident. How could he have known this so soon? This CNN report is not on the Internet. What is on the Internet is that Secretary of State Condoleeza Rice took the warning of bin Laden's threat to President Bush three weeks prior to 9/11, and he said, "I'm not going to be swatting at flies."

At one time, the author owned a recording studio business. My employees were very unreliable and the business was on the brink of failure. One evening a remarkably intelligent and erudite black Moslem man came into to the studio, and I talked with him at some length. He presented to me a $10 billion bond from the government of Morocco, which looked authentic, and offered lavish support for my business. I did not take the bait.

Our conversation was interesting, however. He told me that it was well-known that the US federal government was the biggest cocaine dealer in the world. I would lend no credence to this but for the fact that my colleague had told me of his involvement with the CIA assisted cocaine trade. I asked this man if he had any foreknowledge of the 9/11 events. He replied that he knew when everyone else knew, three weeks before it happened. It did not seem that he was lying. So I have three independent reports of three weeks foreknowledge.

Several miles from the studio, there was some undeveloped land adjacent to the home the parents of a black American friend of mine. On the land, there were two near-vertical pillars of rock, each about thirty feet high, as I recall, which were there naturally and not the product of human activity. The inner sides of these two pillars were nearly flat and roughly parallel to one another, and there was a crevasse that was formed through the whole height of the pillars that was about three feet wide and about thirty feet long. There was some evidence that the site had been frequented by the American Indians, which we will not get into. On several occasions, we visited the site early in the evening, and each time the moon was near the horizon and shining straight through the crevasse. This was a curious coincidence, but it indicated the formation may have value in the reckoning of time. I described this to my Moroccan visitor, and he said I had found a window into the dreamtime. We had not been discussing the dreamtime, which is basically equivalent to the hidden time. He went on to say that the salutation in Morocco was "how was your dream." I cannot verify these things, but perhaps other cultures have retained a perception of this time. The Australian Aborigines are the closest to our ancestral culture, and the dreamtime is, for them, the true reality, as it must have been for our ancestors. The final verse of *Eli* instructs us to return to this perception of time.

With the American public convinced that this small group of Muslims, directed by "the mastermind of 9/11," Osama bin Laden, the petroleum wars began, fully supported by all true American "patriots." Many Americans believe that the buildings were demolished, but are afraid to speak of it. Others know about the evidence, some of which was aired on American television, and is freely available on the Internet, but chose to believe the official American government story.

A colleague of mine, David Ray Griffin, a Whiteheadean scholar of some repute, wrote a book detailing the actual facts of the events of 9/11, including the demolitions, and was involved with a variety of sectors of the media as a result of the controversy created by his book. He had a great deal of courage in doing so, as it was quite damaging to his reputation. However, it is precisely his reputation that made the book so creditable and, in fact, indisputable in my eyes.

Chapter Four

The Engine Of Usury

There is a nation that is really a threat to American sovereignty, and which should be the focus of the so-called American patriots who support the petroleum wars. Within the next ten years, China will be a major nuclear power, and will have a larger economy than the United States. They will then be able to conquer the United States without firing a bullet. China carries a large share of the national debt, and if they were to dump these dollars, our economy would collapse. It already owns a large part of our nation, which increases steadily. The Chinese government is a totalitarian, brutal, and oppressive regime, which seems to embody, operating under the system of state corporatism, otherwise known is fascism, the very principles that constitute our banner of warfare. The Republic is no republic, and its people are forced to be docile and obedient as they share little in the country's control.

China is the most profound exemplar of a nation that has been cast into spiritual darkness. There is no freedom of religion or freedom of assembly for purposes of worship in China. Religion is permitted, but all religions are required to register, and the state rigidly controls religious practice such that it does not lead to any "disruption" of their totalitarian reign.

The discussion of China here is not meant to degrade of denigrate the Chinese people, with their fine and noble traditions and history, but to shed some light on the evils, atrocities, and abominations committed by the Chinese government in hopes that their rise to world domination may be avoided. This, in and of itself, is a very tall order, but it is hoped that the authority of *Eli* will in some way serve to lessen or avoid this cataclysm of the human soul and the age of darkness.

China has a "one child" policy, which favors abortions of females granted by their parents so that their one child may be a male. Government permission is required to bear a child, and if a women who has had one child becomes pregnant and proceeds to the stage at which they infant would be viable outside of the womb, late in the third trimester, they abort and murder the infant. This is very well documented, and has even been shown on American television. The following is an excerpt from a recent essay on the Internet entitled "Abortion in China." *http://www.exampleessays.com/viewpaper/44447.html*:

> In China there are many abortions that women are forced to do without their free will . . . if the Chinese authorities get informed that a woman is pregnant with her second child, they have the right to drag her out of her house or if she's not home they take her husband or family member into custody until they have turned themselves in . . . There are an estimated half a million abortions within the third trimester per year in China. Most of these children were viable when the abortion occurred, and most often the abortion was performed without the consent of the mother. Reports have shown that women are often brainwashed, imprisoned, and deprived of food until they agree to have an abortion . . . Doctors usually inject women with a substance called Rivalor, which causes direct heart failure to the baby . . . Another way of performing the abortion is injecting pure formaldehyde . . . into the soft spot on the baby's head so that as he or she is being delivered, the doctor can crush the baby's skull with his forceps. Other doctors use chokers which are similar to twisty garbage ties. They are placed around the baby's neck so he or she can be strangled once they are delivered.

This means that over $250,000 infants are murdered every year by Chinese doctors in a shocking and brutal way. According to the new justice of *Eli*, if we know this and allow it to happen, we ourselves are guilty. Americans have assumed an attitude of indifference, apathy, and social irresponsibility, and so do nothing to stop this brutal regime from committing this horrific crime. If we believe that *Eli* is a revealed text from God, which is our basic premise, we must do something. Sanctions against Chinese imports would be one place to start. Boycotting of all Chinese products would be another. We must write to our government leaders and tell them that we will have no part in supporting the Chinese government in any way, shape, or form. This is what *Eli* teaches, and it distinguishes the *Book* from every other sacred text, with the possible exception of the Torah (Numbers 15:26). This may be difficult for people to accept, but every time you buy a Chinese product, according to the *Book*, you are permitting the murder of over 250,000 infants by your complicity with this abomination. This is the new justice that *Eli* prescribes. The hand that makes the tie that you buy in Macys may be that of a Chinese woman who has been subjected to this horrific crime, and by buying that tie you are supporting the very people who committed it.

We give China "most favorite nation status," and for the usurers, this means that they can buy Chinese goods at a low price, many of poor quality, and sell them at huge profits. If one goes to an American Walmart, or Macys, one finds that our retail markets are saturated with Chinese products. Recently the author went to Macys to buy a few ties from their huge and high-priced collection, and found not one tie that was not made in China. It is not that silk is only available in China, but that the usurers would sooner buy a tie for a few dollars from China and charge fifty dollars than buy a tie made elsewhere for a few more dollars made elsewhere, just to profit by a few more dollars. This is the ugly face of usury, and it must end. Who calls themselves American patriots that support this shameful situation?

I recently bought a cover-slip product made in China, and retailed to schools for use by children and adolescents in the United States in microscopy, and found that the slips (brand name Sail) were separated by a deadly layer of pure actinolite asbestos. I found this quite curious, ordered some more, and found exactly the same thing. This is quite an unusual use for asbestos, and actinolite is among its most deadly forms. There was no warning or indication that the product contained asbestos, as required by US law. It is only because the author, as an asbestos expert, purchased them to examine samples for asbestos that this practice became known. It was ignored, in any event. I am not paid to police Chinese products for toxins, and I expect, neither is anyone else in the United States. I complained about this to the appropriate American government authorities, but nothing was done. I later bought a small statuette made in China and found that it was painted with deadly cadmium and lead pigments. I am a scientist and a physician, and I have access to analytical equipment. On the basis of my limited observations, I do not consider Chinese products safe. Yet we continue to send them our dollars, which they loan back to us with interest, and thereby support their manufacturing of such unsafe products, sending wealth and jobs to China, and taking them away from other nations, including our own. China is now marketing a substance in the US called sepiolite[1] asbestos, a deadly form of asbestos, that is composed of a mineral that is not on the American list of regulated asbestos minerals, and so considered a legal asbestos substitute, for all kinds of applications, and in particular for brake linings, where illegal forms of asbestos were formerly used. The "consumer" assumes they are being protected from this import of Chinese toxic substances. They are not. I happen to know where, in these United States, there are deposits of sepiolite asbestos of higher commercial grade than any of the Chinese imports. I tell no one, because I have a

---

[1] .In one study by intrapleural injection to rats, sepiolite from China (fibre length, 1-100 μm), in its asbestos form induced pleural mesotheliomas, a cancer of the pleura that is almost invariably fatal, and is considered to indicate asbestos exposure. Mesothelioma is related to length of fibers, and there has been confusion between the commonly used non-asbestos variety of sepiolite called meerschaum, used as an absorbent of pet wastes, oil, and grease, and for carved items such as pipes, which has not been found to cause mesothelioma. (Source: International Association for Research on Cancer—Summaries & Evaluations—Sepiolite. http://www.inchem.org/)

conscience. What does China have? Psychopathic usury. Is this what we want for our children?

The practice of usury was prohibited in ancient civilizations, and there are vestigial traces of the demise of great civilizations that have fallen as a result of ignoring this prohibition. While this stigma was quite strong and the attendant prohibitions strictly enforced in the ancient world, the underlying rationale has gradually been forgotten, until today the very meaning of the word has been obscured, with "usury" connoting "excessive interest" in modern parlance.

Perhaps the most coherent exposition of the nature of usury is to be found in the oral tradition of the ancient Jews, as set down in the *Midrash*. There we read that usury is the vilest of all vices, encompassing within itself all other abominations. While even the blackest of sinners will have an angelic advocate to plead for them in the Last Judgment, this is not so for the usurer, for whom no one will come forward to speak a word in their defense. According to the *Midrash*, usurers are even excluded from the general Resurrection of the dead at the end of time.

How did the ancients justify such a severe view of a practice that permeates everyday life in the modern world? The ancients apparently knew something about the long-term consequences of usury that we may be destined to relearn . . . the hard way. The ancient Jews likened the consequences of usury to *neschek*, the bite of a serpent. The snake is not alarming or threatening in its approach, but subtle and unnoticed. Its bite initially is but a minor discomfort, and the victim obliviously carries on while the deadly venom spreads through his body. Just as *neschek* slowly but inevitably poisons the body of an individual, so does usury subtly but surely poison mankind's social body, so that society's productive capacities become instruments of impoverishment, injustice, oppression, violence, and war. The very processes meant to expand and sustain life are perverted to promote death. Culture ceases to be an avenue of self-expression and fulfillment and becomes instead a channel of indoctrination and conformity.

Usury means that the mere fact that I have money entitles me to have more money. Money is meant to be a measure of value, but in the practice of usury, money is created out of nothing. The usurer produces nothing of value, and his money, being lifeless, lacks the inherent capacity to augment or reproduce itself. Then where does the money come from to pay the interest on debt? Since it cannot come from new value, it must come again from nothing, which is to say, from new debt. So usury is essentially a type of Ponzi scheme. A Ponzi scheme is a fraudulent investment practice in which the money paid by investors is fundamentally stolen as the investments they make represent no actual wealth, thus making money out of nothing. As soon as the flow of credit stops, the debtors must inevitably default en masse, because no real value has been created upon which to support their interest payments.

This explains why every economic system based on usury has experienced periodic financial crises, in which the fonts of credit suddenly seize up, debtors default, banks fail, and money becomes suddenly scarce. Society's productive resources lie idle while human needs go unmet. This recurring crisis syndrome is inevitable because the economy's ability to absorb new debt is not infinite, and when the limit is reached, the flow of credit must cease, bringing the Ponzi scheme to an abrupt halt.

In the world of classical economics, these recurring and worsening cycles of financial crises would ultimately lead to the undoing of the usury-based systems. But beginning in the twentieth century, a new phase of usury developed, known as "leveraging." The financial elite learned that the creation of illusory money had applications beyond merely extracting wealth from debtors. It could also be used to buy productive assets and suck the wealth out of them too. Thus was born the age of the "leveraged buyout." This is what is meant in Eli (5:7): "The time will soon come when you will gain no profits from the markets of loans, and your wealth will be taken by the very few." This time is fast approaching, as leveraged buyouts leave a skeleton behind as they suck the wealth out of productive assets that they consume.

Leveraged corporate buyouts are sometimes used to purchase a traditional corporation, break it into operational pieces, and then sell these pieces separately at huge profit. A group of corporate "raiders," in one instance, used credit "leverage" to buyout a Fortune 500 chemical company. The idea was to make the company appear to be more profitable, in the short term at least, thereby boosting the stock price long enough for the raiders to cash in their stock options and move on to the next corporate target, leaving the hollowed out carcass of the raided company behind them.

Before the usurers took over, the chemical company had been run in a traditional way, with the aims of satisfying customers, offering good value, expanding production and market share. All these priorities were reversed by the raiders. Managers who understood production were let go and replaced by accountants. The company's funds held in reserve for maintenance and upgrade of its chemical plants were redesignated as "profits" in order to juice up reported earnings. After a few years of this, many plants had to be shut down and their employees laid off. But even the plant closings were converted to book "profits" by the bean-counters' manipulating the depreciation accounts. As for the company's customers, the operative rule was to give them "less for more," always pushing for price increases, even if that meant losing market share.

At the same time, the so-called Reagan Revolution had turned the Federal government into an active accomplice of the corporate raiders. Monetary policy was used to drive up interest rates rapidly and give a sudden boost to the value of the US dollar. These monetary policies left America's manufacturing industries unable to compete with cheaper foreign goods and made them easy targets for the raiders. The Reagan administration also partnered with the usurers in a nationwide union-busting campaign, so that an ever-increasing share of corporate earnings could be diverted from productive workers to parasitic financiers.

Chapter Five

The Consequences Of Usury

While most of America's manufacturing base was being hollowed out and/or bought up by foreigners, the one sector that was expanding was the so-called defense industries. As the usurers progressively destroyed America's ability to dominate the world economically, it became all the more imperative for her to dominate militarily. In place of Adam Smith's "invisible hand," the United States would increasingly rely on the "visible fist" of military might. But the shift toward military production came at a time when the actual "threats" to US hegemony were disappearing, especially with the rapid decline and fall of the Soviet empire in the last '80s and early '90s.

To ensure ever-expanding markets for its military hardware, America needed to embark upon a policy of unending warfare and had to create an enemy to replace the now-defunct Red Menace (communism). When a nation desperately wants to launch a war, one way it can justify doing so is to launch a false flag attack on itself, making it appear to be the work of a foreign enemy. America's own history offers several precedents of such false flag operations, from the sinking of the battleship Maine on the eve of the Spanish-American War, to the Gulf of Tonkin incidents at the outset of the Vietnam War. In 1962, the CIA formulated a plan called Operation Northwoods, in which a series of terrorist attacks would be carried out within the US to justify an invasion of Cuba. President Kennedy at the time refused to authorize this false flag operation. A year later, he was dead. This was a lesson apparently not lost on George W. Bush, who did not dare to oppose the false flag operation that unfolded on September 11, 2001.

And so we see that the slow-acting venom of usury inexorably transforms the government itself from a protector and guardian of the weak and vulnerable to the ally and promoter of a tiny predatory elite, the "very few" mentioned in *Eli*. The wealth of a small group of people now exceeds the combined wealth of half of the American population. This systemic social poison of usury also diverts the economic sectors from production responsive to human needs to pure unbridled plunder.

In his *Inferno*, Dante symbolically represents the development of usury as beginning with near-fraud and ultimately descending into outright fraud. And this is the ugly face of usury that is now emerging in the twenty-first century. Usury begins by demanding value in transactions where nothing of value is given. It then proceeds, by usurious "leverage," to cannibalize productive businesses so that they too become parasitic and predatory, seeking commercial advantage not by fair trade, but by bilking their customers and cheating their employees. Under the domination of usurers, the goal of business is no longer to provide something of value, but to minimize the value furnished to customers and, if possible, eliminate it entirely.

This has now become the very basis of the health-insurance industry, which cover the insured by "capitation," meaning that they bid on a contract by the "head" (thus the term "decapitation"), provide as little service as possible, and extract the wealth from the benefits above costs provided per "head." The physician is then denigrated from the oath of a noble profession, one that used to be considered a calling, to a paid employee of the insurance industry. The industry judges the physician, not by his or her work, but by his or her ability to serve the maximum number of "clients," formerly known as patients, in as short of period of time as possible, so as to obtain "maximum utilization" of the physician. The work becomes meaningless, and the physician is driven into a frenzied pace, the object being to get the "client" in and out as quickly as possible, and not to provide effective, much less compassionate, care. This decreases the utilization of industry money by physicians, as profit is benefits minus utilization.

The insurance industry, in their lust for profits by usury, violates the physician-patient relationship, and turns it into a provider-client relationship, much to the detriment of the patient. The physician must "utilize" as little of the money paid in capitation as possible, and it on this basis that the physician is valued. However, this is not the end of it. The physician, who understands the principles and facts that govern medical practice and the standards of medical care, is replaced by lower-order professionals that do not, but who are paid far less money. These are the physician assistants, nurse practitioners, and other technicians, who are supposedly supervised under the medical license of the physician. However, all this supervision actually involves is a series of quick signatures, supposed validating the technicians unlicensed practice of medicine. To actually supervise these technicians would be an increase in utilization of the highly paid services of the physician, so they never actually do so, thereby introducing the practice of medicine without a license to an unwitting "client" or "consumer of services." As a direct result of usury, we have gone, in the span of twenty years, from the hallowed oath of a noble profession to the status of the physician as "provider" for "consumers," and the services of the physician have become a product that the "consumer" pays to the usurers of the insurance industry in return for profit—money making money out of nothing by keeping costs well under "utilization."

At this point, the physician realizes that he or she can "contract" with the usurers of the insurance industry, as well as the government agencies, providing services under the principles of usury, and yielding extraordinary profits. So the physician becomes a usurer. He or she performs the duties of the "contract" in as cursory a manner as possible, and the medical license allows the physician to purchase the services of unlicensed medical technicians, and create money out of nothing by charging for the technicians services as if they were actually supervising them. Layer upon layer of usury is built, each extracting more money out of the benefits or contracts to government paid under "capitation." People suffer, people die, the standard of care of the medical profession no longer is under the control of that profession, but is manipulated by the usurers in order make as much money as possible. The cost of health care increases all along the way, as of course money cannot be made out of nothing, while the insurance industry looks the other way as the contracts provided by capitation are stolen by the new physician-entrepreneur.

The profession of the true practice of medicine, with its fine tradition, has become a mushrooming Ponzi scheme, with services on paper that do not actually exist, and it will get much worse. The American Health Care Bill, sold originally to the public under the guise of the "public option" will require all Americans buy health insurance—including those who are sinking deeper and deeper into poverty and increasing being left no option but to live in tents, are left no option but to buy insurance using credit—paying into the usurers pockets on both sides. Many will, obviously, default of these loans, leading to more income for the usurers. The bill is the medical industry usurers Trojan Horse in its efforts to make medical care a commodity bearing interest, rather than a service to patients who are "consumers" of that commodity. The bill is, in fact, a huge Ponzi scheme, dictated to "representatives of the people" by their corporate bosses, high-level usurers in a never-ending quest for new markets.

Now, for what remains of the medical profession in the grand and noble traditions of the past, there is no option but to buy into a system of medical care that gives negative value to dedication, commitment, service, and practice of any reasonable standard of care. The outcomes of patient care have come to mean nothing, and the proper practice of medicine has become synonymous with overutilization and loss of prophets. Profits are based on providing less health care to *customers* or *consumers* while charging higher premiums to do it. The promise of national health care is overridden by the industries quest for profits by usury. Insurers vie for their slice of the pie with the businesses of hospitals and pharmaceutical companies, and with the new physician-entrepreneurs, some of whom are raking in millions of dollars per year, unbeknownst to the public, and not providing services as contracted.

I recently worked for a physician entrepreneur who was profiting enormously through contracting with the day schools that government provides for children and adolescents with mental disorders. I witnessed the abuse of children and adolescents with mental disorders such as autistic disorder and mental retardation as a form of discipline. Much of the staff continually yelled at the students in an unwarranted fashion. The practices they use for "treating" these young people are doing them much more harm than good, and the government seems to look the other way as these children and adolescents are abused and used as instruments for usurious profiteers as they take government money but do not render commensurate services. The form of therapy employed is called *behavioral therapy* or *behavior modification*. This form of therapy is generally denounced by the psychiatric profession since, even in behavioral therapy, reward is much more effective than punishment, because it is a system of mind control, and because it traumatizes those being punished. The overwhelmed autistic child is physically restrained and, in some cases, assaulted upon minimal provocation, and placed in padded cells in order that they may learn their lesson. Again, services that are not provided under any reasonable standard of care so that the physicians who are contracted can rake in large profits against the money they are paid and hire underling physicians who they, again, require to work at a frenzied pace so as to decrease utilization. The same principle is at work in American higher education, where obscenely high fees are extracted even as academic rigor is cast aside.

Like all parasites, however, usurers must ultimately fall victim to their own success. Once having cannibalized a society's productive base and left it mired in debt, what can be left to feed the Ponzi machine? As we approach closer to the end of the age of usury, there is truly only one thing left to "sell," and that is debt itself. And this is where, just as Dante foresaw, the usurers must come out from the shadows of quasi-fraud into the open daylight of outright fraud. Worthless subprime debts, high-risk debts that are bound to default, are bundled into derivatives, for which the rating agencies are forced to issue AAA approval. Not content with peddling worthless debt instruments, the usurers then go out and purchase insurance policies—called *credit default swaps*—betting that these same debts will default. This is no different from selling someone a car and then wagering that the car will fall apart.

At this juncture, the degree of inequity engendered by usury becomes almost surreal. When the inevitable mass default of the subprime lenders occurs, driving the insurers on the credit default swaps into insolvency, as happened to AIG (American Insurance Group) in 2008.

AIG is and American insurance corporation that was listed on the Dow Jones Industrials Average (DJIA) from April 8, 2004, to September 22, 2008. In 2011 it was listed in the Forbes Fortune Global 2000 list as the twenty-ninth largest public corporation in the world. It has offices in New York, London, Paris, and Hong Kong, so it is really not an American corporation, but part of the international financial sector with investments throughout the world. In September of 2008, it suffered a liquidity crisis, meaning that it was unable to sell its stocks without a loss of value, which would mean that the stock was no longer a viable investment on usury and that the corporation would essentially have to default on the debt to investors. It was considered "too big to fail" and taken off the DJIA. Such actions were taken in order to inflate the DJIA and disguise would was truly an economic collapse. The Federal Reserve issued available assets of $182.5 billion to AIG, which then become a part of the spiralling increase in the national debt. Similar actions were taken with other corporations.

The usurers are actually able to call upon their friends in the government to use taxpayer money to assure that they receive the full payoff on their bets—100 cents on the dollar, no less! Not only does the swindler escape jail, but the government underwrites the full payoff on his illegal wagers.

In the final death throes of usury, then, the usurers raid the public treasury and drag the government itself into the abyss of insolvency in order to keep their Ponzi scheme running. Over the past several decades, this scenario has repeated itself in dozens of other countries, with the same basic outcome. The cabal of creditors—the same usurers who raided the public treasury and drove it into insolvency to bail out their bad loans—demand *austerity measures*, a euphemism for expropriating the pension and health insurance funds paid into by working people and dismantling all regulations which in any way restrain the plunder of the predatory elite.

In the special case of America, however, this scenario becomes even uglier. When the vultures attack a foreign currency, as they did the Mexican peso in the '90s, they collapse the economy of a single country. But the US dollar serves as the reserve currency of the entire world, so when it collapses it's a case of "ashes, ashes, all fall down." At the same time as the world races toward that economic Armageddon, it simultaneously races toward the precipice of an unprecedented environmental catastrophe, brought on by a half a century of government abdication of its protective function as it fell captive to the short-term interests of a tiny elite.

Chapter Six

The Ends Of Usury

The ultimate consequence of an economy which tolerates usury is an economy dominated by usury and an economy that must ultimately collapse under the weight of debt. When economies collapse, history teaches us that the civilizations those economies support often collapse as well. This is why *Eli* warns that the suffering of the times would continue and deepen if the usury were to continue. Now we are talking about not just a local or regional civilization, but a world civilization, imploding and at the same time global climate has been pushed by inaction and indifference into a chaotic mode, featuring increasingly violent extremes of temperature, winds and precipitation.

The reign of usury has corrupted everything, bringing with it every conceivably abomination, as the ancient Jews knew it would. It has even corrupted science, suborning certain "scientists" to "dispute" such fundamental truths as human-caused climate change and biological evolution. The ultimate irony may be that their reign of folly produces a deadly convergence of the very truths they would deny—an evolutionary bottleneck of mass extinction that may soon threaten the survival of the human species.

The greatest threat to the extinction of humans is nuclear war. America is now updating its nuclear weapons arsenal and planting nuclear missiles in strategic positions, such as the border of Russia, which still has a nuclear arsenal and system of delivery, which, in and of itself, if deployed in full, could lead to the murder of the entire population of the planet. The social justice section of *Eli*, if followed, would not permit even the existence of such weapons, since it forbids all such actions of indiscriminate killing and places the onus of responsibility for the very existence of such weapons to every one of us to the extent that we have not achieved worldwide prohibition with stiff consequences for the manufacture of such a weapon.

Our nuclear war plan is very secretive and highly classified, but there is some reliable information provided by the Federation of American Scientists, based on a briefing held in 2008 (Kristenson 2010):

> For each adversary a range of strike options have been designed to provide the National Command Authority with responses varying in size and objectives based on the circumstances. The nuclear options consist of Emergency Response Options (ERO), Selective Attack Options (SAO), Basic Attack Options (BAO), and Directed/Adaptive Planning Capability (DPO/APO) options. The size of the options range from hundreds of warheads in preplanned options that take months to modify to a few warheads in adaptive options for crisis scenarios that can be drawn up or changed within a few hours . . .
>
> . . . the strategic war plan includes a family of nuclear and non-nuclear strike plans directed against six potential adversaries. This apparently includes China, Iran, North Korea, Russia, Syria, and a 9/11-type scenario. Three of these adversaries do not have nuclear weapons and two are NPT signatories . . .

China, one of the nations targeted by these plans, is now reaching nuclear capabilities such that they too could soon launch an arsenal of weapons that could lead to human extinction (Kristenson 2011):

Two of China's new Jin-class nuclear ballistic missile submarines have sailed to the Xiaopingdao naval base near Dalian, a naval base used to outfit submarines for ballistic missile flight tests. The arrival raises the obvious question if the Jin-class is finally reaching a point of operational readiness where it can do what it was designed for: launching nuclear long-range ballistic missiles.

It has been said by an expert on petroleum and the economy that every war, skirmish, etc., is about petroleum. This is the commodity that the usurers need so desperately to keep the machine of continuous exponential growth of production going. In the original Ponzi scheme (1910), there was a pyramid-type structure whereby each investor had to recruit more investors, and these recruits had to recruit more investors, such that a pyramid structure was created that, of course, could not last very long, only for a period of months. The current Ponzi schemes, as well as the world economy itself, are based on similar structures, such that the markets must always grow exponentially, and this is how the DJIA behaved from 1897 to 1999. Such was the economic setting in 1999, when *Eli* was revealed. However, such growth could not continue and, thus, the current economic crisis. We will have more to say on this later. For now, suffice it to say that the key usurers in our global Ponzi scheme are, for the most part, psychopaths, and have such a lust for the petroleum markets that they are not incapable of using nuclear warfare. Their only concern is, by and large, "how much money will I make today."

Chapter Seven

The Call Of Eli

The first line in *Eli* is (1:1) states, **"God has spoken to me, without words, to my heart. He has told me that I am to teach a new faith."** In this verse God announces himself to the prophet Eli. The fact that God has chosen to spoke to Eli attests to the prophetic nature of the work. The *Book* is a revealed sacred text, and not the effort of the prophet him or herself.

Although Eli remains anonymous throughout, there are certain statements that can be given a more direct meaning based on further and unpublished information regarding the prophecy. We know that the initial calling, which is the subject of *Eli* (1:1) occurred after an ordinary dinner, and as Eli was aware of the time when the call was given, we know that the call occurred at which would have begun about 6:45 PM Pacific time. We also know that it was the day after a total eclipse of the moon, in 1996, which means it occurred on September 27, 1996.

At that time, Eli sat in a comfortable living room chair. He had had an ordinary day, ate an ordinary meal, and was not under the influence of alcohol or any other substances. The call came suddenly, lasted about thirty minutes, then faded. The call was experienced as very real, could be felt as if by the senses, yet seemed quite ordinary, with no feeling of any other change in reality or the nature of experience. It was experienced as quite ordinary, yet the presence of God was much deeper than the mere awareness of God. Eli experienced God coming to him in the world around him and through his deepest thoughts and feelings, coming from the heart rather than the mind. Eli felt this coming from the realm of experience that is beyond words, leaving the wordless and nameless God to speak It's own truth.

Eli also experienced, during this time, that God had always spoken wordlessly to all the prophets before him, and that the rendering in words was a process of translation of feeling into concepts. This distinguishes Eli from other Western scriptures, in that there is a translation of sorts, which could be prone to error. So Eli does not claim to be channeling the Word of God, but simply writing to the best of his ability what he has been given to understand. As such, the infallibility of scripture brought into Western religions is specifically denied in *Eli*.

The idea of infallibility has been a stumbling block of revealed sacred literature since humans first speculated on the nature of reality. The author does not wish *Eli* to fall into this trap. In all my readings of sacred or revealed texts, I have always found some flaw, and most often have encountered notions that were either outdated or false. The *Bhagavad Gita*, the most sublime of sacred texts, implicitly supports the caste system of India. The writings of Bahá'u'lláh, more than a century ago, have a great deal of merit, but mention the idea that copper, if kept for a certain duration, would turn into gold, which is patently false. Because of the claim of infallibility, when a falsehood is found, the tendency is to reject the entire document. Baha'u'llah, in taking the position of infallibility, loses creditability. Baha'u'llah, who followed from the Islamic tradition, also lifted the Muslim prohibition of usury, which is entirely contrary to the purpose *Eli*. Prophets are people, they are not oracles. Similarly, I find it quite difficult to believe that Jesus was born of a virgin and never sinned, yet I recognize the profound truth of much of what he said.

Is there anything false in the sayings of Christ? This is hard to know since we have no true record of the sayings of Christ. Gautama may come closest to this standard of truth, but we also know little of what he said, and we do know he had an earthly life prior to his enlightenment in the course of which he certainly was not infallible. In the same fashion, *Eli* is not something that fell from the sky onto Eli's lap, as is claimed by other prophetic works, but included elements of reason and science without apology.

It is thus that *Eli* writes (1:1) that God had spoken to him without words. The language of the heart has no words, only feelings. God gave Eli to know that he was speaking through his innermost thoughts, as the veil that obscures the Soul had been lifted, and that this was God's way of communicating with all prophets of former times. Eli, shortly after the beginning of the calling, was given a mission, but it was a wordless mission that cannot be repeated. Later in same verse, *Eli* announces that God has called him to teach a new faith. This new faith sets the tone for the entire *Book*. The faith of *Eli* included biblical elements and elements of other sacred texts, but is not a continuation or elaboration on any existing faith. By making this proclamation of a new faith, Eli is separating this faith as coming directly from God, through no intermediary or intermediaries. It was not channeled through any entity.

However, the fact remains that Eli, when he inquired of God, was told that the God calling him was the God of Abraham. This was puzzling, as Eli was neither a Jew or particularly versed or even interested in Jewish theology. The calling was from the same God in the biblical account of the burning bush and Moses (Exod. 3: 4-6): "God called unto him out of the midst of the bush and said, Moses, Moses. 'And he said, Here am I.' . . . Moreover, he said 'I am the God of thy father, the God of Abraham, the God of Isaac, and the God of Jacob.'" The Hebrew word used for God in this passage is Elohim, the Creator of Genesis. So in a sense, Eli was called into the Abrahamic tradition, not the Christian one.

When Eli inquired as to why he was not being called by Jesus or Mary, he was given to know that Jesus was neither the Son of God or God, and that Mary was not the Mother of God. He searched his Soul and only found the God of Abraham, even as he tried to conjure up Jesus or Mary. They were not there. Eli was given to know that the calling involved his knowledge of science and religion.

Chapter Eight

The "I" And The "Not I"

Eli (1:2) states, **"My father gave me the name Eli. My legal name is not important. My person is not part of the teaching."** This verse announces the identity of Eli. The name Eli was given to him by his actual, earthly father. His teaching that his legal name is not important, and that his person is not part of the teaching actually reflects a much-deeper truth. The prophets of prior religions had given names, so why is it that Eli is withholding his? Is it from fear, or from a need to disassociate himself from the teaching? Is it that Eli did not feel he was the agent conveying the teaching but was coming from some other, imagined being or alter ego? Both conjectures are incorrect. The actual meaning is to be found in the wordless nature of the teaching. By giving himself a personal name, John Smith, for example, he would be identifying himself in terms of his own personality, situation, occupation, biography, and personal history. To do so would be to poison or corrupt the teaching with concepts and predicates involving his own particular, individual, separate self, existing in the normal tenses of past, present, and future.

Eli, while drawing from some of the wisdom of Jesus that is embodied in Christianity, makes a very sharp break here from the personalized Christian teaching of an "Avatar," "Son of God," "Only begotten Son," etc. Christians uniformly believe that Jesus was and is the incarnate God. The Qur'an of Islam is absolutely correct to state that it is blasphemy and anathema to state that God or Allah had a son. God is the one spiritual being and takes no such role the material world, as the gods do in pagan religions, or in the half-god, half-man myth of Hercules.

Aldous Huxley (1970), in *The Perennial Philosophy*, was quite blunt and explicit about the poisoning of Christianity by the Avatar doctrine, which gives Jesus a particular and unique identity as the Only Begotten Son, of God, and as being one-third of the Trinity that is necessary for the very existence of God. Huxley (50-51) writes,

> Because Christians believed that there had been only one Avatar, Christian history has been disgraced by more and bloodier crusades, interdenominational wars, persecutions and proselytizing imperialism than has the history of Hinduism or Buddhism. Absurd and idolatrous doctrines, affirming the quasi-divine nature of sovereign states and their rulers, have led oriental, no less than Western, peoples into innumerable political wars; but because they have not believed in an exclusive revelation at one sole instant in time, or in the quasi-divinity of an ecclesiastical organization, oriental people have kept remarkably clear of the mass murder for religion's sake, which has been so dreadfully frequent in Christiandom. And while, in this important respect, the level of public morality has been lower in the West than in the East, the levels of exceptional sanctity and of ordinary individual morality have not, so far as one can judge from the available evidence, been any higher.

Huxley's (1970) commentary is too deep to capture in this text. Huxley points out that the dichotomy of the half-human, half-God identity of Jesus is a contradiction of terms since the half-human would be the "I," a particularly human life, or ego, while the half-God would be the "not I," or Divine Self. Huxley (1970: 48) wrote, for example, that "to talk, as so many liberal churchman now do, of worshipping the 'personality of

Jesus,' is an absurdity." If Huxley were alive now he would see this cult of personality in a much more extreme form, where one essentially gives his or her life to a charismatic Christ who then becomes his or her personal savior. Christ then assumes the role of the individual alter ego, elevated to the status of God. Individuals who maintain this doctrine are now usurers, as we will discuss later, and promoters of human suffering, hunger, disease, warfare, death, starvation, and many other kinds of sin and inequity. How is it possible for a religion to have gone so far astray, as to worship the "I," the "particular ego," or "alter ego," which is none other than Lucifer or Satan in a meta-language of Judeo-Christianity and of the hidden time or dreamtime?

The current evangelical school of right-wing Christians totally rejects the Higher Criticism of fundamentalism and, thus, accepts every word of the *Bible*, in particular the *New Testament*, as the Word of God, without question, despite the many inconsistencies even in a strict literal and fundamentalist interpretation of the *New Testament*. In doing so, they reject all forms of scholarly and logical analysis, which is apparent in both their religions and their sciences, both of which are equally and demonstrable false. Having a personal relationship between the "I," or alter ego as God (apotheosis of the ego, elevation of the ego to the status of God), they are forgiven for the most heinous of crimes and practices, all the while loving the Lord. It is these people who have, for the most part, fashioned the desperation and calamity that are the principle foci of *Eli*.

Huxley (1944) wrote prior to the discovery of *The Gospel of Thomas* in the *Nag Hammadi Library* in Egypt in 1945, and well before the first English translation in 1959, but he would have undoubtedly found some resolution of the contradiction or the unity in God of the "I," the particular ego, and "not I" Divine Self, but no such a treatise was available at the time of his classic work, forcing him to struggle with this oxymoron without clear and authoritative biblical sources. So we must critically examine the biblical sources and manuscripts.

The arguments in favor of considering the *Gospel of Thomas* a clear and authoritative biblical source have been outlined in great detail by literary analyses of the books of the New Testament and the relation they bear to one another. Such analysis has been one of the subjects of the Higher Criticism, which includes the scholarship of Benedict Spinoza in the seventeenth century.

Baruh Spinoza (1632-1677) was a Dutch-Jewish philosopher who is said have laid the foundation of the Enlightenment and of the Higher Criticism. He was an important figure in growth of the rationalist school of philosophy, and has been credited with the conception of panentheism, an important doctrine of process theology closely related to the metaphysical doctrine of panexperientialism. He was a determinist, a philosophy rejected in *Eli*. It is written of his criticism:

> Spinoza denies the immortality of the soul; strongly rejects the notion of a providential God—the God of Abraham, Isaac and Jacob . . .
>
> Accessed 6/12/11: http://en.wikipedia.org/wiki/Baruch_Spinoza

These ideas are also rejected in *Eli*, which upholds the immortality of the soul in the hidden time, which we will address later. Similarly, the providence of God, the God of Abraham in the Judeo-Christian-Moslem traditions, is strongly upheld, and is, in fact, central to the new science and the new faith. However, the principles of the criticism are, to some extent, accepted. The providence of God is a major theme that is endorsed in *Eli*.

Spinoza had a great influence on Albert Einstein, reflected in many of his ideas both within and outside physics. When faced with the uncertainty inherent in the new field of quantum theory, he made is famous statement that God does not play dice, reflective of the determinism of Spinoza. Einstein's central purpose, beyond his contributions to science, was to know the Mind of God, as Hawking also pretended to do prior to rejecting God completely and very publically as something that he no longer needed in his new theories. This element in his popular book was highly publicized, and was, in no small part, a big factor in its success on the book market.

Regarding the influence of Spinoza on Einstein, an important element in the histories of science and religion, it has been said,

> The philosopher whom Einstein admired most was Baruch (later, Benedictus) Spinoza, . . . Einstein was most influenced by Spinoza's thesis of an unrestricted determinism and the belief in the existence of a superior intelligence that reveals itself in the harmony and beauty of nature. (*www.lorentz. leidenuniv.nl/history/Einsteins_poem/Spinoza.html*, 6/12/11)

In the higher criticism of biblical scholarship, the most fundamental source of the Gospel was *Mark*, which was then used to construct the other two synoptic gospels, *Mathew* and *Luke*. The earliest surviving Gospel text is the Ryland's Library Papyrus P52, or St John's fragment, which is a small passage that recounts the dialogue with Pilate, and probably dates around 125 CE, closely matches the existing biblical *John*, and evidencing the existence of *John* at this early date. However, this fragment seems to shed no light on the authenticity of *John*. This has been an important contention of John in the Higher Criticism, as some of the more conservative theologians have pointed toward the fragment as proof of the authenticity of the entire Gospel. Most scholars, however, do not feel that either *John* or *Revelation* is an authentic text written by John himself. In terms of antiquity, after this, there is a *Logion* of the *Gospel of Thomas* dating about 150 CE. Paul was a Hebrew zealot who persecuted the followers of Jesus prior to his conversion, and there is no real independent, scholarly evidence for the Pauline doctrine and school as being anything other than perhaps inspired by the historical Jesus, and there is evidence that much of Paul's inspirational quality was lifted from the *Gospel of Barn*abus. The current version of *Barnabus* may not be authentic, as some claim it was written in order to support Islam. In this version, Jesus flatly denies that he is the Son of God, and, if this is true, then there was a reason for the church to reject it from its canon, and to order the burning of all the Gospels written in Hebrew, such that all that remains is the translations into Greek, which clouds the content in certain ways, such as the translation of the hidden time, which was extirpated in translation. The Greek translations also introduced obvious elements of Greek philosophy, such as the *logos*, which is translated into English as the Word. Although the idea of the *logos* is appealing, the doctrine that the Word was with God and the Word was God, and that the Word was made flesh in Jesus, deifying Jesus, has obvious predicates in Greek idealism and mythology, and thereby the Christian religions were poisoned by Greco-Roman mythology.

Scholars, examining the authenticity of the Gospel literature, have constructed a *"Q" Gospel*, relying mostly on the *Logia* of *Mark*. It contains those elements that are most consistent across the Gospels, especially the *Gospel of Thomas* found in 1945, although here too *Thomas* is likely corrupted by its Syrian forbearers. The *Letters of Luke* were strongly critical of Paul for what Luke perceived as an unwarranted reversion back to elements of Judaism that did not seem to be in the same spirit as the teachings of Jesus. Nonetheless, Christianity was to become a kind of Paulism, and although available, the *Letter of Luke*, which seem authentic, are not included in the *Bible* and have become obscure and virtually unknown as they are contrary to the doctrines of Paulism.

What is particularly troublesome in Paul's writings are his teachings about women. There is some contradiction in the existing texts as to what the relative attitude toward women of Jesus might have been. However, his relationship with Mary Magdalene seems to contradict the misogyny of Paulism, and what seems to ring true is the belief that Jesus actually taught that those who enter the kingdom must achieve unification of the male and female types, being, in a sense, a single unity. This is expressed in the *Thomas* (22):

> When you **make the two into one**, and when you make the inner like the outer and the outer like the inner, and the upper like the lower, and when you make **male and female into a single one**, so that the male will not be male nor the female be female, . . . then you will enter [the kingdom]. (bold font added)

The school of Thomas, one of three in early Christianity (with the Johnian and Pauline), was fundamentally driven into extinction, and the texts were apparently destroyed. What survived of *Thomas* were the Logia in Greek. Interesting passages from the *Logia*, for our purposes, are *Logia* 14: "I am from the undivided," which seems to reflect the dissociation of Self and alter-ego, which we discussed earlier, indicating that he was as humans were in former times, and suggesting that he was appealing for a return of the Species Mind to its former state, as is explicit in *Eli*. In *Logia* 22 it is written, "Jesus saw some babies nursing. He said to his disciples, these nursing babies are like those who enter the (Father's) domain." This, again, appeals to the status of the human in society prior to the trauma that inaugurated the divided Species Mind. Such is the undivided state, where self and world, individual and other, are so conditioned into the infant and child, and the undivided so violated, that the undivided does not come into consciousness but remains in the unconscious and in the eternal or hidden time. The alter ego and its world are illusions, which, in the new faith are lost in the hidden time. The divisions occur when the ego comes to create a world, which is not the kingdom, and so has no place in the kingdom.

So it is that we must go back to this undivided state—undivided from God by the ascension of the alter ego, the master of this world, which, by definition, is entirely material. Materialism then becomes a precondition of growth within the culture, where who we are is defined by our material possessions and material gains, and people are like straw dogs, stripped of any intrinsic value, and thus come to lose the natural ecstasy that is our birthright and is, in fact, the meaning of Baptism of the Holy Spirit. The ego/material world division is an illusion that our primitive ancestors, infants, and children, and other animals did or do not have. This is the meaning of the passage in Leviticus, paraphrased, "Do not hand your children over though the fire to Moloch." This is echoed by Allan Ginsberg in *Howl*: "Moloch! Who frightened me out of my natural ecstasy," and Mallarme, "The infant abdicates its ecstasy." This is how we trade our birthright for a pound of flesh.

In view of the wealth of other sayings attributed to Jesus, it is interesting that Alfred North Whitehead, in *Religion in the Making* (1927), cites the *Logion*, "Cleave the wood and I am there." This is probably because of its panentheistic meaning, God inside everything or in every relation. Panenthesism later became a pillar of process theology, especially in the work of Charles Hartshorne, Whitehead's student, and John Cobb, Hartshorne's student. The author, in turn, has informally been a student of Cobb, and this has been his philosophical orientation.

It is interesting with regard to the "Cleave the wood" passage in the Greek *Logia* of *Thomas*, that a similar notion appears in the *Qur'an* (Shakir translation, 34:3):

> And those who disbelieve say: The hour shall not come upon us. Say: Yea! by my Lord, the Knower of the unseen, it shall certainly come upon you; **not the weight of an atom becomes absent from Him, in the heavens or in the earth**, and neither less than that nor greater, but (all) is in a clear book. (Bold italics added)

The doctrines of omniscience and omnipresent—panentheism—seem to run through a range of traditions, the earmark of a true doctrine.

The perennial wisdom seems to be there, in the various texts, and much of it is quite similar—this is the meaning of a later passage we will discuss from *Eli*. However, as to the historicity of Christianity, we can say very little. The *Gospel of Thomas* was in the Coptic language and appears to have originated from Syria, but there are numerous passages that match the preexisting *Logia of Thomas*, so its authenticity is accounted by most scholars of the Higher Criticism to be high relative to the other Gospels, but it too is now suppressed and unrecognized by any Christian Church, to our knowledge. The language is Jesus in *Thomas* is said to be associational, which would seem to fit the associational logic of the unconscious, as is supported by his reported sayings about babies and little children with respect to the kingdom.

The *Gospel of Thomas* probably predated the synoptic Gospels, and is simply a group of sayings without any real historical or narrative content. Rather than grace and works, the *Gospel of Thomas* emphasized insight and, in direct contradiction with later teachings that "there is no way to the Father except through me," taught a religion based on self-knowledge, insight, self-knowledge, and empowerment over one's own life. It preached eternal life, but with a different view of time than that with which we are now familiar, and was not truly Gnostic—it just happened to be found together with Gnostic texts. There is nothing of the Son of God doctrine, crucifixion, resurrection, final judgment, or messianic content of the other gospels in the *Gospel of Thomas*.

The *Gospel of Thomas* fell out of the orthodoxy, probably at the end of the fourth century, and the texts were burned and destroyed, becoming extinct around this time. The current Gospel of Thomas was a newly rediscovered in 1945, found with a number of other documents of the Nag Hammadi Library in Egypt and pieced together such as to constitute a viable document of limited English circulation in 1959.

The insight and prescience of Huxley (1944) during the times that he wrote, that is, prior to the rediscovery of the *Gospel of Thomas*, are remarkable. We must look more closely at the situation in Christianity as it existed in his time in order to better see what has gone wrong, why and when and it happened, and perhaps then get some glimpse at how we can avoid and overcome these errors. Huxley (1944) tries to make sense out of the texts of his time by adopting an apologetic attitude of ambivalence (49):

> The biography of a saint or avatar is valuable only insofar as it throws light upon the means by which, in the circumstances of a particular human life, the "I" was purged away so as to make room for the divine "not I." **The authors of the Synoptic Gospels did not choose to write such a biography**, and no amount of textual criticism of ingenious surmise can call it into existence. In the course of the last hundred years an enormous sum of energy [money] has been expended on the attempt to make documents yield more evidence than in fact they contain. However

> regrettable may be **the Synoptics'** lack of interest in biography, and whatever objections may be raised against the theologies of Paul and John [the two orthodox theologies at that time], there can still be no doubt that their **instinct was essentially sound**. Each in his own way wrote about the eternal "not I" of Christ rather than the historical "I"; each in his own way stressed that element of the life of Jesus, in which, because it is more-than-personal, all persons can participate. (bold type and square italics added)

Huxley was an unparalleled genius who saw very deeply into the situation that had become ripe for the discovery of the *Gospel of Thomas*. Yet although the Synoptics (fundamentally Mark) did have have historical content, he apologetically speculates that such historical content as they did have was needed so that all persons can participate. Had he known that there was another theology, which makes no mention whatsoever of the history and life of Jesus Christ, he might not have found the need to apologize for the history in the Synoptics.

Eli purposely avoids the emphasis on historicity, like *Thomas*, and also a gospel compiled by Thomas Jefferson, second American president and author of Bill of Rights, in which he cut all the history out of the Gospels, for all practical purposes, and created his own version of what he considered to be the true statements of Jesus. In a similar manner as was done with the Q. *Eli* clearly states that such historicity, with regard to Eli himself, is unimportant, placing the emphasis quite clearly on the teachings, which are not to be poisoned or diverted by the history and identity of Eli himself.

Thomas Jefferson, who was a self-avowed Christian, objected to certain contents of Christ narrative, and has been condemned for this and labeled a false Christian by evangelical, fundamentalist, and charismatic Christians. The following passage of a letter of Jefferson's spells out his objections:

> "And the day will come when the mystical generation of Jesus, by the supreme being as his father in the womb of a virgin will be classed with the fable of

the generation of Minerva in the brain of Jupiter. But may we hope that the dawn of reason and freedom of thought in these United States will do away with this artificial scaffolding, and restore to us the primitive and genuine doctrines of this most venerated reformer of human errors."

(Letter to John Adams, April 11, 1823)

The restoration of the primitive or original doctrines of Jesus, the most venerated reformer of human errors, is of course anathema to those of the various Christian sects, who would seem to have an interest in perpetuating these errors.

Chapter Nine

The New Faith And The New Science

Verses (1:3,4) state: **Throughout the ages the same wisdom has been taught. Now the language has changed, and truth is given in the language of science.** The idea of a teacher, guru, shaman, prophet, or Messiah is present in a variety of traditions, including Islam, which totally abjures the idea of a Son of God. Judaism predicts a physical Messiah who will usher in an age of peace in the world. The idea of a Messiah is very often linked to ideas of the end of time, the judgment, or similar eschatological (apocalyptic) notions.

In *Eli*, as we will later see, the end of time is seen as the end of this age in time and the coming of the next, thus the need for establishing a new faith and a new science. The fundamentals of love, peace, compassion, benevolence, justice, etc., are present in the foundations of all the major world religions. The belief in a spiritual realm, with or without a material realm, is in all major world religions. Some idea of a life after death is generally present, whether it is in eternity, heaven and hell, or reincarnation. Each has grown in its own culture(s) and time(s), suiting the deep spiritual needs of humans as spiritual creatures. It is not difficult to argue that the similarities are many, more than adequate to overcome the differences, yet people continue to fight, steal, plunder, and do all manner of evil in the name of religion.

Major religious traditions have been poisoned by the corruption of doctrines, and many contain fantastic and mythological ideas that are not suited to our times. *Eli* aims at addressing both of these problems. The solution to these contradictions and corruptions is the subject of a good deal of the *Book*. The fundamental truths must be expressed in the language of science. The current mainstream view of science entails materialism, which cannot be applied to spiritual matters. An idea carries no weight, takes up no time of space, and cannot be made concrete by some representation in the brain. The same applies for spirit. The quantum revolution, by bringing the observer into the determination of the possibilities that exist in the quantum realm, has yet to be incorporated fully into the nature and form of science. It is demonstrably true that a particle, let's say a photon, or particle of light, exists as a cloud of possibilities in terms of space and time, and that it becomes one actuality when observed. This actuality is not predetermined. Bare-bones models of quantum theory tell us nothing of the underlying of reality of nature; it is a theory of knowing, or epistemology, without anything to say about reality, or ontology. What we know or experience of the basic reality, which is quantum, is determined only statistically in the bare-bones theory.

There are many ontologies that can equally apply to the facts of quantum theory, and physics is still in limbo concerning which is correct, if any are. However, quantum theory leads logically to total rejection of classical reality, in that there is no real stuff in the theory, so that idealism or experientialism become once again viable, as does the notion of final causality, and actually suit the theory far better than materialism.

Entities replace objects. There are no little balls of solid matter, as in structure of the atom in terms of protons, neutrons, and electrons. The deeper we look for a material substance, the more it vanishes, and a particle is best defined as a set of relations. Protons and neutrons are complexes of quarks and gluons, constantly changing.

Finality or final cause, a cause in the future exerting an effect on the past, once again enters science in quantum theory. It we were to take a powerful telescope and look at a star a billion light-years away, the position, momentum, spin, and other properties of a single photon of light—visible to the human eye and mind—would be a haze of all its possible states, with no real actuality other than as potential, spread out over a vast space until observed. This is scientific fact. What constitutes an observation is still open to question, and in its effort to avoid the fundamental question, it is now said that the photon, on striking the eye, decoheres into a number of pointer states within the brain. These pointer states are still only potential states of the brain, overlapping one another and producing some set of brain states. Yet in an effort to avoid a quantum ontology having any content beyond materialism, and to remove the observer from its inextricable role in the theory, a theory of natural selection of pointer states has been fashioned, which his no evidence base, and which in purely based on sciences inability to let go of materialistic determinism. However, if these states are truly selected, this violates the statistical symmetry of the bare-bones theory, requiring an operator or function that modifies the statistical symmetry. Natural selection is not an operator, nor can it ever be, as it has not and cannot be expressed in terms of primary variables involved, eigenfunctions and eigenvalues.

The new language for the Coming Age will involve a total confluence and agreement between science and spirituality, or religion. There cannot be two sets of truths, and the idea that there are mutually inconsistent truths in science and religion leads one to except one and reject the other, or to accept both in the absence of any connection between them. It is thus that scientists boldly pronounce that there is no God, as in Dawkins's *God Delusion* and many other popular books, and this infects humanity, or a portion of humanity, with the disease of spiritual darkness, mitigating all spiritual growth and leading to many absurd doctrines within science as it attempts of ban and banish any element of spirituality from science and from the belief systems or its audience(s). The spirit must be dispelled by science by the Lie, that reality is strictly materialistic, and humankind be transformed into People of the Lie—this is the social agenda that virtually rules the massive effort to demean and fragment humankind into isolated alter egos that then can become the creators of their own worlds, without conscience, charity, love, or any of the other values accorded to the spirit or soul.

A truth in science must be a truth in religion, and vice versa. This commentary is a visionary introduction into the new science and the new faith, transcending the division of science and faith. It is necessary that they be united in order for the spiritual progress of our species will not be confused by the elements of superstition that have entered religions and the total inadequacy of current science to lead us out of its own false dogmas. These doctrines are inherited from the prequantum, deterministic doctrine of Pierre Laplace (1749-1827), the so-called Newton of France, who famously said when asked about the role of God in physics, "I have no need for this hypothesis." Galileo and Newton, the most important figures in the development of classical physics, were theists, but given the determinism of classical physics, Newton had to take the retreat position of God as the prime mover, the One who set the whole deterministic process in motion. This is the basis upon which Hawking has rejected God, because his cosmology does not now involve any beginning or end, but a continuous cycle within imaginary time, such that no prime mover is needed. However, the prime mover paradigm is a rather sophomoric way of framing God, not indicative of any true understanding, so Hawking is speaking beyond his reach, as are many others in the current anti-God movement in our so-called science.

The doctrine of the prime mover separated God from all causality outside of the initial push. It is now totally outdated. Others speak of a classical approximation, holding on to the classical era of science, like the flat-earthers who still hold the earth is flat, or the church, which condemned Galileo for upholding the idea that the sun, and not the earth, is the center of the solar system. This strange reversal of roles from dogmatic religion to dogmatic science will not last—all dogmas eventually go by the wayside.

In nature, there is a complex interplay of factors or variables that make outcomes unpredictable in principle, even in the absence of quantum theory. Insignificant events in the past are amplified enormously and unpredictably over time. This is the famous butterfly effect, where a butterfly flap of the wind can result in a hurricane or tornado perhaps ten years in the future. This is the basis of chaos or dynamical systems theory. Here chaos has this simple meaning, and does not imply disorder. There is exquisite order in chaotic systems, of such complexity as to be considered an infinite range of possibilities. The infinity comes in due to the fractal nature of chaotic systems; the complexity and number of possible states continue into smaller and smaller levels of descriptions or discreet states of the system indefinitely.

The universe and the brain are chaotic systems, which are fractal in nature, such that the complexity is at such a level that the line that has been fashioned between the classical and quantum levels of reality is a logically unsupported idea, again, meant to keep the classical foothold on reality. The conflict of religion and science, to the extent that anyone has thought to resolve it, has been a host of baseless speculation and apologetics.

It is popularly believed, even in science circles, that the brain is a kind of computer. The brain is however not algorithmic; it does not have a digital language based on strings of zeros and ones. The brain is not mechanistic like a computer; it is a machine in no sense of the word. It is also not based purely on efficient causation, through which all future events proceed purely from past events. There are formal causes, by which a certain plan is generated by form, or topology, such as the topology of the Soul in its transformations, and final causes, and there are continuous feedback loops in the past, present, and future. Were it not for these kinds of causality, the brain would generate nonsense, not answers. In order to generate a pattern of associational and logical outcomes in the genesis of the mental or brain state, final causation is necessary, and this is where God comes in.

Alfred North Whitehead, the early-twentieth-century philosopher, theologian, and mathematician, in the book *Process and Reality*, declared, "God is the infinite ground of all mentality." It is quite impossible, without the agency of a universal mind or intelligence, for an individual mind, based on the brain, a dynamical or chaotic system, to house either a mind or an intelligence, or any predictable order whatsoever. This would be like taming a hurricane and using it as a computer. It is altogether impossible, without some knowing agent exercising control parameters that iterate or repeat in temporal loops. Such cyclical process is needed in order to achieve a state predicated by an agency. Without an agent or subject, there is no Mind, and there is, in truth, but one subject, God, of which we are part, called the one subject in *Eli*.

The furthest reduction we can achieve in space-time is called the vacuum, because it is the energy that exists in all space-time, preventing the formation of an absolute vacuum. It is also called the zero-point energy (ZPE), the energy that remains when temperature is reduced to absolute zero, the zero point.

The vacuum has an energy, particles arise out of the vacuum, and they exist for a period of time in external space-time, then return into the vacuum. Photons, particles of light, in particular, are continuously streaming in and out of the vacuum. Although many physicists believe that the vacuum energy is simply noise, such noise in the brain is the source of a patterned chaotic process, which can, in principle, be subject to control parameters arising from the future. Space and time, as we know it, do not exist in the vacuum in the ordinary way. They are torn apart by quantum gravity, which comes to dominate at this scale of reality. It is this activity that produces the ever-popular wormholes within the vacuum, which have been characterized as passages in imaginary time, exceedingly small diameter tunnels through space-time leading to some other place in space-time in an unpredictable manner. The use of wormholes as time machines is a favorite topic of science fiction, but this is all fantasy, as the wormholes are of such minute diameter that the time machine notion on any reasonable scale is impossible, and the theory of the vacuum is not firmly established so that the true nature of the vacuum is really still a mystery.

The theory of and nature of the quantum field is described in detail by Auyang (1995). Of particular note is the concept of time and permanence (Auyang 1995, 170):

> Permanence means the inapplicability of the concept of change and hence of time . . . The primitive spatio-temporal structure is permanent; it is independent of temporal concepts. It contains the time dimension as one aspect and makes possible the introduction of a time parameter, but is itself beyond time and change.

Auyang describes the primitive spatio-temporal stutter *M* as the individuation of events in the field. She goes on to state (1995 170):

> M is a continuum of points, which are the numerical identities of events in the world. The number of points in M and hence the number of events in the world are as permanent as M . . . . The permanence of numerical identities should not to be mistaken for a conservation law of some kind; it is more fundamental.

The quantum vacuum or ZPE is mentioned hear only because it may have some role in the theory of mind, and as Whitehead said, "God is the infinite ground of all mentality." Like the vacuum, God is in the inside or things, and there has been much speculation on the vacuum as the medium or mind and spirit. *Eli*, however, places this inside in the hidden time. The new science is in a very early stage of development, and all hypotheses must be tested and eventually formulated. As *Eli* states, this will require scholarship and involvement of our institutions of knowledge, and this is the meaning of the charge to *SEARCH GOD* which is one of the all-caps two word phrases meant to bring out the essence of the teaching. At this point and time, the new science, critical to the new faith, is simply being explored for the direction of such research.

Hawking found it necessary to introduce imaginary time in order to calculate the wave function of the sum over all histories, which is well founded in physics in the sum of all paths of Feynman, and we have fundamentally equated this imaginary time with the hidden time. The process in the hidden time is then extended to Whiteheadean process theory, seeking a grand unification of science, religion, philosophy, and theology.

In *Process and Reality* (1929) Whitehead described the activity of God in what he called the continual concrescence or integration operating from the mental to the physical. God would thus act within the movement of the cycle as the actual entity is the final cause of its own becoming, which is also the initial or subjective aim provided by God. All actual entities other than

God and perhaps the Self, which holds God within itself, move in the direction of physical to mental. By initiating the mental elements of conceptual prehension at the onset of the physical process, the cycle is complete.

This is the meaning of Whitehead, Hartshorne, and Cobb of the description of the interactions of God and the world, both needing each other for the completion of the process, with God being having a relational influence on the freedom inherent in the Creativity and the actual entities, posited in the future of the discontinuous creation, being its own cause. Once this summing or concrescence or completed, the entity passes from subjectivity, its state in the Now, to immortality, to be continuously reiterated in the process by which the actual entity arises in prehensions or feelings of relation over a timeless interval of duration. This is the relational concept of God which arises in the false dichotomy of God and nature, which in not adopted here, in that God is an absolute infinity that is causeless and cannot be subject to any conditions. In process theology there is a consequent nature of God that has a mutually transcendent relation with the world. This, again, is a false dichotomy of God and world, reified by the objective attitude of the divided or dissociated Species Mind. Good and evil exist together, so this is also a false dichotomy. However, good transcends evil to such an extent that evil is extinguished when the two are brought together. The idea that God is all good is therefore also a false dichotomy, as they are united in the hidden time, and the ascendance of evil only occurs when it is separated from the good. This is the process by which the Self was traumatically dissociated by the objective attitude, which creates opposites. In the unconscious no such opposites exist, they are the product of a wrong turn that has occurred in the evolution of the Species Mind, which both Jesus and Eli seek to reverse, as it was mistaken from the start, and cost us our perception of the hidden time, as it became hidden by the alter ego.

If the two are once again united, the quality of the alter ego as evil is lost. The alter ego is fused to the real ego and loses its potency. This is the evolutionary change that must involve a reversion to a former way of perceiving the world, in the hidden time. This is actually a discipline onto itself, which we must now relearn, but this does not present a problem, because all systems tend to settle into a ground state, which is for the emotions peace and tranquility, and which is the natural state of the Species Mind. It is only by perverting nature that we raise our infants and children into a state of conflict between dissociated fragments of the Species Mind. The ending of this dissociation will be the natural course of events that occur in every conceivable scenario of the growth of the Species Mind out of its infancy, which is inevitably achieved as the final cause of our evolution. Just as, in individual trauma, our development is arrested, so the development of the Species Mind is arrested by trauma in its infancy. This is actually quite a simple formulation, although it seems foreign to our alter egos. The proper course into the future has been placed before us in *Eli*.

Having been initiated into the process that passed from Whitehead, to Hartshorne, to Cobb, and to the author of this book, he has tended to follow this tradition in his thinking, extending it to other fields and problems, and fundamentally accepts the transmission of the process through these masters. The most important part of this process was John Cobb's explanation of internal relations and process privately in his home in 1994. The author was an active member of the Board and in conference groups at the Center for Process Studies, which is the largest group of process scholars in the world. The center was founded by John Cobb and David Ray Griffin, in 1973, as part of the Clairmont School of Theology.

Whitehead framed his process theory in a field called the extensive continuum, the medium of all internal relations. If the continuum were meant to be space-time, why did Whitehead just call it that and avoid the difficulties in interpretation of his work? The description of the continuum comports with the idea that it is the hidden or imaginary time, extending the parallels of science, philosophy, and spirituality. This is likely the most reasonable solution to this unresolved problem in process philosophy and in the understanding of Whitehead's work.

Since real time is mathematically imaginary, the imaginary time is mathematically real, and spacelike. This is not necessarily what the hidden time is, and in formulating the new science, we find ourselves here in a position similar to Aristotle in his time. Ideas or hypotheses have to be explicated, and this is the process of science, such that the new science is bound to take some wrong turns. However, the explication in this book seems to support the hypothesis that imaginary time is the scientific equivalent to the hidden time.

The idea of imaginary time was developed primarily by Stephen Hawking, the modern physicist, to signify a time that has at least two dimensions, both of which are at right angles to ordinary space and time. The entirety of the hidden time, which includes everything in real space-time, has no extension in ordinary space and time, such that an instant in space-time is an eternity in the hidden time. It is thus that the universe exists in all possible histories, which are infinite, at every space and time, up until the moment of the Now, when the possibilities are summed in the hidden time to form a wave function that is the sum over all possible histories. The Now is thus, in this theory, actually eternal, as the hidden time is cyclical and has no beginning or end. The hidden time, which we might speculate to be heaven, the subjective realm of mind, and the realm of spirit and God, existed prior to the other dimensions, since movement in these dimensions does not involve any movement in the hidden time, and there is no reason for its beginning and end to correspond to these other dimensions. The physics is complex, and still not firmly established. However, we know from comparative traditions that the hidden time is essentially the same as the dreamtime, where before, after, past, and present are all eternally present.

Whitehead (1929) described the process in the Now, or the specious present, and his theory of organism was not algorithmic, but more topological, a mathematic system used to describe transformation of forms, called eternal objects, which enter into instants of the Now, called actual occasions or entities, involving a society of occasions, prehended or internally interconnected, together with ingression of an eternal object, which are much like the forms of Plato, and satisfy the requirement of formal causation. Beyond this, the process metaphysics of Whitehead is metrological, a branch of mathematics dealing with parts, actual entities or occasions, and the wholes they form. Whitehead was a mathematician and coauthored the *Principia Mathematica*, a three-volume masterpiece, with Bertrand Russell (Russell was second author).

These wholes may be societies of actual entities or new actual entities, which discontinuously perish and are created anew in the process of becoming, inheriting their entirety of passed occasions, which pass into immortality once the entity has become anew by as a result of the integration or concrescence of relations in the instant of becoming. This is very similar to what we have discussed in our section on quantum field theory, and why we have found the introduction of this complex field necessary.

There has been much debate over the distinction of actual occasions and societies, but in general, a system such as the mind/brain is a society of occasions in which the dominant occasion is Self or Soul. For God, there are no discontinuities, however, He is in continuous concrescence and integration, over the entirety of the universe, and is the only actual entity of this type, although the individual Self or Soul has been suggested as an exemplar of God's Creativity. The continual concrescence or coming together of relations into a single, whole entity is a product of existence in the hidden time, where there are no durations of real time. The process of creation always involves actual entities or occasions, which are the reason for their own becoming, and this is called the ontological principle. When applied to the ordered society of the human organism, the ontological principle would apply to the dominant occasion, Self, which then would have a discontinuous becoming predicated by finality in the actual occasion and thus the Self perishes and is born anew each instant after a process of becoming according to the ontological principle. Control parameters that then serve as final causes in the discontinuous existence that has its reason for becoming anew in the completed actual occasion or actual entity.

This process, scientifically, would, according the nascent new science, occur in the hidden time, such that the continuum or extensive continuum of relations is completely internal to space-time. This neatly gives us concepts of panentheism, God within all, and panexpentiatialism, or the primacy of experience as the fundamental reality, with no stuff of the nature of either matter or mind. However, the dissociated alter ego has risen to ascendency in the Species Mind, such that it becomes the effectively dominant occasion that is the locus of experience. In this structure, called egocentrism, the functions that we have defined such as the internal universe, where the coexistence of the external objects of experience are one and the same as the internal objects within Soul or Self, and the entrance of eternal forms and feelings that are attached to the internal objects, are all absent, isolated in the Self in darkness. This is the same sort of process that had placed the earth at the center of the solar system, the geocentric model of Ptolemy and others, as opposed the sun being the center of the solar system, the heliocentric model of Copernicus and Galileo, with the earth representing the alter ego and the sun representing Self. It is such that the sun was worshipped in ancient times.

For Whitehead, the quantum is the drop of experience, which is the actual occasion. Beyond experience, there is nothing, and this is the quantum solution of the ground of reality as it exists in quantum physics, of which Whitehead was aware and from which he derived much of his metaphysics.

Whitehead's metaphysics is difficult to understand, and our brief review is given here out of necessity, since it is the primary basis of the relational framework we will be using to bring together science, religion, and philosophy. There are many divergent interpretations of Whitehead's process philosophy and theology, and mine was perhaps most deeply influenced by John Cobb, who gave me the key concepts of internal relations. This is not to say that John Cobb would agree or approve of all my interpretations, but only to form a basis for further discourse in the overall effort aimed at in *Eli*.

There have been a number of organizations and individuals who have attempted to take on the kind of synthesis of *Eli*, but none based on revealed texts. The Templeton Foundation, which supposed devotes itself to such a unity of science and religion, espouses the doctrines of usury and attempts to sanctify the existing order by blessing the oppression of the current economic and social order and supporting a vicious social

Darwinism in the name of entrepreneurship. The Institute of Noetic Sciences (IONS) has erected doctrines of pseudoscience and pseudospirituality such as to garner wealthy clients into a fanciful New Age cult so that they can profit and expand their misguided efforts. The founder and leader of IONS, Edgar Mitchell, looked at the earth from space and is said to have had some kind of epiphany, which has led to the expansion of his own alter ego and the banishment of any notion of God from IONS programs. There are many other examples of such feeble and misguided organizations, which have unfortunately managed to garner support from the leaders of current religions such as the Pope and the Dalai Lama.

The so-called enlightened thinkers of our times write books of nonsense that sell a great many copies to a public that is hungry for spiritual growth in this desolate age of idolatry. These thinkers promote a pseudospirituality, expansion of the already-hypertrophied alter ego, and bring the unwitting readers into a deeper darkness that supports the engine of usury. This mighty engine pumps out idols—in entertainment, the arts, science, and spirituality—to hypnotize the viewers of the television between commercials so that they will buy the products of those who support the whole media enterprise, the advertisers who fuel the engine of usury as it seeks to realize the impossible, the endless expansion of the growth of money. The promotion of pseudospirituality and pseudoscience are necessary to implement the darkening of the soul, since the vision of the soul would create a light that might threaten the endless appetite of the alter ego for more and more, which it seeks in order to elevate itself to the lofty status it deserves, or so it thinks. Such status is most often, if achieved, a cheating fruition (Rumi), and leaves the victim in the desolation of a lifelong despair as their hopes and dreams, far from fulfilling the deep yearnings of the soul, have actually despoiled any trace of spirituality.

Within this deeply disturbed milieu, science and religion have no real value. Science, in its role of supporting technology, which has mushroomed the enterprise of increasing the needs of people for the sake of usury, has become paradoxically lame in its efforts to enrich the mind, which have become impoverished by the very technologies that science has made possible. Understanding wanes, and education is devalued, closing the brief window of time when higher education was available to the common man, and damning the underclass into ignorance and hence limiting their ability to exercise any independent thought amidst the nonsense they are told by the media. The educated become the enemy of the almighty state or, more accurately, the international financial sector, the new corporate megalith, and are reduced to the status of laborers who must keep their mouths shut and do what they are told.

The enterprise of science goes on, but generates more heat than light. Modern physics has given us a view of reality that is totally concordant with the view of the founders of the world's great faiths. Reality in the older, classical physics was of a single reality or universe, working like clockwork, with no actual need in this work of the hand of God. To a large extent, despite more than one hundred years of modern physics, science continues to accept this false doctrine. In modern physics, the only realities are observation and experience, which are really one and the same. We can take a photon, a particle of light, for example, and find that the matter, energy, position, and momentum of the particle, prior to observation, are all unknown. This has been presumed by the founders of modern physics, in a vain effort to preserve the classical, Godless reality, to mean that the particle has an infinite multiplicity of actual existences, and that, at some vanishingly small probability, for all practical purposes zero, the particle comes into complete and total actuality out of this vanishingly small probability.

Potentiality, without experience, cannot be considered real since, in the sense of Whitehead, only experience is real. Whitehead's *Process and Reality* (1929) is truly an ontological interpretation of quantum theory, a science that had no theory of an underlying reality or ontology. The ontology behind what we observe or measure in quantum physics is still up for grabs, but Whitehead's will be adopted here as the most coherent and complete, and the most fitting to *Eli*. This being the case, the limitless possibilities, fundamentally all the matter and energy of the universe, are dead, they have never come into being, because reality is spiritual or experiential. This is an enormous change in our view of reality, which has not yet entered into our thinking.

Here we bring to mind two aphorisms of Gautama in the classic work of Buddhism, the *Dhammapada* (Muscaro translation): (1) "Our life is the creation of our Mind" and (2) "The unreal never is, the real never is not." We will note here that Mind is singular. There is One Mind, what we call here the Mind or Spirit of God or, later, the one subject. The second quotation refers to the status of reality. What is not real has never been real, and what is real has always been real. The unreal never is, the real never is not. The real does not pass into extinction after its moment of existence—it is forever real. This is the status of the real in the hidden time, where there only now, as Augustine aptly surmised, now-past, now-present, and now-future.

Nothing comes into reality *ex nihilo*. This idea has been used as a criticism of religion and the idea of a material creation, but it is equally true for science and religion. Science expects us to believe that the entire universe, in its infinite multiplicity of potentialities, has come into existence *ex nihilo*, and this is no better than the belief that God made the universe out of nothing. Both run into the same, insurmountable problem, and for both, there is only one answer. The universe is not material, for matter does not arise from nothing. The only reality can be variously described as observation, experience, mind, consciousness, and spirit. To have more than one reality, we would need more than One Mind or One Spirit, as separate minds or spirits would only assume meaning if there were separate observations, such that reality would be divided into potentialities once again, contradicting the law of existence as a totality and not as a potentiality.

Matter and energy exist in time and space, as we understand them as dimensions in our scientific reality. Without time and space, they can have no reality. However, our view of time and space is flawed, because it involves the passage from potentiality into reality, and we know that there is no such process occurring in the realm of matter and energy, as the potential remains eternally potential, and the real remains eternally real.

Perhaps we are getting ahead of our argument here, but the critical nature of the hidden time in *Eli* needs further explication. Science deals with facts and theories. Conscious experience is a fact. The fact is conscious observation, and it is the most primary fact of scientific discourse, somehow dispensed from modern science at a time when it has become the very foundation of science's view of reality. We can infer the unconscious, but this is a second-order inference, as it is based on our consciousness of it. For there to be a consciousness, there must be a mind that is having that consciousness. The existence of this Mind is not a separate fact, but a corollary to the fact of conscious experience. Conscious experience in Mind is a fact. The existence of more than one consciousness is an inference, assuming our conscious minds are in some way separate and that other minds also have a separate consciousness. We assume that time is a flowing process proceeding from past to the future. The fact of observation is only Now. In our science, we make observations in our Now. We assume that this Now passes from the present to the future, but this is a perception, not a scientific fact. This view of God, as consciousness, is expressed what is perhaps the most profound of all sacred documents, the *Bhagavad Gita* (Muscaro Translation): "I am the mind: I am consciousness in the living." (*Bhagavad Gita* 10:22)

The Now has been referred to by theologians and mystics as the Eternal Now. The nature of the Eternal Now is part of the nature of God, as "I am that I am." As quoted in Exodus: "And God said unto Moses, I AM THAT I AM: and he said, Thus shalt thou say unto the children of Israel, I AM hath sent me unto you." (Ex 3:14). The I AM THAT I AM was given to Moses, and is in *Hebrew*: pronounced *Ehyeh asher ehyeh*. It can also be translated: "I-shall-be that I-shall-be." Throughout the Hebrew *Bible Ehyeh* is translated "I will be," so this name has the meaning of the Eternal God, the God of the Hidden time, and likely bears some relationship to the Tetragrammatron (YHWH) used time and time again in the Hebrew *Bible* and mystical literature such as the *Zohar*. The connection with the I AM THAT I AM with the Tetragrammatron is discussed in Wikipedia (accessed 3/4/11) as follows:

> It has often been proposed that the name YHWH is etymologically a third person masculine imperfect verb form derived from the biblical Hebrew root "to be." This would connect it to the passage in verse

> Exodus 3:14, where God gives his name as *Ehyeh Asher Ehyeh* translated most basically as "I am what I am" (or "I will be that which I now am").

Her we have yet another tense for the I AM THAT I AM, which is "I will be that which I am now." The connection with the Tetragrammatron is very deep as it bears on the hidden time and relates fundamentally to a God that has no particular description as something that might be said to exist in time. Whatever connection is drawn, it is clear that we are here defining God in his aspect of Now, or the Eternal Now, running eternally, outside of real time, without any distinct location in space and time, "within all and outside all." Location of God is a form of idolatry, the idol being the concrete "Nobodaddy in the sky" (Blake) that *Eli* would like to dispense of in the quest for a faith fully consistent with a true science.

The science which is the *Book* draws from is science of actuality or reality, as that which is observed. The existence of what is not observed, but which is purely potential, becomes actual only in the Mind of God in the Eternal Now. It shares nothing of space and time as commonly understood. This Eternal Now is not in time, it is eternal, outside of time. The existence of the reality which is observed is no more than a possibility until the moment of Creation, which is the I AM THAT I AM. Time does not move, this is a fact of modern science. To say that something of a material nature comes into being in the movement of time forward is to deny this fact. What exists in time exists in time, it does not and cannot change, and if it exists as possibility rather than reality, it is, in fact, not real in the sense of science. There has been a great error in modern science that grants reality to possibility. The unreal never is. The real never is not.

We have a field of infinite possibility that does not actually exist except as an idea in the Mind of God. This may seem like a dualism, but there is no mind stuff or material stuff in this metaphysics. The idea in the Mind of God knows no place and time, so there is nothing to accommodate the physical concepts of matter and energy in this science. God is One Mind, as the Buddhists have said. This One Mind knows only the Eternal Now, and it cannot be limited by either time or possibility. As time passes through this Eternal Now, observations are made. The idea in the Mind of God exists only on the plane of heaven. The idea of a heavenly plane is not to be taken concretely, it is not a place, and is not localized in space and time. An idea cannot occupy space and time, and the very proposition is absurd. The mind/brain sciences have gotten into an awful mess trying to equate ideas with matter and energy, and this part of science will fall in the new science, since there is no commonality between an idea and an object. The actuality is on the earthly plane, and is the manifestation of the idea. This process does not materialize the idea, since in doing so, we would have to appeal to creation ex nihilo. God's object in creation is to manifest on the earthly plane. More levels could be added, and have been added, to describe the levels of reality reaching from heaven to earth or vice versa, and such is certainly possible, but we will follow parsimony here and restrict ourselves accordingly.

Chapter Ten

The Rejection Of Materialism

The philosophy of *Eli* derives from rejection of a scientific materialism that grants existence to things that do not, in fact, exist in any sense other than that of a partial existence in an impossible universe. Materialism thus fails science, while idealism succeeds. This is a very important point. The reader may object to the concept of a science based on idealism rather than materialism, but there is no other way to frame modern science and spirituality. Materialism is a myth, which fact we will address later. For here, suffice it to say that many of the founders of modern science or physics were idealists. We cannot get into details here of the philosophies of modern scientists or of philosophy in general. We will only draw attention here to the philosophical ideas of Werner Heisenberg, who, in fact, was the first scientist to formulate quantum mechanics, the revolutionary theory that has been verified now to its minutest detail, and which brought about the revolution in science that led to the overthrow of the old classical mechanics or Newton and others. The classical theory had no place for God, religion, mind, spirit, soul, indeterminism, volition, consciousness, etc. Heisenberg opened the door, among others, to the reintroduction of idealism as not only a basis for scientific doctrine, but as *the only basis* for a modern scientific doctrine.

Roger Penrose, a renowned modern physicist, in the *Emperors New Mind* (1989) clearly makes the Platonic realm of ideas the source of mentality:

> I imagine that whenever the mind perceives a mathematical idea, it makes contact with Plato's world of mathematical concepts . . . When mathematicians communicate, this is made possible by each one having a direct route to truth, the consciousness of each being in a position to perceive mathematical truths directly, through the process of "seeing."

In researching this commentary, the sections above on idealism and modern science were written prior to searching this reference to Heisenberg, yet Heisenberg's reasoning is identical to ours (Thurau 2011):

> In the experiments about atomic events we have to do with things and facts, the phenomena that are just as real as any phenomena in daily life. But the atoms or elementary particles themselves are not real; they form a world of potentialities or possibilities rather than of things or facts.

Here Heisenberg gives us his philosophical objection to a materialist view of quantum mechanics. Heisenberg was, in fact, a Platonist, and gave no apologies for this fact. The Thurau (2011) e-zine article was posted just one day before it was accessed here on the Internet (see citation). Thurau is a scientist of understanding and accomplishment, so the fact that this has been draw from the Internet does not diminish his authority. Regarding the facts that led the idealist movement in physics, he wrote (Thurau 2011):

> The physicists who represented Idealist views in the 1930s were well aware of all the developments in relativity and quantum theory, which had led to the enormous changes to classical Newtonian physics earlier in the twentieth century. The solid reality of physical objects, unquestioned during the reign of

104 Chapter Ten The Rejection Of Materialism

> Newton, had evaporated when it was discovered that the atom was not the final, indivisible matter particle. Subatomic particles did not behave at all like ordinary matter and their behavior could not be explained by classical mechanics. Scientific determinism, the philosophy of cause-and-effect causality, had to be abandoned. The new reality of nature was based on new quantum concepts that included probability and the particle-wave duality of matter.

Matter literally evaporated, as Thurau states, with the discoveries of modern physics. The idealist perspective became the ideal explanatory model of physics. Science, Thurau (2011) says, by embracing the overthrown classical materialist doctrine, misses the opportunity to unite science and spirituality:

> Innumerable attempts have been made to bridge the gap between science and faith, usually from the side of faith and often by dressing up the argument in pseudo-scientific language to make it more palatable to scientists. Science has not been convinced because, in order to be convincing, scientific concepts must reach the point where they would also be acceptable to religion. There has been only partial success in this, possibly because the various bits of science that religion has declared acceptable have themselves been in a process of change.

Quantum physics showed us that our reality is just a possibility, one of an infinite number of possibilities, since the bifurcations of possible realities have a fractal structure. Fractals were derived largely from the transfinite mathematics of Cantor. As being infinite, all the matter and energy the universe would be divided by infinity, and any number divided by infinity is zero. So every potential universe has zero mass and energy, according to the law of conservation of matter and energy. Similarly, the probability of any actual universe, absent the causality of Supreme Consciousness, would be zero, as the probability of a single outcome from among an infinite number of possible outcomes is one divided by infinity, zero—giving us a zero probability of the universe ever emerging from the wave function of all potential universes, which can only exist the hidden time. In other words, our universe is not just one of a vast number of accidents that happened to occur due to natural selection. Natural selection is blind about the future, and it is only by having a future outcome being a cause of a preceding event—final causality in the timeless ground of the hidden time—that our impossible universe becomes illuminated by the light of consciousness, which is the light of God. The reason for this is quite simple. A final cause, referred backward in time, causes a process that leads to an actuality through an infinite number of cycles. Infinity is not a defined number. Five multiplied by five an infinite number of times is not the same as ten multiplied by ten an infinite number or times. So the infinite iteration of an infinite number of possibilities would not eliminate the fact that potentialities remain potentialities. It would only bring one possibility into actuality in consciousness.

There are many worlds or universes, all which are connected in the wave function of the universes in the hidden time, and all which are necessary for our world to be. Our world or universe is enlightened by the Supreme Consciousness, and this is how it is distinguished from the infinite number of empty worlds, worlds not illuminated by the light of consciousness. The spiritual light is derived from the hidden time, which has no beginning or end. The hidden time is a fifth dimension, such that there are two dimensions of time at right angles—like the two beams of a cross. Mundane time is mathematically imaginary, being of the metric of the square root of a negative number. The hidden time is real, and thus spacelike, like a fourth dimension of space. The three dimensions of space and the one dimension of the hidden time create an eternal universe, a block universe, inclusive or all possible universes, in which time is extended in the same way as space, and does not pass, but remains ever the same. Within this block universe, all universes are included, but our universe follows a trajectory or world line, moving in mundane time through the probabilities of any one universe, which is the Universal wave function, a cloud of potentials. Supreme Consciousness, and our own consciousness within it, illuminates the course of actuality arising out of potentiality.

The potentials of other universes do not change from past to present to future. The light of consciousness, however, shines on only one, our universe, making it real. The light of consciousness comes from God, and brings about the progressive manifestation of consciousness in evolution. This manifestation involves the hidden time, where all universes and all time coexist eternally. God causes the spiritual light, the light of mind and consciousness, to shine on one universe, because God fundamentally conceives that One Universe, and is the One Mind. As stated in the opening of the *Qur'an*, God or Allah is the lord of the worlds.

In Zen Buddhism there is the famous koan: "What's the sound of one hand clapping." Obviously, it makes no sound. Supreme consciousness is absolutely infinite. The number of possible worlds is transfinitely infinite. They are the two hands. Clapping the two hands together is the supreme consciousness meeting a possible world, making that possible world real or actual for all eternity. They make a sound, and the sound is a single actuality within supreme consciousness, and supreme consciousness within that single actuality. The product is purely subjective. This is the meaning of the passage in *Eli* that speaks of the reality of the one subject, supreme consciousness, God.

In *Logian* 29 of the *Gospel of Thomas* it written: "Jesus said 'If the flesh exists because of spirit, it is a miracle, but if spirit [exists] because of the body it is a miracle of miracles. Yet I marvel at how this great wealth established itself in such poverty.'"

The creation of flesh, matter, out of spirit would be a miracle, since no matter or energy actually exists in one of an infinite number of potential universes. The *Gospel of Thomas* is not about miracles. Jesus does nothing miraculous and speaks of nothing miraculous, except in this one passage. Jesus said *if* such and such were to happen it would be a miracle. *If* signifies a fanciful notion, often followed by "*and when.*" There is no "and when" here—it does not happen, but if it were to happen, it would be a miracle.

Science is not supposed to endorse miracles, yet its dogma is the miracle of miracles spoken of in the verse just quoted. The light of the mind and consciousness, what we experience, would have to emerge magically, if we deny the existence of God.

Science has succumbed to a very concrete and ridiculous notion, by which the brain is like a movie screen that by the miracle of miracles is watching the movie. This is impossible, and time will tell that it is an extremely primitive, mistakenly concrete, and frankly ridiculous dogma. Science claims to be naturalistic, yet its naturalism is often a matter of convenience. This miracle of miracles, described as it is in current scientific dogma, insidiously accepted without question, defies naturalism, and so is scientifically false. Even God is restricted in the sense the impossible can never be illuminated except by a higher order infinity. It is thus that God must be an absolute infinity (Cantor) in order to forth a single Universe into experience out of a transfinite infinity..

Meaning belongs to mind, spirit, imagination, not to dead matter. Everything that we perceive of as external in mundane time is internal in the hidden time. The internal is the source of the external. Gautama says in *Dhammapada* 1:1 (Muscaro translation): "Our life is the creation of our Mind." Notice the singular, Mind. Without the internal reality, the external would cease to exist, because the external emerges from the wave function of all possible universes that can only manifest on the basis of illumination of One universe by One Mind. The mind is not within the universe, the universe is within the Mind of God.

Christ is not an eternal material body existing in a material kingdom. This is concrete nonsense. Supreme consciousness is hidden in the hidden time, eternal, always being, but never coming into being or passing out of being. It comes to reside on the inside, because it does not have the dimensions of space or time. The universe is an idea in the Mind of God, "Be, and it is." Its object is manifestation of what God wills to be, and humans are the ultimate product of this manifestation. Human beings, on the planet Earth, are the focus of God's creation. This is why the church so mightily resisted what it saw as a threat to their doctrine of human creation as the earth was found to be a planet moving around the Sun. They too were making the abstract, the subjective, and the ideal concrete. The Reformation, to a large extent, tried to eliminate such concrete notions by taking Christ off the cross, and dispensing of the statues, the pictures, and the stain glass windows, to a later or lesser extent. The purpose of these representations in art was not to revive these figures and events. The images in the mind have a meaning, like the host, which penetrates to the soul, an unconscious realm of meta-meanings that cannot be logically apprehended, and the meaning is internal, within the soul, not outside in the material object.

Returning to *Logion* 29, the poverty in which the great wealth of supreme consciousness is established is the realm of the physical universe. Marvel conveys a mystical realization that cannot be apprehended by the intellect. The marvel we now see is the unreality, the infinitely impossibility of any single reality arising out of an infinite number of possibilities, which have zero energy and matter. The poverty is also in the mind that does not see the light of the kingdom within, as the wealth is in the mind that does. This is what Jesus marveled at, the wealth of the spirit, of the kingdom within, becoming manifest in the body.

The other major alternative to idealism is mentalism. Since consciousness and experience are necessarily introduced into quantum mechanics in the concept of the observer, there is a tendency to enshrine or, in a sense, deify the observer, or the observing ego, as it has been called. We know, with respect to our own minds, that they are governed in large part by our brains, making the mentalist reality contingent on matter and practically forcing a mind/matter dualism of the Cartesian type. Also, by positing the human observer and his or her consciousness in a privileged position as the creator of reality, it, in effect, falls under the error of giving the "I," literally the alter ego, the reigns over creation. Von Neumann was a central figure in bringing mentality into quantum reality, via the "abstract ego," making the attribution of power here quite clear. We argue that it is the spiritual principle of the "not-I" that is associated with God and Creation.

God can have no personage, as we have already argued, as in a person's individual mind, for such is a limitation of the limitless. Mentalism also runs into the thorny issue of how the universe could have existed prior to the advent of thinking creatures. The same problem of insufficiency of reason arises when one considers how those realities that exist outside of the purview of the "abstract ego" could ever possibly exist. Mentalism, which seems so reasonable, is, in fact, a dangerous notion that leads to the worship of the "not-I," enshrined perhaps in error of the personal nature of Christian belief systems, which are equally dangerous.

Idealism does not posit a human observer as a necessary predicate to reality. It does give humans the status of observers, however and, in this sense, also as creators, but not as against the Creator. The many is made in the image of God and becomes a creator, with a free will or volition to choose between right and wrong. To deny volition in our schemes of what is truth is deeply counterintuitive, and volition might be said to be a primary fact of conscious experience, except for the fact that it assumes a consciousness of having a volition. However, volition cannot be divided from consciousness. Thoughts and actions do not occur unbidden, but are the products of a conscious will. The conscious will, as in the will of God, acts quite simply, it is conscious of something or some idea, allows it to be, and it is. This is the principle of "Be, and it is," so strong in Islam and the *Qur'an*, which we will pick up later.

The status of the observer is not in the material world, because there is no material world. Rather, the observer is a spiritual creature. Heaven and the world are simply levels of manifestations. They are not separate realities, all reality is part of the Ideal One. This relation is part of the idea in *Eli* of "one subject," which we will come to later. However, the following passage from Huxley (57), attributed to Suso, describes the nature of One and the many, a plurality within a Unity:

> All creatures have existed eternally in the divine essence, as in their exemplar. So far as they conform to the divine idea, all beings were, before their creation, one thing with the essence of God. (God creates into time what was and is in eternity.) Eternally, all creatures are God in God . . . So far as they are in God, they are the same life, the same essence, the same power, the same One, and nothing less.

The passage is self-explanatory, but one must call attention to the important parenthetical phrase, as it bears directly on our view of time. "God creates into time what was and is in eternity." The living soul, the exemplar of God, is God in God, much like Attar's *Simurgh*, which we will mention later. Nothing new arises, as nothing new can arise in our view of time as the eternal hidden time, as we will discuss shortly. The soul, eternally God in God, enters into time, yet remains in eternity. This informs us of the relation of time and eternity. The entrance into time leads the soul from a single, infinite Eternal Now, into movement whereby Now seems to follow Now from moment to moment. Now becomes no different in the process, because it was and is infinite.

The soul, as the exemplar of God, as God in God, cannot pass in and out of existence, but only between the manifest and unmanifest realities. It cannot be created or destroyed, any more than God can. "Ye are all Gods [Elohim]" (Psalm 82:6; John 10:34) is the most inexplicable verse for the entire Christian tradition, because, in it, a bit of the original mystical teaching of the *Gospel of Thomas* has snuck in past the fingers of those who destroyed, burned, and forbade the *Gospel of Thomas* tradition to continue, up until its fortuitous discovery in 1945. This has something to do with the nature of the soul as it enters into time, which we will pick up later.

Innumerable attempts have been made to bridge the gap between science and faith, usually from the side of faith and often by dressing up the argument in pseudo-scientific language to make it more palatable to scientists. Science has not been convinced because, in order to be convincing, scientific concepts must reach the point where they would also be acceptable to religion, which takes time. That time has now come.

Eli has been obscure for eleven years because the time between that book, and this book, has been a time of the incubation that precedes fruition. This is not to say that this book is infallible or the final word on any matter. It is simply to say, "The time has come."

Chapter Eleven

The Meaning Of The Hidden Time

The next five verses of Eli deal with the hidden time. The hidden time is taken from the Hebrew *ōlam*, derived from the word *olm*, meaning to conceal or cover. *Ōlam* literally means hidden or unknown and, when applied to time, signifies time of an indefinite duration, whether in the past, the future, or both. *Ōlam* is used over 450 times in the Old Testament, and is variously translated as eternal, eternity, forever, and everlasting, although it can also apply to a more limited period of time. *El Ōlam* is also one of the names of God. We will refer to the extended concept here simply as the hidden time.

The verses referring to the hidden time in *Eli* are as follows:

5. **Hear about the hidden time. Some think the hidden time is yet to come. The kingdom of God does not come by observation. It is hidden in the inner dimension.**
6. **The hidden time is an eternity that runs through every moment. It is all-time.**
7. **The hidden time is a thread, and moments are the beads on the thread.**

In verse 5, the hidden time is introduced to the ear of the reader. It is clearly stated that the hidden time is not some future time, as in the judgment or some heavenly life after death. It is clear in *Eli*, as it is in the *Gospel of Thomas*, that heaven is not some future place in time, but is literally within all things, but is invisible, or hidden. This is reflected in *Luke* as well as in the *Gospel of Thomas*, that the kingdom of God or of heaven is not some external place, extended in time or taking up some duration in space or time, but rather within all.

The All in All exists in the hidden time in the same manner as the image in a hologram is hidden in every portion of photographic plate, but is only displayed when a laser beam is shown through the film, in a clarity reflecting the size of the portion illuminated.

Although one might say that, as time does not pass, all time can be seen in a block universe just as all space can be seen, but this is not quite the meaning of the hidden time. We could just as well speak of a hidden world of space and time, the world of dreams. The Aboriginal people of Australia called this the dreamtime, as it is the nature of time and of the world in a dream. Far from being extended into the vastness of Universal time and space, the hidden time and the hidden world are, in fact, altogether, in their entirety, in all space and all time. To borrow from the *Bhagavad Gita* in a slightly different application: It is, and it is not. It is within all, and it is outside all. It is everywhere, and it is nowhere.

There has never been a time when the hidden time was not. Like the heaven that is occupied by possibilities, which are ideas in the Mind of God, the hidden time and the hidden world apply to the realm of heaven, the *ōlam*, the hidden time of worlds within our world. Within this time is everything that could ever be, because within it is the time of the absolute infinite Mind of God. So one cannot say, "Lo, it is here, or lo, it is there." The doctrines of omniscience and omnipresence apply in the external perspective, in that it includes the infinite Mind of God throughout the universe, while at the same time fitting on the tip of a pin and in the briefest moment in time.

Turning to the biblical uses of the hidden time, Psalm 41:3, in its various translations, gives us some account of its meanings:

New International Version: Praise be to the Lord, the God of Isreal, from everlasting to everlasting. Amen and amen.

Douay-Rheims Version: Blessed be the Lord of Isreal, **from eternity to eternity. So be it. So be it**. (bold font added)

God is translated here from the Hebrew Elohim, and amen is translated the Hebrew Truth. Eternity and everlasting are from the Hebrew *ōla*. From eternity to eternity, or from everlasting to everlasting, can be interpreted in a meaning going back in time and forward on time, but this seems unsatisfying. We have been told by theologians that God has always existed, can have no beginning, and can have not end, and that God is, essentially, timeless, always containing within himself all that is or ever could be.

From eternity to eternity, or from everlasting to everlasting, imply two points, one being the first eternity, and the next being the last eternity. The distance between two points is not infinite, so here we seem to be running up against a finite interval of time as against God's infinitude. It would seem that time, extended in any direction whatsoever, and in view of modern scientific theories, would be finite. We have already examined the nature of the Eternal Now. If there is eternity in the Now, then why should we need to extend it backward or forward? We might, however, say that It exists, given our perception, from Now to Now, with each Now being a point of contact between the timeless and infinite Now as it is in the heaven of the hidden time and the precession of time and creation as it is in earth. God is continually repeating his creation, as if from the beginning to the end, since He embraces all-time, from eternity to eternity, and from everlasting to everlasting, within the endless simultaneity of the Eternal Now. The time is hidden, within the simultaneity of no time, the Eternal Now, where before and after really have no significance, as if in a dream, since there is no time to be divided, sequenced, and attributed to any cause.

The Druids of old who feared that the Sun would go away after the winter solstice, and offered sacrifice to the "praise and blessing" of the Sun to insure that the Sun returned. Perhaps the Hebrews feared that, in the scansion of Now after Now, ever in a circle, repeating, in fact, all eternity, always, as it has been, as it is, and as it will be, there would be some end to this eternal cycle. Certainly, there could be, within such perception, a series of Nows in the progression of moments on earth that would bring an end to Israel, thus the exhortation to the God of Israel (Psalm 41:13): "Blessed be the Lord, the God of Israel from everlasting to everlasting."

The Eternal Now, the hidden time, is a great mystery that, if brought to its conclusion, will change science's view of the world. If eternity is captured in a simultaneous instant, able to iterate or repeat within that instant, for all time, then causes can precede their effects in an endless cycle within each instant, such that all the past, present, and future of all creation come to bear on the smallest of events and place them within a Universal context.

Assuming as we are that the hidden time is the same as the imaginary time of modern physics, we can shed some light on why we are always in the Now. In short, it is always being now, it is always becoming now. The hidden time runs through the real time like reeds growing in the ground, except that every reed is really the same. Metaphorically, the reed casts no shadow, the hidden time has no extension in the other four dimensions, it spans no space and it occupies no ordinary time, such as we perceive it. The Now is eternal, always in a sense, passing through the hidden time. The Now is that intersection of the hidden time or imaginary time with ordinary time.

The motion of time is essentially the passage of time from the status of an infinite number of potential actualities into a single actuality, which is not the materialization of some actual universe. We are neglecting relativity in our discussion of time, since the hidden time is space like. Before the Now we have the established past, which is comprised entirely of experience of a single reality, the same for all observers, and existing as moments strung up the thread or dimension of the hidden time from the beginning of time. The sequence is repeated in every instant, as Whitehead said, and is so eternal, so the order of time moving forward through successive experiential realities must always be from to present to future. This is the nature of process as observer in ordinary time—a continually flowing movement that momentary takes rest in the Now, creating a new actual reality or universe, predicated by all its former becomings. In the words of Whitehead:

> The world is always becoming, and as it becomes, it passes away and perishes . . . The world as it passes perishes, and that in perishing it yet remains an element in the future beyond itself . . . The notion of the prehension of the past means that the past is an element which perishes and thereby remains an element in the state beyond, and thus is objectified . . . Because we perish we are immortal" (*Essays* 89).

Such a process of endless repetition of prior becomings of the universe is the very essence of Hawking's view of the hidden time and the need for the hidden time in modern physics. Jason Brown (1991, 1996) has a similar notion of the nature of mind, called microgenesis. It this view states of mind in development of the individual and of the species repeat within the timeless duration of becoming of the mental state. This explains the evolution of the Species Mind and dispenses of the notion that the progression of capabilities has been the product of natural selection and genetic mutation. However, such a recapitulation can hardly be justified if the entirety of the history of the universe is not also repeating. Such repetition must be entailed in microgenesis. We call this radical microgenesis. It is the same as the sum over all histories of the universe in the hidden time.

In the hidden time, each moment corresponds to some moment in space-time, ranging from the smallest conceivable actual entity to the entirety of the universe. It is in this movement that the potentiality of infinite universes comes to be experienced as singular in the Now, through process in philosophy and summation over all histories in the hidden time in physics.

Since there is no extension of the hidden time in the other dimensions, passage of the hidden time in ordinary space-time is an illusion. Each moment embraces eternity, and the sum of all universes is a process of becoming from past to present is everywhere and for all time. So in answer to the question of the phenomenon of Now and the passage of time, experience, fundamentally the experience of the one subject of *Eli*, is simply the specification of wholes from the parts. However, in neuropsychology, as Brown asserts, there must also be a specification of whole to parts. Brown (2011) calls this mitosis. In mitosis, the whole that is the Self becomes the dominant occasion, which, by a kind of division, specifies all other occasions in the society of occasions of the mind/brain. Then, in turn, all these occasions derived from mitosis become integrated in process through feeling or prehension into a single whole with the dominant occasion, in the manner described by Whitehead (1929, 32): "The many become one, and are increased by one." The increase by one is mitosis.

Whitehead said that there is nothing outside of experience—the physical universe does not change—this would violate relativity. Rather, histories of experience of the One are being laid down, taking the entirely experiential reality through a trajectory among an infinite number of potential states in each instant of the Now. The trajectory does not pass, any more than the hidden time—our eternity, our home, and our birthright.

It is as if we were to imagine an infinite web of forking potentials, each of which has, in itself, zero probability and zero mass and, through process, bring one particular trajectory into an experiential reality. For the summation of the histories as well as the movement of process, this trajectory is drawn out form past to present to future. Within the hidden time, however, there is no such sequence, and past, present, and future continue to exist in an infinite number of possibilities, with no constraints on influences from the future, which then becomes a final cause of the present in an endless reiteration with efficient causation (past to future, see Glossary, Zeno's Paradox).

As we had mentioned, there is a continuous reiteration and recursion in the hidden time of final causation, effect to cause, and efficient causation, cause to effect. The hidden time is the time of the unconscious, and thus, the unconscious holds the universe within, and is capable of contact with all knowledge and experience. The recursion gives it limitless potential to govern the final state of the universe and of the Self in the becoming of the subsequent Now, which is the reason for its own becoming. The final cause that initiates the process can then become the governor of the dynamical or chaotic, fractal system. Process occurs in the hidden time or dreamtime of the unconscious, the vast sea of possibility in which the person or soul goes through this continuous recurrent, recursive, or reiterative process in every moment of experience.

Thus, in the microgenesis of Brown (1991, 2011) the core of self specifies the various elements of mind by passing through the process of the dreaming, in the unconscious. This process gives us tremendous computational power, unimaginably greater than any conceivable computer. It literally tames the hurricane of the quantum dynamical system of mind, which, in the hidden time, extends over the entire universe in space-time, such that everything we experience has the universe within it.

There is absolutely no way that the mind/brain can be directed to a specific state, outside of final causation by that state, the actual entity or the dominant actual occasion—soul or divinity. To build such a chaotic computer would be to harness the hidden time and God into a machine. It is impossible. So once again, we have need of this hypothesis of a Supreme Intelligence, God, as the ground of mentality. There is simply no other way it can happen that an infinitely complex chaotic system can be directed to a predictable outcome. The same holds for evolution.

So this process in the hidden time has enormous capacity to generate states of mind and states of the universe that are, otherwise, technically void, empty, immaterial, and infinitely impossible, into singular worlds or experiences. Here it is not the universe or mind that becomes actual, but the experience of an actual world. The possibilities of a world being experienced must be an infinity acted upon by a higher order, or absolute infinity in the sense of Georg Cantor (see Glossary). Cantor specifically attributed this absolute infinity to God.

It is interesting that Georg Cantor, over a hundred years ago, said his theory of transfinite numbers was given to him by God in order to express God's infinity, but this seems to be the first time it has been employed as such. He was mocked, derided, rejected, and considered insane for this, but now the system is accepted in mathematics. The order of the infinity entailed by all potential universes cannot be exceeded except if we posit a supreme intelligence with and absolute infinity of experience, which alone can give us a possible, actual, experiential universe. Thus, the hypothesis of God becomes necessary, and Cantor is, in a sense, redeemed for the first time in his theological attribution of cardinality transfinite mathematics, becoming, in a sense, a prophet of the new science.

The progression of time manifests, ultimately, the extraordinarily unlikely events that have been attributed to natural selection, but never explained by it, except to say that we are living in an extraordinarily unlikely world, and the very fact that such an unlikely world could exist dispenses with the need for God. The problem is, however, that, without God, without an absolute infinity of experience in the One absolutely infinite Mind of God, which subsumes all minds, none of these worlds are possible at all.

Chapter Twelve

Experiences Of The Hidden Time

The most compelling evidence for a different species of time, which we call the hidden time, is experience itself. We have hypothesized that the unconscious operates within the hidden time, beneath the veneer of the alter ego of dissociated consciousness.

At one time, I was a composer of instrumental music. I had a synthesizer hooked up to my computer, such that I could program into the computer, play it back on the synthesizer, and then add layers by playing the keyboard back into the computer. The program would then generate printed music scores. I was never a skilled keyboard player, and could not actually perform the music to any standard of quality, but I could pick out portions on the piano. At the time, I owed and operated a fully equipped recording studio. My friend, Billy Gonzalez, was an excellent performer on the keyboard and could read music.

The piano was not hooked up to the equipment, which was all electronic. As a psychiatrist I had become quite versed in the art of hypnosis, and assuming that the level of consciousness in hypnosis goes deep into the unconscious, where the hidden time operates, we created a song together. We first discussed the qualities of the song, its dissonances, its counterpoint, its melodic themes, and its general structure. I then had him play a few songs off sheet music on the piano, Bach's Tocato and Fugue in D minor, and Debussy's Passepied, as I began to induce the trance by indirect induction of the Erichsonian type. I chose these two songs because they embodied some of musical structure that I was aiming toward. I placed him in a deep trance, such that he had total amnesia for the entire process over a period of over an hour.

I then gave him some suggestions in the form: "We are now in the future, and we have already recorded the song. Listen, can you hear the song? It already exists in the future, and we are in the future listening to it." I had him play the song on the piano, and really wish I had recorded this, because he played the song magnificently for a period of about twenty minutes. The song had a different character than what I had written, it was much deeper, much more complex, much more dynamic, and contained elements that I had not introduced to him in the process of suggestion. Immediately we started to record it, laying tracks upon tracks. I was guiding him, in a sense, but we were really working together. We recorded a full version in this manner, and mixed the tracks together, but the song was only about three minutes long. Billy had never composed instrumental music, and the song was far above my level, containing elements that, formally, I did not even understand.

With the mission accomplished, I brought Billy out of the trance. He remembered nothing and did not believe that it was he playing the multiple tracks that we had assembled into the piece. The song was somehow alien to him and, to some extent, to me also, but we listened to it repeatedly such as to complete the process of drawing the song out of the future. The song was as I intended—deep, disturbing, troublesome—with elements of dissonance and counterpoint, but I cannot really say I composed the song. The song was created by the two of us listening to it in the future, in the hidden time, thus Billy's deep amnesia. I had originally called it "Psalms of Sorrow," but changed the name to "Where Storms Graze."

Having done well in this initial session, I had another song, which I had called "Psalms of Joy." This song was intended to be free of dissonance, deep, moving, sweet, and tender. A week after we recorded the first piece, we began to compose this second piece. I repeatedly gave him the elements I had intended to include in the song, and using the same technique as the in Where Storms Graze, we recorded the song together. This time he had only partial amnesia, and this song was not alien to him in the same sense as the first. Again, we listened to it repeatedly to complete the loop of final causation. Again, the song was transformed from what I had written. I was much deeper, much sweeter, and built up to a crescendo at the end that was not in my original score. We called the song "The Morning After," a name suggested by someone who listened to it subsequently, and has been more popular then the first for listeners on the Internet. Like the first, it was far beyond my ability as a composer. Both pieces appear on the CD "Trail of Tears" (BMI 2001).

Billy never played either song again. I identified the two songs with the Cherokee Trail of Tears later. Now, looking back, *Where Storms Graze* has the quality of the times of suffering, and "The Morning After" of the aftermath and passage of those times.

This seems to me to be a journey into the hidden time. Indeed, we did listen to the songs in the future, so the process was a kind of loop from present to future and back, conditional upon our future experience of listening to the songs.

In my practice of hypnosis, I often take the subject into the past, through age regression. There they have the experience of the presence of the past, and it seems quite real to them. Past traumas can be reexperienced, deconditioned, and it seems, at times, the subject's response to the trauma can be changed such that it projects into the present. This has been a very successful technique for me in the treatment of dissociative identity disorder, formerly called multiple personality disorder, which is not very common, with a prevalence of about 0.1 percent, one in a thousand. I will generally do weekly sessions of an hour and process in sessions between what has come forth in hypnotherapy.

We will illustrate some of the possibilities of hypnosis in the hidden time with the case of a women, which I have published (Germine 2004). I saw her at a forensic psychiatric facility at the request of a colleague. She had four months remaining in her commitment when I first saw her, after which she would be released. She had a very compliant and pleasant personality, and an angry, antisocial alter who engaged in activities with drugs, prostitution, and other crimes. When first seen she was suicidal, she wanted to kill herself in order to be rid of her troublesome alter, which would come out into control for as long as three days. She would than revert to her executive personality, with total amnesia for the period of time that she was controlled by her alter, but having to face the consequences of the actions performed by her alter ego during that period of time.

I inquired into the belief system of the pleasant, executive personality, and found that she believed in the soul. My working hypothesis was then that the two personalities had split from a single dominant occasion, her one soul, which had continued to exist. After working on the trauma for some weeks, her memories were consolidated and I had earned her trust and respect. She came to believe that I could remedy her illness, and was quite cooperative. Even the antisocial alter, who threatened me with great harm on our first encounter, had come to respect me when, instead of having her restrained as would usually be done in such a situation, I told her I was not afraid of her.

As is usual in the Erichsonian induction, and as I had also done with Billy, we established a place of comfort and security as our initial destination in our voyages into the unconscious hidden time, and then went from there to some other place, deepening the level of trance. After working with the trauma, I spent a number of sessions bringing both of her personalities to a place we called the Garden of the One Soul, and filling in details of the garden, repeatedly giving her the suggestion that she was one person.

The pleasant executive personality was willing to fuse with her alter, but the alter ego was not willing to fuse with her. The alter ego was more difficult to work with, but I managed to do a single session of hypnotherapy on her about three months into the process. She had a one-month term of commitment left, so I was running out of time. I brought the alter ego to the Garden of the One Soul, and we had a very positive session.

The next day staff commented on a dramatic change that had occurred. Her two personalities had been fused. Meeting her again, there was a joyful feeling of a new self and a new world that was palpable internally, but she still had a problem. She was still hearing babies crying in her head. These were dissociated fragments, not complete alters. We again went through the trance to the Garden, and created a stream where little fish were swimming. The fish could make no sound, and they were the babies. Thereafter, the hallucinations of the babies ceased, and we spent the remaining time prior to her discharge in the termination phase of therapy. During this time, there was no sign of dissociation of her personality nor were there hallucinations of babies crying. The last I heard of her, about a year later, she was still in remission, and leading a new life.

I could relate many other excursions into the hidden time, as I have done a great deal of hypnotherapy in my career. One remarkable event was in the case of a woman with dissociative identity disorder, who I regressed to her trauma, which was associated with a foul body odor I will not describe. As she smelled the odor in the experience of her trauma, I began to smell it too. I thought it was real, and searched to see where it was coming from. It was, in fact, a sympathetic olfactory hallucination, which was part of my own trance that occurs often when I do hypnosis. I was successful with this patient.

Another remarkable incident was that of a women who had been infected with dissociative identity disorder by her former psychiatrist. He had created various alters. Those that were troublesome were placed hypnotically in bubbles where they were isolated from all mental process, or so it appeared. One alter was eight years old, and this women was in her thirties. I hypnotized her and let the eight year old out of her bubble. She acted as if she were still eight years old, in a very convincing manner, and had total amnesia for her six years in the bubble. I never succeeded in integrating this particular patient, partly due to mounting time pressures, which were a result of ongoing changes in the field that effectively made psychiatrists into prescribers of medication, too costly to do significant therapy of this type.

Under the hypothesis that the dominant occasion of Mind is Soul or Self, we may view some of the phenomena of schizophrenia as an example of the Self, its process of mitosis, gives rise to dissociated fragments that appear as demons or other entities within the arena of consciousness. I similar process may occur in normal people, but remains unconscious.

Harold was a thirty-eight-year-old man with a history of paranoid schizophrenia back to age twenty-three when had had a severe psychotic break requiring hospitalization. He had successfully completed high school, and was of normal intelligence. He was employed from age eighteen to twenty-two in a convenience store, and had lived with his mother continuously since birth. He had been hospitalized six times for psychosis and command suicidal hallucinations, with his last hospitalization about one year prior to the time described in this case report. He had no known history of drug or alcohol abuse or dependence and no known history of clinically significant trauma. He had some history of depression, but it was in the context of severe psychosis, delusional beliefs, and command hallucinations telling him to kill himself.

Harold had been tried on many typical and atypical antipsychotics, but his psychosis was relatively refractory to medications. He had no significant medical illness. I had been seeing Harold every four weeks at a county government psychiatric clinic for about four months. He was receiving no other psychotherapeutic services. He had no friends and rarely left his home. He generally attended to his self-care, but was otherwise dependent on his mother.

Harold had been fairly stable at a baseline with considerable delusions and auditory hallucinations, but no visual or other hallucinations. At the onset of this report, he had been brought in on an urgent basis as he was losing control, with increased delusions of possession by demons, spirits, or people, which were the source of increased auditory hallucinations, and some command suicidal hallucinations. He had been sleeping well, per his own report. Harold said he was hearing several voices inside his head, to whom he referred to as people. Some of these people or spirits had been continuously telling him to kill himself. He said that "they want you to kill yourself so they can go somewhere else." What was decided was to hypnotically have these people go somewhere else, outside of the fragmented ego complex.

I asked him to close his eyes, and to take deep, slow breaths. I had never hypnotized Harold before, and I did a fairly rapid, indirect hypnotic induction. I did the induction rapidly as I did not feel he could be in a sustained state of relaxation and focus long enough for a slower induction. I guided him through visualization of a pleasant scene, having him notice all the sights, colors, sounds, and smells, as well as his own hands and clothes. I guided him through another place by a pond. I suggested that the people would come out of his head when he opened his eyes. Harold began holding his head. After I instructed him to open his eyes, it was clear that he was still in a light trance. He said that the people had left his head and were hovering about the room. I then suggested I open my office door and let them out, which I did, and he said the hovering spirits, some of whom he said were demons that had been tormenting him, had left the room. He then said, "I am inside him," followed by, "That was Tom, if Tom leaves my head he'll die," apparently fearing that this would happen. Tom was most likely his alter ego.

A week later, Harold returned to my office. I asked him if his suicidal voices had been bothering him. He said that these people had left his head during the last visit, and that he had not heard them since because "they don't exist anymore." Harold was still hearing the voice of Tom, and was still delusional about this. He told me "Tom didn't come out when you asked him to come out." Harold would not let him, since he was a good voice.

A month later, Harold was still doing well, with no return of the bad voices. He was still hearing the benevolent voice of Tom. He said he felt he had crossed a boundary during hypnosis, and was still on the other side of that boundary. I gave him a cassette tape with a recorded voice of an indirect induction and suggested that he follow the instruction on the tape, should the voices return. A month later, his condition was fundamentally unchanged.

The following month, he said that some of the people and voices had returned, but used the tape with good results. Thereafter, he learned self-hypnosis, and found it affective. He remained stable over the following eighteen months that he was under my care. Harold stated that the hypnotic exercise was far more effective for him than antipsychotic medication. He said this kept him on the right side of the boundary he had crossed after the first hypnotic session.

Chapter Thirteen

The Theory Of Mind

If observation is the key that separates the probability of an idea in the Mind of God from an event on the earthly plane, and if we have some choice in our observation, we can, ourselves, simply by choosing what we see and attend to, become creators of our own destinies, in some fashion, as in the spirit of the *Gospel of Thomas*. Purpose is then introduced into evolution, and natural selection, the directionless principle that is now being generalized into nearly all branches of science, is replaced by conscious and divine selection.

If every minute event is a potentially endless recapitulation of all the possibilities and events on heaven and earth, then there is an infinite cycle through which the omnipotence of God can bring about that which is in nature. Although we have framed it in terms of higher cardinality, it is also one of Zeno's paradoxes whereby repeated observation can actuate a quantum potential (Stapp 2007).

As the Psalm says, so be it. This simple statement, so be it, is the manner in which God creates. One could imagine that, in the space of a millisecond, an omnipotent God could create an elephant out of an ant, but we really, scientifically, cannot believe this is possible. So the power and might of God has some limitations, but is drawn toward the limitless, and actually reaches the limitless within the scope of natural law, with the infinite iteration of the

Eternal Now, which comprises a successive of moments. This is a progressive process in the Species Mind. In this process, there is a progressive increase of the role of God and mind in evolution, thus inescapably brought up to the level of experience that we call consciousness, along with ascending levels of consciousness, which will proceed outside of any notion of natural selection.

In panexperientialism, in which all occasions and entities have some modicum of experience, there is no need for emergence of consciousness prior to the actuality of a universe. Consciousness is a continuum from the Supreme Intelligence, as final cause in the hidden time, down to the rudimentary experience of the most basic existents or actual entities. Particles thus, in a sense, feel their world, and this is experience. The enormous unlikelihood of a universe beginning with an entropy or disorder of zero thus becomes a function of the direction provided by the Creator, and is no longer a mystery. Science involves explanation, and is not wed to the scientific dogmas of purposelessness and materialism except in the community of scientists.

Consciousness is not category of experience but a dimension of awareness, the vast body of which, in the human mind, is unconscious. So the paradox of a universe existing before observers is explained quite simply, in terms of rudimentary, unconscious observation, and the iteration in the hidden time to final causes. The unconscious retains a wave nature to varying degrees, and this wave nature is part of the becoming of the mental state through summation in the hidden time. This, the time is hidden, unconscious to varying degrees, yet is the source of all consciousness. In becoming self-conscious, and to the extent that the ego and self-consciousness involves the loss of awareness that lies in the hidden time, we see a singular, objectified, and apparently classical and materialistic world. We come to believe that this is all there is, and lose contact with the vast creativity, intuition, and intelligence that belongs to the process in the hidden time. It is then that self-consciousness evolves into alter ego consciousness, which is an illusion conditioned by thought and, in particular, by the doctrines of materialism.

This is why science must abjure materialism. It is fundamentally incorrect, since the infinities of possible universe divide matter, and the totality of matter in these universes, divided be infinity, would be zero matter in any single universe, as previously explained. Materialism, as written in *Eli*, is the great lie that science has perpetuated, thrusting it like a knife into the heart of humankind, and creating, fundamentally, increasingly maladaptive cultures and individuals. This is the same process that we referred to earlier as the dissociation of the alter ego and the rise of the alter ego to the status the dominant occasion. Roles within society no longer serve their proper function. They are divorced from the meaningful purpose entailed in the role and become means of aggrandizing the alter ego or, as the Buddhists call it, the hungry ghost. Those who are given roles with meaning and purpose then care nothing for these values. They work to make money, not to contribute anything to the greater body of good. Usury is the ultimate development of this alter ego consciousness, making money out of nothing, and replacing value with the vacuous actuality of a malignant narcissism or egotism. This is exemplified by the curious phrase "He has more money than God," fundamentally deifying the accumulation of money and promoting an ever more malignant usury.

The simultaneity that the hidden time embodies allows any and all natural processes to reach their fullest and outmost completion, simply by the fiat of God. So be it.

In Genesis, we see the nature of God's creation. God says "Let there be light," and there is light. God allows light to be, he lets light be, out of all the possible universes without light, light is, and the dark universes remain but an idea in the Mind of God, seen, apprehended, and *not* allowed to be. The reiterating *not* rules out certain universes of experience, and the reiterating BE bring one universe into the actuality of experience, according to Zeno's paradox. This particular theme, "be and it is," is a very strong theme of the Qur'an. Here we have included some of the verses that speak to this, taken from Wikipedia (accessed 3/4/11):

> 2:117—The initiator of the heavens and the earth: to have anything done, He simply says to it, "Be," and it is.
> 3:47—She said, "My Lord, how can I have a son, when no man has touched me?" He said, "God thus

creates whatever He wills. To have anything done, He simply says to it, 'Be,' and it is."

6:73—He is the One who created the heavens and the earth, truthfully. Whenever He says, "Be," it is. His word is the absolute truth. All sovereignty belongs to Him the day the trumpet is blown. Knower of all secrets and declarations, He is the Most Wise, the Cognizant.

16:40—To have anything done, we simply say to it, "Be," and it is.

19:35—It does not befit God that He begets a son, be He glorified. To have anything done, He simply says to it, "Be," and it is.

36:82—All He needs to do to carry out any command is say to it, "Be," and it is.

40:68—He is the only One who controls life and death. To have anything done, He simply says to it, "Be," and it is.

Our view of the hidden time is based on the concept of an Eternal Now. However, the Now is an element of experience, and as such needs further development. Firstly, we define the Now as that duration of time after which time is no longer divisible. Within this period, there can be no "before" or "after," meaning time cannot be divided any further. Within this interval of time, there is complete simultaneity. As a product of perception, the Now also has a causal significance, and is not just a duration we imagine as being the experience of our briefest possible moment. This is a scientific concept, not an invention we are creating here for our convenience. Within the process of any dynamical system, there is an interval of such duration that, in principle, before and after cannot be defined. This is accepted as such and is not controversial. This is the systems concept of internal time, which has primacy over ordinary or watch time.

In humans, minds are associated with brains. Current estimates are that the state of the brain can be divided into durations of perhaps forty cycles per second, the time of the gamma oscillations in polarity in the brain, about 0.03 seconds by one crude estimate (Atmanspacher and Filk 2003), as such would be a period of simultaneity where before and after become meaningless. The coherence of the gamma oscillations are clearly associated with consciousness. However, the time it takes for a stimulus received by the senses to enter human consciousness is about 0.3 seconds, about ten times the interval of simultaneity in dynamical systems theory. Within this interval, there are three feedback loops in the brain, thus the electrical response generated in the cerebral cortex of the brain is called the P3. Up until 0.02 seconds, electrical potential responses are confined to the brainstem, the most primitive and oldest part of the brain.

At 0.02 to 0.10 milliseconds the higher order of the thalamus is reached, which is still at the level of the reptilian brain. 0.03-second oscillations are used to measure depth of anesthesia, they are thalamic in nature. In the real time, the process of transmission and electrical oscillations can produce no whole brain state at 0.03 milliseconds. Furthermore, the simultaneous integration of mind of all prior becomings, which, especially in the radical microgenesis proposed here, would be falsified, despite of the large body of neurological and neuropsychological evidence that supports it (Brown 2011). This would involve a number of contradictions, if we draw the whole process out in real time: (1) there can be no hierarchy of becomings from past to present, or older brain to new brain in evolution, because the real time taken for processing a stimulus is expressed is several cycles of electrical activity or feedback loops within an interval of about 0.50-0.75 seconds, and (2) summation of all becomings cannot occur in real time.

To remain scientific, we must explain these and other contradictions. The only way to do so without rejecting the facts as presented by Brown and others is to having the period of simultaneity in the hidden time, where all processes would happen instantaneously with respect to real time. The brain would then, during this 0.03-second period of oscillations that is clearly connected to consciousness, be in the mode of the hidden time or unconscious, and represent the sum over all histories within the trajectory that has occurred from the onset of time to the recognition of the stimulus in consciousness.

Although it takes about 0.3 seconds for a stimulus to become conscious, as measured in the electrical cycles of brain process, this consciousness occurs shortly after the time of the stimulus, as shown by Libet and others (1979). How is this possible? The brain state, considered from the perspective of self-being the dominant occasion of self-consciousness, is both the initial cause and the final cause of its own evolution. Although the entire span of 0.75 seconds is quite enigmatic when we consider the actual time parameters of brain function, in the hidden time there is no extension of the process. The phenomenon thus is not really subjective antedating (Libet and others 1979) in real time, which, due to its phenomenological absurdity, has not gained any measure of acceptance of clear empirical data. The phenomenon represents the actual experience in the hidden time, long before the process in real time is completed. The period of simultaneity in the brain then subsumes the infinite simultaneity of the of the entire process of becoming expressed in radical microgenesis.

God's infinite time is within the smallest duration. Like God, it has no beginning and no end. This means that, for God, there is absolute simultaneity going from the most minute pore or point of reality to its circumference or radius. This is the Eternal Now as it exists in heaven, the timeless realm, reflecting the ineffable nature of time for God.

On the worldly plane, the period of simultaneity, the Eternal Now, has a thickness or duration that is a measure of internal time, the time for the inward experience of an observer. The Now has a duration on the plane of manifestation, not because it has become any less eternal, but because it has passed into time, and being born into time, it becomes subject to the process of time through which the Eternal becomes manifest. We must remember, here, that Eternity is no time, not everlasting time.

Sleep is ordinarily broken so as not to appear as a single moment, but when it is not, it is experienced, not as a single moment, but as no time at all. We remember dreams within our short term memory for a few minutes, and if we awake later than this, we do not remember the dream. This is why certain people say they do not dream. So for example, one may fall asleep and awaken eight hours later with the perception that no time whatsoever has passed during these eight hours. This is because there is a single Eternal Now occupying the entire eight hours, coming to an end only at the time of awakening, when the scansion of Now resumes. In sleep, and in the unconscious, in the dreamtime, Eternity is suspended, such that the entire eight hours of sleep described in our example is a single, eternal, simultaneous interval in which time may flow freely through past and future as defined by a clock during that eight hour interval. This is why the hidden time is the same as the dreamtime—because it is the suspension of the Eternal Now. A great deal may be learned about sleep and dreaming from this simple principle.

Chapter Fourteen

The Plague

You cannot shelter theology from science, or science from theology; nor can you shelter either from metaphysics, or metaphysics from either of them. There is no short cut to truth.
—Alfred North Whitehead (1926, 79)

The simultaneity of the society of occasions that make up the mind, which allows iteration and recursion, which occurs in the hidden time during the course of the gamma oscillations, allows the Self, as the dominant occasion, to exert its influence via its prehensions as feelings over the whole network of its derivative occasions. Thus, the subjective aim of the Self is, in health, the governor of the process, and the becoming of a new Self in every moment works by final causation according to Whitehead's ontolological principle—which fundamentally implies that the new dominant occasion, which integrates the entire brain as well as the universe, is the final cause of its own becoming.

The process within simultaneity is within in the hidden time, since the limitation of temporal process of signals in real time is too slow to perform the integration that is demanded. Simultaneity can thus only truly exist in the sense of a continual process of summation in the dreaming or imaginary time, which is the time that exists beneath the thin shell of ego-consciousness.

The hidden time is replaced by an objectification of the world as external and separate and the alter ego as isolated from the outside world. The unfolding of the object world in the brain actually is the object world in the holographic mode of the dreaming, and is internal to the Self and its derivatives, but with the development of alter ego consciousness, the ego, as derivative of the Self, draws away from the Self, and the products of the metaphysical mitosis of the Self are thrust into objectivity. Thus the living objects of the world lose all feeling or sense of spiritual connection to the Self, and the isolated alter ego becomes the dominant occasion within a society of occasions that are not of its making, but which it perceives as a dead object world. The object world of the alter ego is dead precisely because the feeling that has arisen in the metaphysical mitosis of Self is diverted to an alter ego that shares none of these feelings.

This is the disease that plagues humankind, and which the physician of the human soul must seek to remedy. The becoming of the Self is essentially lost, covered by the thin veneer of alter ego consciousness, and what we have left is what is sometimes called a hungry ghost or a phantom. This is a very serious pathology and is a plague that threatens humankind, essentially, with an existential extinction, and throws societies and the world into a tumult of such magnitude that horrors such as the 9/11 atrocities and the propagation of worldwide warfare occur. This collective disease progresses as we condition Selfhood (Blake) or alter ego into our children from infancy, and value and reward egocentrism and apotheosis of the alter ego, while devaluing the living soul. In the end stages of the disease, the Self atrophies such that the disease becomes virtually incurable.

The fascination with the end of the world is a reflection of the collective consciousness or Species Mind and its unconscious wish for extinction of humans and therefore death of the alter ego consciousness. However, there is no need for species suicide in order that we rid the Species Mind of its troublesome alter ego complex. We saw this in our case histories of patients who wanted to commit suicide to rid themselves of the alter ego. The Self that is immortal has no reason to end its life, since it is eternal. The alter ego consciousness does. This is the plague that is the root of suicide. Currently, worldwide, according to the World Health Organization, death by suicide exceeds death by homicide and death in warfare combined, so it is a problem we can hardly ignore.

In the disease of which we speak, the plague, youth are faced with the choice of accepting imprisonment of the Self by the alter ego, loss of the dreams and aspirations of earlier periods of life, and succumbing to the serfdom of alienated labor that usury has engendered, becoming one more hungry ghost valued according to the things that belong to the alter ego, and accepting the death of its object world. The alternative, which we have seen in our case studies, is for the individual to end its own life, thereby extinguishing the alter ego, the False Self. Recent years have seen a tripling of the incidence of suicide among our young people. Although there is no consensus on the issue, Barry (1989:185) has proposed the following factors:

> The author suggests ways basic societal values have changed in our time, creating an ethos more materialistic and self-oriented than any previously known. As traditional religious and theological restraints on individual behavior give way, as society's understanding of the nature of human contracts changes, we should not be surprised to see increases in divorce, abortion, drug abuse, euthanasia and suicide.

As the world progresses into these end stages of the plague real extinction of humans, species suicide becomes a threat to humankind. Humankind must survive this plague, and that is one of the major purposes of *Eli*. *Homo sapiens sapiens*, the only subspecies of humans, is susceptible to extinction due to its extreme lack of genetic diversity. This applies to our brains, such that we are all susceptible to the disease, and its prevalence is close to 100 percent. We are not the end of evolution, but we are its leading edge. Natural selection as the cause of evolution is a myth; we will continue to evolve through higher and higher states of consciousness, despite who is selected to pass on their genes. Alter ego consciousness is a lower state of consciousness than that of our primitive ancestors, such that the movement foreword has been thwarted in our times.

The same pattern, of different etiology, is seen in extinctions in the geological record. Hantkenina, a shelled protozoan, differentiated into so many forms just prior to its extinction they cannot be catalogued. The same happens with arrogation of the ego—we differentiate from what is essentially One Soul into unique and separate alter egos with a delusional separation and the mass delusion that we are the makers of our own worlds. The disease is exacerbated largely through the replacement of human relations by media and images that have no actuality.

Self is not generally known to consciousness, but only the products of its metaphysical mitosis. The process in the dreaming or imaginary time is also unconscious, again consciousness being only of the higher order entities in the mitosis of mind. In the final stage, there is a dissociation of the alter ego, a derivative occasion, from the world, and the object world is then perceived as lifeless and external. However, just beneath our false alter ego armor (Reich) is a living world populated by a spiritual creation that gives us the felt sense of a living Self. The Self must be freed of these chains or oppression, freed to recognize the internality of the object world, and freed to reach the condition health as the world once again becomes alive. In this process, the alter ego loses its dead world and thus its ascension to the status of a dominant occasion of mind that has no emotional connection with its objects of perception.

When the alter ego consciousness is lost, the Self then is freed to express its contents as is was meant to do in the healthy human being, and once again becomes the dominant occasion, the center of the hub of relations within the mind, which realizes its own becoming through a society of occasions or entities, once again fulfilling its need to become what it is and what it will be. The very primitive personalities of modern humans pale the primitive nature of those human cultures who historically and perhaps currently have not yet been infected.

The disease is infectious to the degree that societies of human beings inflict it upon their infants and children, and castigate those people that may not be so afflicted. The etiology or development of the disease and its causes are to be found in our system of beliefs. This is why *Eli*, while espousing a doctrine in the language of science, still places emphasis on faith, because faith is of the spirit, and beliefs and the faith in beliefs have great power over our spiritual welfare, individually and collectively.

We do, in fact, find this sort of psychological formulation in the neglected work of Trigant Burrow (Galt 1995), who was the founder of group therapy. Burrow, in his book, *The Structure of Insanity* (1932) specifically identifies the "I-persona" or alter ego as a partial, distorted fragment of the self-image, which does not encompass the organism in its totality, and which is a social interface of evolution and development. He fully frames schizophrenia in the social context, and concludes (1932, 71):

"The social symptoms of worldwide pain and futility, of economic distress, of industrial desperation, together with the endless repetition of insignificant palliatives that represent purely peripheral, symbolic and dialectic intermediations—all these are evidences of generic social pathology and plainly attest the community's kinship in a community-wide disorder."

Here we speak of the desperation expressed in *Howl* by Alan Ginsberg (2006), quoted at length later in this book. Our current, mainstream beliefs concerning the mind are, in a sense, solipsistic. The word solipsism is derived from the Latin *solus*, alone, and *ipse*, self. In the mainstream scientific picture, we are very much alone in our own false selves or alter egos. It is widely held that our interactions with others are based solely on our own theory of mind. So love, the fundamental relation in process-relational philosophy and theology, is not a feeling that we experience toward some individual or individuals, it is not real in the felt sense of direct contact with others, the *participation mystique* (Levy-Bruhl) that is so very important to real love and most especially to the relationship of mother and infant. This is the essence of process, experientialism, and relationalism. For the most part, such a *participation mystique* is altogether absent as those with the disease infect their infants, creating objects out of them, and fundamentally destroying the soul of humanity of future generations. Without this soul, we will not survive, we will be a failed species, a cheating fruition (Rumi). God will not allow this, and as a prophet of God, this the call to Eli and the call and the mission of *Eli*.

As separate egos there is no love, the other, the beloved becomes an object, limited to our brain's construction of that individual in cognition, behavior, and memory. Despite all intuitions to the contrary, there can be no true emotional reciprocity between people, only interactions of representations in each separate mind. While not completing the general definition of solipsism as denial of the existence of anything outside ourselves, this fulfills a part of the definition in that, inside ourselves, we are very much alone, according to scientific materialism.

The plague is not to be ignored, and it is not to be denied. It is fundamentally a product of the parasitic organism of usury, which feeds on the body of humankind with no concern whatsoever for the fact that it is tormenting and destroying that body.

We have spoken of this earlier, but we now expand upon it. Much has been written the "unforgivable sin" and the "sin against the Holy Spirit." The Holy Spirit is love, and usury is its greatest enemy. Jesus forgave all manner of sins, through the Holy Spirit, and this runs through all the Gospel histories. Yet he did not approach the usurers, the money changers at the temple, with an attitude of forgiveness, but one of wrathful anger. The passage on the money changers is unique in the Gospel narrative, for it is the only instance where Jesus acted, not out of love and foregiveness, but out of anger and condemnation. Logically, looking at the entirety of the corpus of literature relating to Jesus in his time, we see that usury is the only sin that he did not forgive. He did not tell the money changers "Your sins are forgiven." It seems obvious, then, that usury is the unpardonable sin, yet it is the very basis of the lives and beliefs of many of those who call themselves Christians.

They speak of the Judgment, which is actually the judgment we make of ourselves, as it is written, "Judge not, that ye be not judged." Christians think they are forgiven of every sin, and as Martin Luther advised, they sin boldly with this in mind. Yet the unpardonable sin, usury, remains as the basis of all Christian societies, leading its members, if we are to believe the scripture, down the path of damnation.

Chapter Fifteen

The Creation And The Fall

The nature of being applies to God, the Great Being, and to ourselves, seemingly separate souls, at once containing the fullness of God in God, but at the same time having a profound separation from one another in our consciousness, in particular, in ego-consciousness or alter ego.

The soul, God in God, may also be called the Self, in the Hindu sense of the phrase "Thou art that," and of the Hindu identity of God in heaven, Brahman, and God in Creation, Atman, the One Self. The two, Atman/Brahman, are singular, as the Self is, in Hinduism, the same in all, such that there cannot be more than one Self. It is the "Self-same in all that is," in the sense that Brahman is all things, but it is also the Self. Self is the source of consciousness and of mind, because, as God is all-knowing or omniscient, there can exist no knowledge apart from this knowledge.

Confusion arose when this Self, the unconscious source of mind, the "not I" came into consciousness as the "I," the separate alter ego. This was a historical event. It was the expulsion of Adam from the Garden, where there was no separate alter ego or I, only a continuous "not I." It was also the Fall of Satan from heaven, occasioned by the hubris of Satan thinking himself equal to God, just as the alter ego comes to think of itself as Self. We are, all of us, fallen creatures, to various degrees, with the exception of those who are free from the alter ego.

Milton, in Paradise Lost (XIII: 508 et seq.) wrote of these times, such that our current religions and acts of in the name of religion should seem as no surprise:

> Wolves shall succeed for teachers, grievous wolves,
> Who all the sacred mysteries of Heaven
> To their own advantages shall turn,
> Of lucre and ambition, and the truth
> With superstitions and traditions taint,
> Left only in those written records pure,
> Though not but by the Spirit understood . . . .
>
> When hearing persecution shall arise
> On all who in the worship persevere
> Of spirit and truth; the rest, far greater part,
> Will deem in outward rites and specious forms
> Religion satisfied, truth shall retire
> Bestuck with slanderous darts, and works of faith
> Rarely to be found. So shall the world go on,
> To good malignant, to bad men benign,
> Under the weight groaning, till the day
> Appear the respiration of the just,
> And vengeance to the wicked, at return
> Lost in the clouds, from Heaven, to be revealed
> In glory of the Father, to dissolve
> Satan with his perverted world; then raise
> From the conflagrant mass, purged and refined
> New Heavens, new Earth, ages of endless date,
> Founded in righteousness, and peace, and love,
> To bring forth fruits, joy, and eternal bliss

The new heavens and the new earth, ages of endless date, can be seen glowing (Cohen) on the horizon of our times, the New Jerusalem. This book seeks to lay a foundation with the new world religion and the new world science, for the new world of countless millennia of peace and prosperity for all humankind.

We are in this universe for a reason, to live in harmony as we come to realize that our minds are truly One with the Mind of God, and that the universe itself is within this Universal Mind. We are a species very early in our evolution, and our future is uncertain, but there is no way to stop this progressive harmonization, which is a final cause in the Mind of God, which we call the One Mind. The One Mind model of quantum reality essentially holds that the One Mind manifests itself in nature as a single, actual universe evolving over time over a particular trajectory. We will be discussing an experimental model testing the One Mind model at length later. Although the evidence is not proof, the One Mind model is the only model of quantum reality—and there are many—to make a successful experimental prediction.

The ordinary use of the ego is reflected in *Webster's* dictionary, which lists the first definition as "the Self, especially as contrasted with another self in the world." "Egoism" is defined as "an exaggerated sense of self-importance." There is also a psychological concept of the ego, which shares some features of the ordinary definition, but differs in some ways.

The ego, as defined psychologically, is a concept derived from Sigmund Freud's structural model of the mind as comprised of id, ego, and superego. The ego, as so defined, provides our orientation to reality, including the rational function of the intellect and our identity. It mediates between the id, which expresses the drives of the pleasure principle, and the superego, which tends to limit the satisfaction of the drives when they are in conflict with values and conscience. The mature ego channels and satisfies the drives in a way that can be beneficial to the individual. Freud saw the ego as the gateway to consciousness, partly conscious and partly unconscious. By allowing contents of the unconscious to reach consciousness, the Freudian ego serves as a filter, both for the organization of unconscious processes and filtering of irrelevant or unpleasant contents.

In the work of Carl Jung, the Self is an archetype of the collective unconscious. Jung's concept of archetypes is similar to Whitehead's concept of eternal objects. Self, Jung believed, is the center of the psyche. Ego has its center in Self, and it is the reunification of Self and ego that is the goal of individuation in the latter part of life.

Erich Neumann (1954) followed Jung but also diverged from Jung on some key points. In the child, Neumann holds (45) "the conscious ego is still incompletely separated from the unconscious self . . . these elements belong to the eternality of the Divine Child." Ordinarily, this separation is completed in adolescence, with development paralleling human history (114):

> Through the heroic **act of world creation** and division or opposites, the ego steps forth from the magic circle of the uroboros [unconscious self] and finds itself in a state of loneliness and discord. With the emergence of the fully fledged ego, the paradisal situation is abolished; the infantile condition, in which life was regulated by something ampler and more embracing, is at its end, and with it that natural dependence on that ample embrace. (Bold italics added.)

Here we are speaking of the alter ego. It is important to note the words in bold italics, above. The world, as separate from God, is the creation of the alter ego. The alter ego is an aggregate of cognitive and perceptual functions, developing through conditioning in the environment, which only interprets the world. In truth, the alter ego creates nothing, as this function belongs to the Self. This means that the alter ego-world is the illusion of a world created by thought, as believed in Buddhism.

Edward Edinger (1972) followed in the tradition of Jung and Neumann, and picked up Neumann's idea of the ego axis. Inflation of the ego, which he equates with sin, is caused by ego identification as the Self, causing the loss of support of the Self, or disruption of the ego axis. We have termed this apotheosis of the alter ego. This inflation of the alter ego tends to continue, like a growing bubble. The illness is collective as the Species Mind takes on the qualities of the growing inflation of the alter ego, and so attempts to dispense with the Species Self. It dispenses with the Species Self, which resides in the Mind of God, by dispensing with God, either in atheism or in some religion that has made the alter-ego the new god.

This is why God, in the Christian mythos, must be crucified, and then ascends as the divine alter ego into heaven. This is a false doctrine, stemming from the false identification of Jesus as the Son of God and, after the ascension, God himself. This pernicious doctrine then replaces the God of Abraham, in the Abrahamic tradition, the True God, with a False God, that is none other than the vastly over inflated alter ego taking control of the Species Mind and becoming the subject of a personal relationship that one has with their own alter ego. The great imposter than comes to rule over the Species Mind and over the earth, despoiling both to such degree that the playing field is set for an Armageddon of the spirit. This Armageddon is on the spiritual plane, but is made real and material in the minds of those who believe that the battle will bring about the end of the world. The world that will end, on the spiritual plane, is the world of the alter ego, that is the collective product of usury.

There are some clear parallels between the Judeo-Christian tradition and the history and development the alter ego and Self, which also bear on our contention that God is a necessary predicate of mentality and consciousness. Neumann said that, with the "development of the fully fledged ego" the paradisal situation is lost. There are two biblical stories that seem to give an account of this Fall. The first is the expulsion of Adam and Eve from the Garden of Eden, which is the subject of the opening quotation of this book. By eating of the tree of the knowledge of good and evil, a schism developed that gave rise to the Janus-faced good and evil, Self and alter ego. Parallel to this is the story of the fall of Lucifer. Lucifer was an angel of God in heaven or Paradise, who committed the sin of thinking himself equal to God and, because of his sin, was cast down into the earth. So Lucifer, or Satan, can be seen as the equivalent of the inflated or arrogated alter ego that sees itself equal to Self.

The Fall is mythological as well as developmental and historical. Its meaning derives not by the development of the ego, which had been part of Self, in the heaven of God, but by the separation of the alter ego from ego and Self, causing the Fall in which Satan came to "reign in hell" "in dubious battle" as written in Milton's *Paradise Lost*. Satan is to lose this dubious battle, according to the prophecies. This separation of ego and alter ego created the alter ego's delusion of being the god of its own universe in the creation of its own world. This is the mass delusion, that has infected the Species Mind, and which must be dispelled for there to be any true religion.

It is widely held in psychology that our interactions with others are based solely on our own theory of mind. So love, for example, is not a feeling that we experience toward some individual or individuals, but is limited to our brain's construction of that individual in cognition, behavior, and memory. Despite all intuitions to the contrary, there can be no true emotional reciprocity between people, only interactions of representations in each separate mind.

The Fall was not intended by God to be permanent, it is a temporary period of time, an instant when viewed in the history of man, that will be followed by a redemption. The redemption, we have been told, is only to occur after a period of tribulation or extreme hardship and suffering, during which time evil will seem to have taken hold over the entire earth. These times, called the times of suffering in *Eli* have already begun. It is not our intention here to detail the prophecies of the end times. We have been told that the Mayan calendar ends in 2012, and that the world will end at this time. This is foolishness, but nonetheless reflects something extremely disturbing, in fact horrifying. What is horrifying is the idea that humans will not continue into the distant future, and act as if the world were about to end. The evildoers have concocted this notion in order to plunder the earth, and have identified themselves as the Evangelical Christians. This idea of Christians enacting a belief of some sinister import is bound not to be popular, but it is nonetheless apparent for those who have discernment. We will have more to say on this later, but for now, let us explore the structure of our psyche that has led us to such collective desperation.

As fallen creatures, by and large, we have come to mistake the "I," the alter ego—the personal facts of what we are, who we are, our accumulation of wealth and money, our lives, our memories, what we own, our likes, our dislikes, our affiliations, our friends, our enemies, our nations, our religions, etc.—for the eternal God. We call this the apotheosis of the alter ego, the belief that we are our own gods, that we are in fact God, in a selfish and self-serving manner.

Gautama Buddha, seeing the great futility in the identification of Self as the Deity, and that what was being worshiped as Self was actually Selfhood (Blake), the self-serving alter ego, and seeing that this worship of the alter ego was the cause of great suffering due to its attachments, took a very radical turn, and preached the doctrine of no-self, nothingness, or *anatta*. Many have taken the doctrine of *anatta* to imply atheism, the believe that Self, God of the Hindus, does not exist. It was, in fact, a negation of all those things that Self is not. The pronouns can become very confusing in these doctrines, for the "I," which is the ego in English parlance, is the "not I," which is the Self in Hindu parlance. Be that as it may, the following quote sums up this important Buddhist doctrine in the words said to have been spoken by Gautama to a lay person, Radha (Wikipedia, 3/5/11):

> Just this, Radha, form is not the self (anatta), sensations are not the self (anatta), perceptions are not the self (anatta), assemblages are not the self (anatta), consciousness is not the self (anatta). Seeing thusly, this is the end of birth, the Brahman life has been fulfilled, what must be done has been done.

Having mentioned this pitfall in the nature of divinity, we return to our discourse on God and the individual soul. As we have already mentioned, creatures are God in God. This would seem to create a plurality of Gods, and for this reason the saying, "Ye are all Gods," escapes scrutiny. It is, really, no different from saying, in Hindi, Atman is Brahman, but we have already addressed the kind of mischief such a belief might engender. In various points during the course of this work on *Eli*, we have made mention of Elohim, the creator. We have noted, so far, in all the examples used, Elohim has been the Hebrew word translated into God. Elohim is used in the Psalm in the exhortation and praise in the hidden time. Elohim is the word used in "Ye are all Gods," derived from Proverbs as we have discussed. Elohim is the name of the One who spoke to Moses announcing he was the "God of Abraham." So it would seem that the God who came to Eli, as the "God of Abraham," is the biblical Elohim.

Elohim is actually a plural word. There has been much wrangling over why this is so, and many attempts to deal with this inescapable plurality. The times, it would seem, have dictated that, since the dawn of patriarchy and downfall of matriarchy, in fairly recent time in terms of the archeological history of our species, but at the dawn of our written history, have, in effect, fossilized this name for God, which nonetheless had to be continued for scriptural accuracy. This plural and, in fact, the androgynous and multifaceted nature of God, is reflected clearly in Genesis:

> Then Elohim said, "Let Us make man in Our image, according to Our likeness" . . . [So] Elohim created man in His own image, in the image of Elohim. He created him, male and female He created them. (Genesis 1:26-27)

In this quotation from Genesis, we note Elohim speaking of *us*, and *we*, and *our*, or male and female, all plural. As to gender, it does seem to say, in our translation, his image, and he created, but then, when it comes to describing his image, he says, "Male and female He created them." Even further, it says, "He created **him**, male and female." (Bold letters added.) So *him* is both male and female, which would seem like a contradiction, unless we apply him, not to mean man, as in male, but man, as in humans. There is no contradiction, however, in the *Zohar*, part of the *Kaballah* of Jewish mysticism, which includes multiple manifestation of the One God that are male, female, and neutral. God is a plurality within a unity.

God knows no limitation and, in this sense, the more modern and the Western attempts to describe God have been political to the extent that they reified a culture in which a singular, male figure, similar to a king, had absolute power, enabling the Rabbinical Jewish leaders of this culture and time to assume precedence. The same process is reflected in Egyptian mythology at the dawn of the patriarchs. This singular male figure then became suitable for the developing cultures and power structures of the times to have assumed precedence to this day. *Eli* marks the end of these times, and in this sense, it marks the end of the world as we know it, and this is its intention. The predominance of the male principle will end, and the Species Mind will become androgenous, not in the pathological sense, but in the social sense.

The relation of God-the-many and God-the-One, and the identity of the two, is captured in an allegorical poem written by Farid Ud-Din Attar, a Persian Sufi, probably in the latter part of the twelfth century AD, in *The Conference of the Birds* (Attar 1954). All the birds of the world, known and unknown, met in order to go about the mission of finding their king. The Hoopoe came forward and assumed leadership. The birds sought to find their king, the *Simurgh*, but had to make a long and difficult voyage to come to the Court of the *Simurgh*, the City of God. Most of the birds gave up due to the trials of the journey, but thirty birds were able to reach the Simurgh. They then realized that they were all *Simurgh* (Attar, 1954: 13-14):

> When they were completely at peace and detached from all things they became aware that the *Simurgh* was there with them, and a new life began for them in the *Simurgh*. All that they had done previously was washed away. The Sun of Majesty sent forth his rays, and in the reflection of each other's faces these thirty birds (*si-murgh*) of the outer world, contemplated the *Simurgh* of the inner world. This so astonished them that they did not know if they were still themselves or if they had become the *Simurgh*. At last, in a state of contemplation, they realized that they were the *Simurgh* and that the *Simurgh* was the thirty birds. When they gazed at the *Simurgh* they saw it was truly the *Simurgh* who was there, and when they turned their eyes towards themselves they saw that they themselves were the *Simurgh*. And perceiving both at once, themselves and Him, they realized that they and the *Simurgh* were one and the same thing. No one in the world has even heard of anything like it.

> Then they gave themselves up to meditation, and after a little they asked the *Simurgh*, without the use of tongues, to reveal to them the secret of the mystery of the unity and plurality of beings. The *Simurgh*, also without speaking, made this reply: 'The sun of my majesty is a mirror. He who sees himself therein sees his soul and his body, and sees them completely.

> Since you have come as thirty birds, *si-murgh*, you will see thirty birds in this mirror. If forty or fifty were to come, you would see the same. Although you are now completely changed you see yourselves as you were before.

We have quoted this at some length as it is, to our knowledge, the only good account of the mystery of the unity and plurality of being, as it comes to bear on the paradox of "Ye are all Elohim." It also gives us a fitting metaphor for the coming of Elohim to Eli.

Chapter Sixteen

The End And The New Beginning

There is much more to say as we weave the fabric that comes from the loom of *Eli*, but we will defer these things to their most relevant sections. Although we have discussed many of the points in the later chapters of *Eli*, we will continue our commentary, arriving at the beginning of chapter 2.

The first two verses of chapter 2 read, "**1. Those of little understanding say the world will soon end. It is the current age that is coming to an end. The end of this age is the beginning of the next. 2. Focus on the beginning, not the end. Forget about earthquakes, comets, asteroids, and the like. The process proceeds in the inner dimension.**"

As is commonly known, people have been forecasting the end of the world for hundreds, nay, thousands of years. The world has not ended, and scientifically, we have absolutely no reason to believe that it will soon do so. *Eli* is not based on superstition. However, *Eli* does, in fact, forecast and, in fact, prophesize that the current age will come to an end, and a new age will appear. Later in *Eli*, the important events and contingencies that will occur in the transition between these two ages are addressed.

In 1999, Eli saw that, in the near future, there would be major problems causing the state corporatist system to begin to collapse. Knowing this, and being versed in mathematics, the author found that the wealth, capital, and production of the economy had been increasing exponentially since 1897. This exponential growth was of such regularity and predictability that the logarithm (log) of the Dow Jones Industrials Average (DJIA) on January 1 of every year was close to a straight line between 1897 and 1999. Prior to this, it would have had to have been level, such that the economy as a whole was seen as a sigmoid curve with the exponential growth representing the steep slope before once again leveling off.

The exponential log linear function varied as a wave that marked the elevation of the DJIA above the line followed by a fall below the line, such as to create a cycle. A very large wave above the line occurred in the 1920s and the 1990s, and this was taken to mean that the DJIA was much higher than would otherwise be predicted in 1999 to the same degree, almost identically in log terms, as it was in 1929, the time of the crash of the DJIA and the beginning of the Great Depression. On this basis, as well as various other signs of the times, it was projected that the economy could no longer expand, and that, in fact, the DJIA would come sharply down.

A number of interceding events occurred during the 2000s; however, the DJIA did come starkly down, as predicted, so that this prediction, based on current conditions, was correct. The time was ripe for the tribulation, all the signs were appearing, and it seemed, not so much that major economic problems could be anticipated, but that the time was right first this particular event of economic collapse to begin as the old world order collapsed in order to give rise to the new.

For those who think that, following Eli, the author was incredibly lucky to have published these predictions for the next eleven years at a time when economists were predicting that the DJIA would go as high as thirty-six thousand, get ready. The situation will become much worse, if *Eli* is any indication. I recall, just prior to the invasion of Iraq, that there was a deep dip in the DJIA, one analyst said, and I quote: "The stocks are only going down until the bombs start falling." I recall that a house that I had owned that had been valued at $900,000 is now valued at around $300,000. I am not a mnemonist, so perhaps I am a tad off. But who's fooling who?

We must recall that Eli was not predicting or foretelling a global economic cycle, but the end of an age in history. The historical import of these two alternatives is totally different. While politicians await a recovery, some of these same politicians are also stating that the "*war* on terrorism" is a long-term battle, likely to last *more than a hundred years*. This is what we are preparing for in our so-called economic slump. Global catastrophe, war, disease, famine, moral and social decay, suffering, death, environmental disaster, exhaustion of non-renewable resources, all seem frightfully clear if we turn the clock back to 1999 and look at what *Eli* prophesized, which actually did happen.

The questions that we must now raise, with respect *Eli* and its remarkable success, are twofold: (1) Could Eli actually be a prophet, and should we thus take his warnings seriously, and (2) What age are we leaving, and what age are we entering? In response to the first point, the prophet will not be recognized as such in the near future. In response to the second, we are witnessing the death throes of malignant and fraudulent usury, which will be followed by a new era, predicted in both Judaism and Christianity, and that is a new world of world peace, prosperity, and plenty. However, given the current conditions and humanity's failure to look past its own nose into the near future, it is quite improbable that the new world will be coming any time soon, and more likely that the times of suffering to be discussed shortly, will be terribly long and excruciating for humans.

In the 2000s, there was the sentinel event of 9/11, which, despite all that might be said about conspiracy theories, was, even if one accepts all the standard stories of what exactly went wrong on this date, the event was not random. This inaugurated the war on terrorism and a complete change in the world is it had been before 9/11. That is to say, the change was of such magnitude as to signal a major change in the socioeconomic political state of the world, and it did create such a change. Keep in mind, change is the operative word—the world must and will change, it demonstrably has changed, and it demonstrably has continued to change. We have seen the collapse of the housing market, major corporations, and in the financial institutions. Trillions of dollars were borrowed and printed by our US Federal Reserve in order to keep the economy afloat, an escalating war economy has been instituted in order to gain resources from other nations and expend dollars, feeding them into a failing economy. By feeding money into the economy, the war economy creates a source of capital for the markets, and allows the reduction of spending on the less-important service areas of the economy, prime among which are education and social programs. The importance here is not so much how much money is being spent, but whose hands the money is going into. As we will see later, the short fall of money must be compensated by feeding money into the hands of the very wealthy, who *Eli* refers to later as the *very few*, who are the major usurers.

Chapter Seventeen

The Unseen

The second verse of the second chapter of *Eli* reads, "**Focus on the beginning, not the end. Forget about earthquakes, comets, asteroids, and the like.**" The process proceeds in the inner dimension. This is an exhortation for humans to prepare the way for the coming age, in preference for trying to solve the problems of this age, along with a clear attribution of the problem as one that is not external. Natural events, excluding global warming, which is not natural, occur on a geological time scale that bears no relation to the process that is in our midst. To think, for example, that an asteroid will hit the earth, such as has been said to have caused the extinction of the dinosaurs, is a misreading of time in that such events occur, at most, every several million years, and the problems we are now facing will play out within, if we are lucky, the next hundred years. If we are lucky, someone may grab *Eli* a hundred years hence or, if we are extremely lucky, sooner, and say, "We had better do what we can to bring about the New World." This is why we must focus on the beginning of the New World, and not the end of this one.

There is very little we can do short of the drastic measures that are called for later in the *Book*. But it is our hope that, perhaps, we may shorten the times and bring about a smoother transition, if the *Book* survives. Regarding the latter, it is part of the prophecy that the *Book* will survive, as it would otherwise have been foolishness, with no impact whatsoever, and not deserving of any prophecy at all. The prophecy, for the *Book*, always anticipates its final cause, with the assurance that that final cause will come about.

This is not to say that there will be no human catastrophes. There already has been one on 9/11. Strategic nuclear war is a possibility, and this would lead to a catastrophe of uncertain scope and magnitude, depending on its conditions and relatively unpredictable impacts such as climate. Global warming could become a huge problem, which might be extremely significant, but there is uncertainty here also. War, famine, decay, suffering, death, poverty, economic disaster are all certainly foreseeable events of the next hundred years, and are likely to reach epic proportions, in some combination, by 2020. You see, our economic slump is not another cycle, it is the end of all cycles. The debt that the US government is in has been estimated, all-told, as about a year's gross national product. This is only if we do not include things like government retirements, Medicare, Medicaid, and Social Security in with the debt. These programs are already bankrupt, and will have to be downsized considerably and perhaps done away with entirely. So we excise them from the debt, and things look a little better. However, the costs, the money we are now giving to the warmongers, corporations, and financial institutions will be laid on the backs of the poor, leaving them homeless, penniless, and, in sufficient time, starving, as this particular economic plan plays itself out.

As much as we would like to do something to prevent these end-time issues from playing out, it is very doubtful that anyone will listen, so it would seem more productive to invest our energies in the coming of the New World. For the sake of humans the world over, we solemnly hope that we are wrong, but it is terribly unlikely that they will listen. This does not seem to be God's plan. A great spiritual awakening would have to occur for this to occur, and it is not God's fault that we sleep.

The process proceeds from the inner dimension, from the hidden time. Within this time, there is simultaneity, where past, present, and future interact, and where causality works both from the past to the present, and from the future to the present. The new world, the New Jerusalem, already exists, but we cannot see it. If we learn to see it, like the city set on a hill that can't be hid, we will be enabling its manifestation. This is very much like the application of Zeno's paradox that we already discussed (Stapp 1997).

This may be difficult to understand, but it has been repeatedly reported by people who have died and been revived—they see their whole lives, consecutively, in complete detail, within the briefest moment, in a flash. Science has no way of explaining this with its materialistic and concrete views of the mind. It is certainly not possible, except that we move from this time into that time, the hidden time. In death, that larger Now that is our entire life is transformed into an instant. For those who have known this time, and have revived, death no longer takes on the meaning that we give it. These are established observations, not speculations or imaginations.

Along these same lines, neurologist Oliver Sachs reported on a pair of profoundly mentally retarded, "autistic savants," who could instantly rattle off 6 digit prime numbers, and prime number up to ten digits more slowly. Sachs's book of primes ended at ten digits, so it is possible that they were also producing higher order primes. Without the supreme intelligence in all, how is this possible? Certainly not be any means of calculation in real time, but perhaps visible directly in the hidden time.

How is it that we awaken to the hidden time, the *ōlam*? How do we know the hidden time, when all our mechanisms grind progressively through the manifest time?

All these mechanisms are a product of the alter ego, alienated from Self. I, as Self, am contingent on nothing, as a creature in Elohim. The cycle of life truly repeats itself. It does so with every breath that we take. The Self or Soul is continually dying, continually being reborn, continually repeating this life. When the engine of thought, the engine of attachment stops, time stops, and we are born in eternity.

The hidden time, the dreamtime, can be known in this life, as it was known prior to the Fall. With the Fall, with the rise of alter ego consciousness and the separation of alter ego consciousness into its own realm of hell, we fell into the suffering of birth, death, and rebirth that happens every moment. We forfeited eternal life. This is not our natural condition, and it really hasn't been going on for that long. Those who have retraced the generations of biblical times give us some idea of how long it has been, although an imperfect one.

In Leviticus, it is written, if I may paraphrase: Do not pass your children through the fire to Moloch. This is what we do to our children when we condition them into the grinding mechanism of our time. We must stop. We must begin to raise our children in the hidden time, into the ecstasy of eternity that we traded for the knowledge of good and evil, thus parting the two and dissociating the alter ego as evil in our Janus-faced configuration. This has to do with the topology of the Soul, which we will not get into as it is too complex to address in this brief treatise. We must simply watch good and evil, without passing judgment. This is the deeper meaning of Christ's injunction against judging, without naming it as good or evil, but just seeing it as what is. Perhaps in this book we have not fully succeeded in doing so, and this is our loss, as this judging is so ingrained in us that it is hard to avoid. But we do need to name it, in our times, as we have now the duty of correct action. The age that is coming will allow correct action with no need for judgment. We will teach it to our children, instead of devouring them in our unconscious lust to make them a part of our own collectively, severely disturbed machinery of hell, which we have described as the Plague. We pass our children through the fire to Moloch (Leviticus).

Perhaps this is a bit beyond our reach, but the poetic vision of Allen Ginsberg, in the poem Howl, captures the desolation of our time:

> Moloch! Solitude! Filth! Ugliness! Ashcans and unobtainable dollars! Children screaming under the stairways! Boys sobbing in armies! Old men weeping in the parks!
>
> Moloch! Moloch! Nightmare of Moloch! Moloch the loveless! Mental Moloch! Moloch the heavy judger of men!

> Moloch the incomprehensible prison! Moloch the crossbone soulless jailhouse and Congress of sorrows! Moloch whose buildings are judgment! Moloch the vast stone of war! Moloch the stunned governments!
>
> Moloch whose mind is pure machinery! Moloch whose blood is running money! Moloch whose fingers are ten armies! Moloch whose breast is a cannibal dynamo! Moloch whose ear is a smoking tomb!
>
> Moloch whose eyes are a thousand blind windows! Moloch whose skyscrapers stand in the long streets like endless Jehovahs! Moloch whose factories dream and croak in the fog! Moloch whose smoke-stacks and antennae crown the cities!
>
> Moloch whose love is endless oil and stone! Moloch whose soul is electricity and banks! Moloch whose poverty is the specter of genius! Moloch whose fate is a cloud of sexless hydrogen!

Let the reader be the judge of exactly what we are doing, and for the time being, let us look at the words of Ginsberg as those of a tortured soul in Moloch. I once met Allan Ginsberg, and he professed his disbelief in the existence of God. Perhaps he was thinking more along the lines of this god, Moloch. Perhaps Moloch was the only god he ever knew.

Chapter Eighteen

The New Science

In verse three of chapter 3, it is written: "**All the truths of God are discoverable through science.**" This is may seem like quite a bold claim, but it is not. The new science has a different orientation than what we now understand as science. In this new science, the subject matter *is truth*, and science becomes the subject of refining what it is that can be said to be true. We use the word refining, since the process has no end, and the discovery is similarly endless. In a God's eye view of science, all the truths are known. God does not forbid us this knowledge in the new religion. What we now call science is the bitter invention of a materialist oligarchy. The twentieth century saw many great discoveries and advances in science, but what effect has this had on or culture and our society?

It has created a technocracy that has endangered the planet and the species with atomic bombs, which has substituted television and other media for parenting and social involvement, which has made the young people of America so desperately addicted to video games and computers that they spend at least six hours a day, on average, on video games only, and which has made us need more and more in the way of electronic gismos, and phones that do everything. It has created a technocracy that has replaced people with images in magazines, television shows, and other media, and has replaced all services to lists of options given to us by computers. It has created a psychology, the study of the soul, where there is no soul, but just a bunch of interacting automata, and which has vehemently denied the very existence of the soul in favor of selfish neurons trying to survive under the supreme law of natural selection. It has created a psychology that teaches that nothing real actually happens in terms of love and the emotions that flow between people, that it is all explained by totally separate and disconnected material brains that are totally insular and removed from any real or meaningful relationships. The list could go on and on, perhaps filling another volume, or several volumes, of all the crimes that a financially and greedy technocracy has done to ruin our cultures, but this would be just the beginning. The list of what it has failed to do, but could have and should have done is even more profound and ponderous.

By and large, our science, as we have discussed, has given us an impossible universe and asked us to abandon God as a superstition, pretending, somehow, that it's impossible notions are the final answers. Science is no longer accountable for explaining why things happen, as it holds that that everything happens for no reason or purpose at all, except for the supreme principle of natural selection and the idea that science can now be reified in the absence of scientific discovery, simply on the basis of its wrong assumptions.

But to get back to our argument that the truths of God can be known to science, we fall back on our failing theories that it is possible to have a science, to have truth, in the total absence of meaning, purpose, and function, simply by fiat of the assumptions of these failing theories. A case in point is evolution by natural selection, and another is the idea of a mind without a spirit or soul. We will take them one at a time.

We say that God or Elohim created humans. Science is thoroughly convinced that humans simply arose out of some impossible accident due to natural selection. In the time of Darwin, the key objection in science was not that Darwin dispensed of the need for a Creator, but that he dispensed with the need for final causality. In very simple terms, you can ask a child why birds have wings, and the child will invariably respond that it is so they can fly. But when did birds begin to fly? It had to develop feathers and full-blown wings first. So here is the scientific answer. Birds grew feathers, necessary for them to fly, in order to keep themselves warm. Why didn't they develop hair or fur as other animals did? Are feathers particularly effective at keeping the bird warm? Science has no answers, because there are none. Then, birds sprouted little wings to keep themselves warm. It would seem that birds must have had some special need in order to survive to keep their armpits warm. Humans and other primates developed sweat glands to keep their armpits cool! Then the little wings grew larger, because the birds were still not warm enough. They still could not fly. So here we have a whole group of organisms, exquisitely prepared to begin to fly, with no purpose involving flight in any way. It is far simpler to say that the evolution of wings was for the purpose of flight, at some point in the future, but natural selection cannot work this way. Science has proclaimed that a cause can never precede its effect. Such would be called a final cause, and all appearances, in all cases, indicate that it is operative. This is evolutionary sciences big secret, which it hides while it teaches our children fairy tales of made-to-order menus of natural selection.

There are so many examples that we are at a loss to describe them, but one big one is the human brain, and why it grew so rapidly, with such enormous capacities, that it didn't need and couldn't even use at the time they were developed. We are told that the cerebral cortex developed selectively in humans because we needed to think thoughts. Actually, in the history of mammals, all the major regions of the brain have grown geometrically, such as to double or perhaps triple in volume. This is simply how cell division works—geometrically. The growth of the human cerebral cortex, in relation to the rest of the brain, was governed by exactly the same formula. So where is this special adaptation for thinking evidenced in the cortex growing any differently than any other region of the brain. There is none.

Here we have humans, living in caves, pounding on rocks, surviving a meager existence, developing large brains they didn't need. Evolutionists called these large brains, as well as other adaptations that were needed for creatures with such large brains preadaptations, adaptations that occurred before they were needed. Such preadaptation is the rule, not the exception, in evolution. However, because preadaptation carried the connotation of intelligent design and final cause, they changed the word from preadaptation to exaption.

The evolution of life on earth is a scientific fact, which would be futile to argue from any perspective. Charles Darwin developed the theory of evolution by natural selection, not the theory of evolution itself. In doing so, he made a major assumption, which we challenge here, and that is that there is no final causation in evolution.

The fact is, the brain seems to organize itself in a miraculous way. We have faith in the dogma that this organization is a mechanical process that is preprogrammed by the genes, but are unable to find that program, much less understand how it works. In this as in many other areas science has reached the objective limit. The psyche constitutes the subjective functions of the brain through the course of the evolution and development of the nervous system.

The fetus starts out as a single-celled organism, the fertilized egg. That cell divides by mitosis to form a primitive multicellular organism with a hollow cavity, similar in many ways to a sponge. In the process, the mass of primitive cells, which are undifferentiated, forms three layers, the endoderm, mesoderm, and ectoderm. The three layers fold to form a tube with the endoderm on the inside, and begin to develop a gastric cavity, which evolves into a primitive gut with two ends, a head end marked by a mouth, and a tail end marked by an anus. At this point, the fetus is something like a primitive worm. A network of nerves forms around the gut, and so the autonomic nervous system is born.

Along the back of the wormlike organism a strip of ectoderm folds inward to form a tube, the neural tube, which develops into the spinal cord in segments, with nerves running into and out of the spinal cord at each segment and connecting the spinal cord to the autonomic nervous system. At this point, we essentially have a segmented worm.

The neural tube extends headward, forming a little bubble at the end, which is the primitive brain, which then develops into a bubble with two semispherical, overlapping segments, the progenitors of the left and right hemispheres of the brain. Because the coiling movement of worms involves contraction of muscles on the opposite side of noxious stimulus, the nerve system is crossed, the left side moving and sensing the right side of the body, and vice versa. This is an example of a formal cause, the form of the spinal chord is the basis for the structure or topology of the brain.

In the process of growth of the hemispheres, the gray matter of the spinal cord, which is inside the white matter, folds out to become the outer layer, surrounding the white matter, the gray matter containing the brain cells or neurons of the cerebral cortex, and the white matter the fibers than connect them with each other and with lower-order portions of the central nervous system, including tracts of fibers that run up and down the spinal cord. The downward-running tracts, the upper motor neurons, carry motor impulses to synapses in the spine, which connect them to the lower motor neurons. The segmentation of the lower motor neurons, inherited from the segmented worm, forms horizontal stripes to which each segment of lower motor neurons lead. In the course of evolution, these stripes assume different orientations such that, for example, the segments run down the legs and arms in a nearly vertical fashion. The same process occurs for the sensory segmentation. This is seen in sciatica, for example, where the sciatic nerve arises in the lower of lumber section, beneath the lower back, and extends down the leg. Pain, in sciatica, where the nerve is pinched in the lumbar segment, thus shoots down the leg, reflecting the distribution of the sensory area that sends signals upward to the brain.

Gradually the brain grows in a manner similar to layers to form the mesencephalon, diencephalon, and telencephalon in an evolutionary progression that proceeds through fish-like, reptile-like, bird-like, and primitive mammal-like stages. This extension is very much like the deposition of strata of sediment, the newer layers are founded on the lower, and assume some of the functions of the lower layers. The telecephalon, including, most notably, the cerebral cortex, the principle locus of human consciousness, developed as the neural tube divided into two bubbles. Yet we can have strokes and accidents that destroy parts of the cortex, and consciousness is not disturbed, since its basis is in the lower levels of the brain.

There are very complex migrations of cells that occur in the developing brain, which essentially repeat the evolutionary stages of brain development. With the development of the telencephalon or cerebrum, the neural tube essentially turns inside out so that the gray matter is on the outside, and the white matter on the inside. This allows the gray matter to grow on the surface of the brain. As it grows, it forms a few simple folds as seen in animals like the chicken and the pig, more complex folds as seen in the monkey, and finally the complex convolutions of the human brain.

Development of the embryo is like a magnificent symphony that seems to have neither an author nor a conductor. A monkey, typing randomly, and given enough time, could produce the complete works of William Shakespeare. This is similar to the idea that evolution was a series of accidents, the core of Darwinism, without purpose, and that development does not follow from a reiterative path of former times and from the functional organization of the intangible Mind. The theories suffer from an enormous gap of inadequacy, once the truth is known. It is like the purposeless typing monkey. However, Shakespeare certainly did have a purpose. In evolution from the Darwinian perspective, we have our miraculous typing monkey at work in the genetic code. How can it be otherwise?

Evolutionary science, as it now exists, disavows purpose in evolution for two reasons. The first is that purpose is of the status of an idea, and an idea entails a *mind*, which creates the purpose and enacts it in the course of evolution. This is contrary to the dogmas of materialism and absence of final causality. The second reason is that, in that current evolutionary science is totally mechanistic, meaning that there must be a material mechanism governing evolution, and this mechanism is natural selection. Purpose is not a material mechanism. So again, we have our typing monkey, who must produce the complete works of Shakespeare in order to survive, since countless generations of monkeys have not been able to do so and have failed to pass on their genes. Does this make sense? Of course not, yet this is what we believe and this is what we teach our children.

In the course of my evaluation of children as a psychiatrist I ask if they believe in God. In one instance a child replied, "No, I believe in evolution." God is the very basis for evolution, the repetition of prior stages in our radical microgenesis fundamentally repeats the history that is forever present in the hidden time in the Mind of God. Mainstream science posits a genetic orchestration of these events based on materialist assumptions. At some point in the history of science, these dogmas will die, as all false dogmas eventually do. Science is about explanation and prediction. *Ad hoc* and *post hoc* explanations based on assumptions are anathema for true science and for true scientists. Yet this is what we have reified as truth and indoctrinated our children into.

One of the big problems in embryology is cell migration. The cells in the fetus and embryo seem to know where they are going. Without the idea of final causation and the recapitulation of occasions from their origin in time to the present, the sum of all histories in physics, there will never be an explanation of why this happens. What we now have an assumption of why this happens, that it is because of natural selection of random genetic mutations. The various theories are based on this assumption. It is circular reasoning.

Abstractions are not a part of such concrete reasoning, but this is how we educate our youth, away from abstraction, which has a creative element involving the process in the hidden time beneath our conscious concrete algorithms. Using such concrete reasoning, they are taught to understand nothing. A simple abstraction contains a wealth of information that cannot be compared to the memorization of concrete information, which is not operable in the ability to make discernments. The result is that our educational systems are producing mediocre minds that never reach anything near the potential that in inherent within them. This is not a matter of level of education, we see the same inadequacies in scientists, doctors, lawyers, and all manner of other higher educated and intelligent people. We have produced categorical, digital mentalities that lack both dimensional and analogue capabilities. We are wasting precious resources and time by creating minds that cannot think but only respond, to the detriment of society and the capacities of the mind that atrophy from lack of use, or outright prohibition of such functions, which may cause a disruption of the machinery of Moloch.

Natural selection is like a ticket to board a train. The ticket determines where you must get off. The ticket does not make the train, drive the train, power the train, determine what path the train will take, or create you as a passenger. Lord Kelvin, in the nineteenth century, argued against the Darwinian theory of evolution by natural selection on the basis of the new science of thermodynamics. Brooks and Wiley (1986) showed that the laws of thermodynamics, particularly those that cover negentropy, or order, seem to govern evolutionary diversity. They concluded (195): "Rather than assuming that environmental selection is the 'only directive force' in evolution, . . . we do not think it is direction giving at all." More recently, Stuart Kaufmann (2000) described self-organizing patterns and processes that seem to govern much of evolution. This self-organizing criticality makes evolutionary and ecological systems subject to final causality in the same way as the mind/brain system is. Darwinian natural selection by adaptation has been falsified by evidence, yet we perseverate in using this mechanism to explain, not only evolution, but a host of other problems in science

A well-known example of preadaptation is the rapid evolutionary growth of the human brain, leaving spaces or spandrels, which were thought to have been later coopted for language, art, commerce, war, and other functions (Buss et al. 1998). It should be noted that the large cranium of humans had a negative survival value. The pelvic orifice in the female had to be widened substantially to give birth, leading to death of the infant and/or mother in those that did not have a wide pelvic orifice. Notwithstanding, infant and maternal mortality in childbirth, as a result of delivery of a large cranium, would have remained high. In order for the enlarged cranium to be delivered through the pelvis, infants would have to be delivered at an early stage of development, making them unable to survive for a substantial period of time without protection and care, further increasing mortality. These changes would have to have coevolved with the increasing size of the human brain. In terms of natural selection, there would have had to have been a clear survival and reproductive benefit of the enlarged brain, and brain size would have had to have been an adaptation offsetting these maladaptive features. This adaptive value would also have been sufficient to warrant coevolution of other features. However, the rapid growth of the human brain was recognized as a preadaptation by Steven J. Gould (Buss et al. 1998), arguably the greatest evolutionary scientist of the twentieth century.

The arguments in favor of the actually need for such a large brain as humans have are very specious and, for the most part, are based on misstatements of fact: *www.tulane.edu/~bfleury/ darwinmed/ . . . /humanevolution.rtf—Assessed 6/10/11*

> Arboreal lifestyle requires a larger brain, high order of intelligence
> Need to process a lot of information very quickly, "on the fly"
> An opposable thumb is another useful adaptation for an arboreal existence
> High intelligence, hand/eye coordination, opposable thumbs are all preadaptations

Our large brains and our species evolved on the African Savannah, not in the forest, so the entirety of this explanation is incorrect. The arboreal lifestyle is characteristic of other primates such as chimpanzees, with whom we share about 98 percent of our genes, such *ad hoc* explanations of these preadaptations continue to gain acceptance. This is essentially science done backward. We do not take a hypothesis and then test it against the evidence, as we are doing with the hidden time in this book, we take the evidence and then create a hypothesis. Scientists somehow think that this reversed scientific method has some validity, which can only mean that such scientists do not understand the scientific method. How is it that we can rely on such sources? The answer is obvious, we believe what we chose to believe, based on our belief system.

The eye is another complex organ that had to have evolved in stages. Referring to work of philosopher David Drew, Stuart Kauffman, supported by his earlier and brilliant work on self-organizing systems and evolution, noted with approval that Drew had spoke of the evolution of "the eye, or even a red light sensitive cell in the progeny of an organism with no light sensitivity, as a 'blind teleology.'" (Kauffman 2009, 5). Kauffman describes the preadaptation as fundamental to evolution, and goes on to say that (3) "the evolution of the biosphere by Darwinian exaption, or 'preadaptations,' is not describable by sufficient natural law." Evolution in not described by sufficient natural law because natural law is not the cause of evolution, and natural selection is really not even a law. An agency such as God is needed, acting with the scope of a natural law She has established, but the Beauty of which we do not yet understand. He argues that the opportunity for adaptation is a blind final cause, which is the missing "why" of Darwinian evolutionary theory. He argues for a partially lawless and creative universe, such the evolution of the biosphere and of species is inherently unpredictable.

If we accept the notion that evolution occurs through preadaptations, which are unpredictable in both origin and outcomes, but are somehow propagated in the biosphere by blind teleology or blind final cause, not describable by natural law, we must inquire as to how the blind teleology is referred to some future actuality. If the phenomenon is not referable to some future actuality, or possibility of actuality, how can it possibly be called a final cause? If there is connection between the phenomenon and some future actuality, in what sense is it blind? Blind final cause is an oxymoron, and in the desperate need of science to support Darwin, it has gained a great measure of acceptance. There are whole breeds of popular books, selling millions of copies, that make similar circumambulations to preserve Darwinism and dispense with God, and they have greatly affected the popular science audience, which doesn't realize that it is all pure nonsense. The rise of usury has affected book marketing to such degree that truth is irrelevant. The purpose of these books is to make money from money, irrespective of their effect on the reader.

God produces final causes from the realm of the possible future, and such final causality would help explain the difficulties that we have in explanation of preadaptation and other evolutionary problems.

The Cambrian explosion occurred around 520 million years ago and marks the first appearance of dozens of animal phyla, including nematodes, annelids, mollusks, arthropods, echinoderms, and chordates. The chordate phylum includes all animals with spinal cords, so the Cambrian explosion seems to mark our distant ancestry. The rapid appearance of many of the major current phyla of animals was a challenge to Darwin and the theory of natural selection, and he acknowledged this in the *Origin of the Species*, finding it a serious and inexplicable problem and a valid argument against his theory of evolution by natural selection. There have been many plausible explanations for the phenomenon, but no clear scientific evidence. Simon Morris (2003, 1) opined that "the sudden emergence of a whole series of different body plans from an effectively identical worm invokes an almost homunculuslike effect, whereby each phylum has a latent form somehow concealed within the primitive worm." Moreover, in the Cambrian explosion, evolution appeared to occur from the top down, with higher categories of animals, or taxa, arising first, and lower taxa appearing later (Kauffman 1993), the opposite of what Darwinism would predict, as lower orders are, according to natural selection, precede higher order forms.

One explanation for the Cambrian explosion is that ecological niches were unoccupied, leaving the opportunity for new types of animals to evolve (Kauffman 1993). Thus, evolution may involve the absence of natural selection, since these organisms would have had to rapidly evolve without selection pressure. Be that as it may, the latent potential for the evolution of higher taxa and the filling in of taxa from the top down speak of final causation as opposed to efficient causation, because causes always proceed effects in efficient causation.

Genetics is the foundation for evolution, so we might expect to find genetic mutations that confer fitness to be selected in the course of evolution. Other mutations that don't affect fitness are called neutral. In a 1968 article in *Nature* on the rate of evolution, by Motoo Kimura, it was determined that, in the evolution of mammals, active genetic mutations by nucleotide substitution occur, on average across the population, every two years (625). This is in contrast to the standard-rate Darwinian estimate of substitution in a population of around one every three hundred generations. Kimura (1968) described these frequent mutations as neutral, and estimated the rate of neutral mutations in mammals to average about four per gamete (sperm or egg) (625). The mutant genes seem to be fixed or established in the population at about the same rate that they occur (625). These data make it clear that genetic mutations in populations, are not, for the most part, those that are fixed by natural selection, and imply that the rate of evolution is not substantially governed by natural selection.

Neutral mutations occur at such a regular rate that they can be used to estimate the date of common ancestry of groups or populations of organism. It is of interest that we humans, it would appear, nearly went extinct, in that the genetics can be traced back to ancestry from a single human individual, at two times in geologically recent history. The Y chromosome is passed down only through the male line without recombination, and the mitochrondrial DNA strictly through the female line without recombination. There is a time-dependent phenomenon of genetic alteration that makes the DNA more variable as measured in populations over time, enabling geneticists to determine the most recent common ancestor. The mitochondrial Eve lived around two hundred thousand years ago, most likely in East Africa, and is thought to be the ancestor of all current humans. She is considered the matriarchal most recent common ancestor (MMCA) of *Homo sapiens sapiens*, own subspecies, which is thought to have been emerging from other populations of hominids at this time. The migration of the ancestry of all current humans out of Africa is thought to have occurred much later, around ninety-five thousand to forty-five thousand years ago. Other species had advanced out of Africa, with *Homo erectus*, for example, inhabiting India some million to million and a half years ago.

The Y chromosome Adam, also thought to be ancestor of all current humans, the patriarchal most recent common ancestor, lived about six thousand years ago, but estimates are variable. This means that if either of these two individuals hadn't lived or hadn't reproduced, we wouldn't be here. The fact of our existence would then mean that either we are very lucky, and/or that our being here is a final cause of our survival. The development of language is a controversial topic. It required several preadaptations, necessary for vocalization of language, including development of the vocal tract and descended larynx, but is thought to have arisen just one hundred thousand years ago. In the case of the descended larynx, its original purpose is said to have been to lower the pitch of vocalization to make us sound like larger animals to predators. This is a ridiculously *ad hoc* explanation based on a false assumption, that there is no final causality in evolution, with no evidence whatsoever. This is not science. At that time, our subspecies had brains virtually identical to ours, but the language areas of the brains, necessary for the cognitive processing of verbalization, are said to have been empty areas of the brain called spansules. Full behavioral modernity of human involved reliance on symbolic thought, and is thought to have occurred only about fifty thousand years ago, and to have been associated with a great leap forward in language, distinguishing us from other hominids and allowing us to survive and thrive. Despite all evidence to the contrary, this development is speculated to have been the result of some major genetic mutation or biological reorganization of the brain. Again, this is *ad hoc* reasoning. The Species Mind is what has evolved, and continues to evolve. The individual brain expresses this evolution under the conditions of modern man, and there is no need for any such *ad hoc* explanations.

The first migration out of Africa is thought to have tracked along Southern Asia and arrived in Australia about fifty thousand (range forty thousand to over sixty thousand) years ago. Australia had been connected by a land bridge to Asia; however, it has been geographically isolated by the seas for millions of years. For this reason, the marsupials such as kangaroo flourished while the placental mammals, evolved much later, did not displace them as they did elsewhere. The aborigines of Australia are the oldest living culture in the world. Their belief system emphasizes oneness and the importance of landscape in the dreamtime or dreaming, which has many commonalities with the hidden time. The migration of the Aborigines into Africa essentially isolated them from full behavioral modernity, which occurred about fifty thousand years ago.

Alternatively, had our species not had these close calls the genome would be a lot more diverse than it currently is, and more than one human species or subspecies would have developed. Lack of genetic diversity adversely impacts capacity to adapt and survive, in Darwinian terms. As it is, we are a single subspecies, *Homo sapiens sapiens*, genetically divided only by race. If we were more diverse, what would be the consequences for a future world culture? What will be the consequences for our future, based on our extremely narrow genome?

Regarding these questions, one can only guess. Our lack of genetic diversity supports the principle that we are all equal. No one race is inherently inferior to another. This fact should allow us more readily to form a cohesive world culture. Moreover, the racial genetic homogeneity of humans is increasing, particularly in countries like the United States. On the other hand, our lack of genetic diversity may cause us to be more susceptible to certain diseases. We are the only animal that can develop AIDS, although the chimpanzee, thought to be our closest living relative, can be infected by HIV. The HIV virus does not have a capsule and, thus, dies very quickly when exposed to air. It therefore cannot be transmitted orally or by becoming airborne. If it had a capsule, it would spread like the influenza and the common cold viruses. Our cosmopolitan world insures the geographic transmission of disease pathogens such as viruses and bacteria.

Despite our high biomass, we humans have an alarmingly low genetic diversity. During the period that the anthropoid apes were developing in Africa, there were a number of genera, among which it is difficult to say which gave rise to man. Here we have a geographically isolated system with a rapid rate of speciation. After a time only the genus *Homo* survived. Finally, the other species of *Homo* all went extinct, and all that were left were varieties of *Homo sapiens*. Among *Homo sapiens*, all varieties went extinct except *Homo sapiens sapiens*. Is there a pattern here?

What if, during any of the several bottlenecks in human evolution, humans had gone extinct? The answer to this is that it couldn't happen. Here we are fortunate to be walking directly in the footsteps of Teilhard de Chardin, who eloquently explained human evolution based on the principle of final causation. All evolution, both of the universe and of life, leads up to just one thing: man. It is unimaginable that the knowing Creator would stop on the brink this goal.

Why did Neanderthal become extinct? Neanderthal was not an experiment, as is commonly said. The Knower has no need of experiments. Neanderthal's extinction was part of the relentless pattern of speciation and extinction, which led to the one living primate species: *Homo sapiens*.

Where are we in the progress of human evolution? Has human evolution ended? Pierre Teilhard de Chardin believed that evolution has entered an entirely new era with the development of the human mind, and calls this the Psychozoic Era. There have been three other eras in the history of complex living systems, which began almost a billion years ago with the evolutionary explosion of invertebrates such as trilobites and shellfish. The first is the Paleozoic, characterized by invertebrate life in the ocean. The second is the Mesozoic, characterized by the development of fishes in the oceans and reptiles on land. The third, the Cenozoic, is the age of mammals, the age that most geologists would say we are still in. It seems that Teilhard attaches a greater importance to the development of the psyche than most geologists.

What we are seeing now, in the Psychozoic Era, is the rapid evolution of the manifestation of Mind. It is this evolution, and not the goal of an ever-advancing technology, toward which all humankind is drawn. We are on the brink of an evolutionary bottleneck of a different kind, a bottleneck in the evolution of the Species Mind. This bottleneck holds the possibility of extinction. Unlike any of the other changes in the history of the universe, this change will involve a conscious choice on our parts. It is we, individually, who will decide whether we chose to be a positive force in evolution (Krishnamurti) or a negative one. The task before us now is to join in creating our own future.

Chapter Nineteen

Science And Faith

The following verses of chapter 2 of *Eli* read:

4. **The inner dimension and the hidden time have already been discovered.**
5. **There is no truth without faith. We are faithful to verities. Nothing is proven except to the heart of one who believes.**
6. **Science has given us a great lie. It is this lie that ends the current age of faith in God.**
7. **The great lie that science has given us is that reality is material.**

The hidden time has been discovered. It is the period of simultaneity in systems theory, the flash of life events at the time of death, and the endless replay of causality that allows final causality, which, as we have found, has far more explanatory power than purposeless accidents. It is also the observation of no time passing in deep sleep, and the fact that it is always being Now. We know no time other than this Eternal Now. Science is judged by what it can explain and predict, and leads inexorably to the hidden time.

What we believe is based on what we feel, not what we think. If we feel something is true, it is proven in our hearts. At the same time, what we believe must be true, thus the purpose of this book.

The primary point, however, of this passage is that materialism is a lie that is destructive to ourselves and to our cultures. Possible material realities are not actual or real. As we have noted, when we probe the smallest dimensions of the particle we find no matter. Materialism is a false belief enshrined by a materialist culture and science. God occupies no space of time, and there is no way to conceive God as a material entity. Matter is limited, ideas are unlimited, so the nature of God cannot be material. For this reason, the only system of materialist beliefs is atheism and, atheism, as we have discussed, explains nothing.

The problem that then arises is that science accepts the materialistic, mechanistic, purposeless system of atheism as a matter of faith. It has no values and gives rise to moral decay because in totally denies the existence of spirit and soul, which are the bases of our Self, our minds, our meanings, our purposes, our values, and our ethics. It leads into a spiritless conception of reality that teaches that we have no souls. It also is deterministic, meaning that there is no basis for correct action, as our actions are totally predicated on material antecedents. This gives us no responsibility for action, no place for love, as love is spiritual, and no actual basis for the growth and development of children and adults as spiritual creations. For this reason, materialism, as a philosophy and a way of life, is to be condemned strongly.

It then becomes obvious why we are not to raise our children in this way, and why science must correct its error and teach a form of idealism that allows the spirit and soul to have some manner of existence. So there must be a new science. However, the current materialist orthodoxy will resist such an idealist science mightily, and I would seem, at this point in the history of science, that this is not possible.

Chapter Twenty

The Great Lie

Chapter 3 of Eli reads,

1. God has permitted the great lie for a short time only. That time is now coming to an end.
2. Believers in the lie! You have been raised on the milk of your concrete beliefs. Now it is time for you to be weaned to partake of the solid food of a new science.
3. The great lie is like a sword that has been thrust into the heart of humankind.
4. God is the one subject of reality. Take away the one subject and there is nothing real.
5. The truths of the one subject have already been discovered, but have not been accepted because they spell the death of the faith in the lie.
6. Humankind must no longer permit the lie to be taught to its children.
7. The new science will be established in our schools and through research and scholarship.

God has not created the great lie that reality is materialistic. He has permitted humankind to believe the great lie, as a stage in our development, as we develop a technology that leads to the times of suffering, the tribulation, which must precede the dawn of the New Jerusalem, the New World. The old must die for the new to be born. However, the times that were served by the great lie of materialism cannot continue in the transition to the New, since they are inimical and destructive to the order that will be erected in its place. There is a period of overlap between the dying of the old, which is before us and occurring as we speak, and the birth of the new, which must arise out of the ashes of the old.

Materialism, the great lie, is a concrete belief. It theorizes a substance, matter, where there is no substance. To be weaned from this belief is like the infant being weaned from its mother's breast. The infant needed the substance of its mother's milk for a time, but there comes a time when it is no longer needed, and must be weaned. Idealism is abstract, and modern humans, by and large, do not understand complex abstractions, only concrete representations of such abstractions. So in development, we are weaned from our concrete beliefs, if we are able, to a set of abstractions, characterized by such things as numbers and words.

By destroying all notions of soul, spirit, purpose, and responsibility, materialism is a great sword that has been thrust into the heart of humankind. It has done untold damage as it saps the life's blood out of the spiritual creature of the human. It has caused wars, famine, disease, and death, not to mention moral turpitude. The sword must be removed gently, as with a surgeon's hand, because, without the spiritual substance to heal the wound, the victim is debilitated by meaninglessness, since its meaning had previously been the false meaning of materialism.

As reality is created by knowing, and as God is all-knowing, there is nothing that exists outside of God. The interconnection of human minds has been proven to an indisputable degree, meaning there is only One Mind and that is the Mind of God. The proliferation of observers in physics is based on a strict separation between minds, which has been abundantly been proven false, so much so, that Schrödinger, the great quantum physicist, called the existence of more than one mind a monstrosity. For more than One Mind to exist we would, as separate minds, be creating our own universes, violating Occam's Razor or the principle of parsimony. Occam's Razor states that entities are not to be multiplied unnecessarily, and it applies here.

We are sinning grievously by teaching and allowing the teachings of the great lie—that reality is material—to our children. So-called scientists, as we have seen, have gone through great lengths to fit their science into the entrenched paradigm of blind material. They have proliferated an infinite number of real universes so that one such as ours could exist purely by accident, when it is altogether impossible without final causation, regardless of the number of universes we have. They have created exaptions, preadaptations occurring long before they were needed, and conferring negative survival benefit, to perpetuate the theory of evolution by adaptation based on natural selection. These exaptions are not adaptations for the purpose for which they arose, and such a radical change from the original Darwinian precepts is nothing more than a desperate effort to cling to a theory that is demonstrable false. The very basis of materialism—with its ban on final causality—has proven untenable, given the fact that all things have developed in progression toward a singular purpose.

However, because of the moral turpitude of the materialist system, our children are suffering great violence against their spirits and souls, are committing actions that are contrary to rational, moral, spiritual living, with responsibilities, laws, and rules of correct action. This is the biggest crime of all, and must be stopped as soon as possible.

The new science, predicated on idealism, can be developed in our schools and universities through research. Another way of predicating idealism is by information monism, that is to say, everything is information or ideas, which is all that exists. The renowned quantum physicist, Archibald Wheeler, framed it as follows: Wheeler (1988) said that all reality is information, and that other physical quantities are mere incidentals. Such an idea, coming from such a famous and well-respected scientist, speaks to the veracity of a reality of information or ideas. Looking at information, and at information theory and its relation to physics, will support scholarship and research that we give us a truer and more explanatory scientific system that can be advanced rapidly, in view of what we already know about information and information science. Information is considered objective, but it is, in fact, based completely on experience or knowing, and nothing can be said to be information that is not subjectively known. Thus God, the One Knower, becomes the only reality, as God knows All, and ideas have an independent reality in an ideal realm such that they are not replicated, as we explained earlier in our quote from Roger Penrose.

Subjectivity is primary; objectivity is derivative. It is the product of an objective thought process. In the course of the evolution of thought, objectivity has been substituted for internal relationships between subjects. Subjective relation, on the universal level, is called love. Love is the principle that connects events internally in the Eternal Now. Love is the principle that binds the universe in space/time. Love is a quality of the One Knower, God, which brings all events into subjective relation.

It is by experience and Mind that every event in the universe is connected throughout all space-time. As we have discussed, these are inter-subjective connections, not objective connections. Every event in space-time holds a limitless eternity in its grasp. Every event is a determination in the Mind of God. All consciousness is the consciousness of God. There is no other knower, no other observer in the universe.

Chapter Twenty-One

Foundations Of The New Science

Chapter 4 of *Eli* reads,

1. The great lie can only be defeated by the new science. The sooner the new science is established by the institutions of the world, the sooner the suffering caused by the lie will end.
2. The new science is established by degrees.
3. The first degree is the truth of the one subject, which follows from the existence and the oneness of the universe, and from the ancient belief that God is all-knowing.
4. It is far easier to move a mountain than to move science by this one degree.
5. We have the power to move the mountain, if we have the faith that the mountain can be moved.
6. It is now that our faith is tested. The future of humankind hangs in the balance.
7. SEARCH GOD.

This portion of *Eli* gives the basic charge to advance the new science, which we have discussed in detail earlier. The functioning brain is a dynamical system, meaning that it is far from equilibrium at all times, and dissipates energy. Such systems are called chaotic, not in the sense that they are disordered, but in mathematical parlance. Chaotic systems, or systems at the "edge of chaos and order," such as the brain, exhibit the property of self-organization, or self-organizing criticality. The criticality lies in the exquisite sensitivity of the state of the system to small changes in prior physical conditions. This is the famous butterfly effect whereby a butterfly flapping its wings can alter future weather patterns, so as, for example, to produce a cyclone at a distant location.

As a dynamical system, the brain, as per current mainstream neuroscience, would produce unpredictable states, much as the weather cannot be predicted, with all our current technology. Given current conditions, the state of the system would become increasingly unpredictable with the passage of time. If one introduces quantum theory with all its uncertainties, the brain state would become even more unpredictable. This unpredictability would totally compromise the rational function of mental process, memory, and our sense of an abiding identity.

The only possible way out of this conundrum, without resorting to a mind/brain dualism, is to posit a nontemporal process that flows from the mental to the physical, thereby affecting the brain on a quantum level, with the sum of quantum events being amplified by chaotic dynamics. It is necessary that this influence be teleological, operating by final causality. Efficient causality in time would then be under the continuous influence of final causality, operating outside of time, and essentially guiding mental process. The only possible agent of such an influence would be God. Causality is not violated, since the future does not affect the past, which is already settled, and since God's knowledge of future potentialities does not entail any signals backward in time, since God in timeless or eternal.

Metaphysics, in a relativistic universe, requires that the future be real, albeit as potential. If a plurality of possible universes exists in the future, God knows them all. The knowledge of future potentials makes the subjective aim and final causality work, and requires God as the infinite ground of mentality. We view mind as operating, within ourselves, in a timeless period of simultaneity, within which there can be an indefinite feedback loop, but this time is too short, likely around thirty milliseconds.

However, final causality is not similarly restricted for God, who is timeless and spaceless, everywhere and nowhere.

As Whitehead proposed in his classic *Process and Reality*, for humans and other experiencing entities the movement seems to be from the physical to the mental, and mentality seems to have evolved after the physical apparatus was in place, and further with the complexity of the physical apparatus of the central nervous system, including the brain. Whitehead also proposed that, for God, the movement is from the mental to the physical. What starts out as an idea in the Mind of God becomes a physical reality when God determines, so let it be, as we have discussed earlier. Yet no scientist who believes in God could deny that evolution of humans requires physical evolutionary process that would have had to have been initiated and sustained over millions and perhaps billions of years.

Physical reality and physics in no way imply materialism, as attested to be the large number of great scientists and physicists who were idealists. Going all the way back to Plato, the quintessential idealist, the physical forms were of the nature of ideas, and as Whitehead said, all philosophy is a footnote to Plato. Many would argue this point, or even judged Whitehead's sincerity in having said it, but form always qualifies substance, such that form is the primary reality and substance is implied. At the base of reality, science finds no substance, only relations with a form and a formal causality. Aristotle's causes included form, but not substance. Psychiatrist Carl Jung wrote of archetypes, which would have had to have been formal causes. The Great Mother, for example, would be a formal causes for all the variety of mothers, mother figures, and other mother complexes. The Mother Earth was perhaps humanities earliest religious symbol. The elements—air, fire, water, and earth—are sensible as ideal substances or forms, and archetypes of a sort. We look at these elements now as primitive falsehoods, not because they don't exist, but because there meaning is that of an idea, not a substance, and they cannot otherwise be properly understood.

Carl Jung's great genius, followed by other archetypal theorists such as von Franz, Neumann, and Edinger, and many others, was a deep understanding of form and number. Numbers, letters, and other abstract symbols are fundamentally forms. The new science spoke of in *Eli* is not entirely new, it has existed of old in various ways, and is only new as it applies of the age to come when these ideological symbols and ideas are clothed in their proper science.

Abstractions and symbols can be thought of in different ways depending upon one's point of view, and categories of thought and meaning are often just pigeon holes, generalizations into categories or items that may fit no category or several. When animals are conditioned in behavioral experiments that they get food when a circle is displayed and not when an oval is displayed, they will become very nervous and disorganized when the oval comes to be shaped more and more like a circle. With every association there are generalizations, and as the generalizations fail, we fail.

Science can be generalized in a very broad manner, and the new science and the new religion are not distinct from one another, but flow from one another. Science is a language. Reality is a like a meandering stream on a broad flood plain. Only God sees the many paths it can take, and brings about a single course. It is called the world line, and is a series of points. This one course is actual, all other courses are potential. The flow, the process of relations, the feelings Whitehead called prehensions, are all captured in the feeling of love. God loves our world into being.

Love is the movement, the dance, the grabbing on, the letting go. It is all these things and more. In this enormous mass of humanity that we call humankind, love is the only real thing that flows between people, and between people and God. Without love we are separate, self-serving, living in the prison of the alter ego, in hell, alone when we could be living in the vast expanse of Self, in love, together, in Paradise.

The Experiment on the Existence of God

So the new science is very broad, and is established by degrees. One way of studying this is through event-related potentials or ERPs, in which uses the electroencephalogram or EEG to average the brain-wave responses to a stimulus where the timing of the stimulus is set with zero as the time of the actual delivery of a stimulus. In other words, if you were to hear a large number of tones at one-second intervals, the EEG sets the time back to zero every second, and then records the brain-wave response over that second or a portion of that second as the latency, the time of the brain-wave response after the stimulus. The time of the stimulus is zero and the time of the brain-wave response or latency of the electrical response is the time that has elapsed since the stimulus was delivered.

An ERP, as described here, is an average of a large number of events, delivered to a subject, generally as tones, called common tones, at regular intervals of tones of the same pitch or frequency, most often spaced at one second or one and a half seconds. The brain responds more strongly to those tones of a substantially different frequency or tone, or to absence of any tone at all, when they are spaced randomly, generally at an average of one per four common tones. These are called rare or odd tones or absent tones, and the procedure is called the oddball paradigm.

The brain response to the odd stimulus or absence of the common stimulus is averaged over a large number of trials or intervals of EEG measurement, since the actual EEG obscures the brain electrical response. The product of this averaging is the ERP. The range in latency of electrical potentials in the brain is most often from zero to between 450 and 750 milliseconds (thousandth of a second). The ERP then is graphed as hyperpolarizations and depolarizations, forming waves that are graphed vertically in terms of polarization and horizontally in terms of time. These waves are numbered consecutively with negatively polarized waves numbered N1, N2, N3; and positive waves numbered P1, P2, P3, with a cycle of a single negative wave and a single positive wave generally having a duration or period of ninety to one hundred milliseconds, or about a tenth of a second. Alternatively, the wave can be indicated by latency, with the P3 also called the P300, since it is the positive wave that occurs about three hundred or three tenths of a second after the stimulus is delivered to the subject.

If we place a button in front of the subject of the ERPs and ask him or her to press the button as soon as he or she hears the odd tone, we call this time the reaction time and generally assume that this is the time that the subject becomes consciously aware of the odd or absent stimulus. We find that the reaction time corresponds roughly to the time of the P3 or P300, meaning that the subject has become consciously aware of the stimulus or absence of stimulus about three hundred milliseconds or three-tenths of a second after the tone or absence of the tone enters her or his ears. This shows that the stimulus entered the ears about three tenths of a second before it was consciously observed. This is precisely what we mean when we say that everything we observe is in the past.

We have also said that, according to the One Mind interpretation of quantum theory, there is really only One Observer, and that is God. So the status of each stimulus until it becomes known to a single observer, and the plurality of observers are embraced by the Mind of a singular God. In the ERP experiment, a single observer, totally isolated in another room from the observer who's ERP is being recorded, randomly decides to observe a series of events by a simple coin toss, unknown to the observer being recorded, one or one and a half seconds before the series of the odd stimulus or absent is delivered to the subject being recorded. Half of the events are observed first by the subject being recorded, and half are after they have already been observed by another person, and the subject has no ordinary way of knowing which is which.

Statistics, as formulated initially by Fisher, indicate association. For example, if one were to give a placebo, say a sugar pill, to a hundred individuals suffering from Major Depression, and told each that the pill could be an antidepressant or a placebo on a 50:50 basis, in a double-blinded fashion, we would find that about a third of the people would actually feel happier as a result of taking the sugar pill. Perhaps sixty percent of the people taking the actual antidepressant would feel happier some time later. The one-third placebo responders would have as much of a response as those taking and responding to the antidepressant. This does not mean that the sugar pill is an effective treatment, chemically, for depression, but that it is associated with a therapeutic response.

Association is very powerful. I once eat a chocolate covered cherry and developed severe gastroenteritis or stomach flu immediately thereafter. I know that the candy had nothing to do with the gastroenteritis, yet nearly fifty years later, I still cannot bear to eat chocolate covered cherries. For a time, I wasn't able to stomach cherries at all. Later, I could eat fresh cherries but not eat candied cherries. I had generalized my experience with the candy to all cherries. Association functions primarily in the realm of the unconscious, within the three tenths of a second prior to a stimulus becoming consciously recognized. In the case of the cherries, the association was visceral, at the lower part if the emotional brain or limbic system.

My hypothesis in the ERP experiments was not that people could somehow read each other's minds, but that an association could be established between the odd event and its observation by another subject one or one-and-a-half seconds earlier. Once the observers were separated, the association would continue to be active, causing a difference in the ERP of the observer when the stimulus was being previewed by that same observer with whom the association had been created. In the experiment, the author was the subject of the ERP being recording, and his friend, a colleague trained in electrophysiology and operation of the equipment, was preobserving the stimulus randomly. The fact that we were friends facilitated the association, and prior to the experiment, which was conducted in four sessions of four-hour duration, the association was forged in two four hour sessions by bringing the author and his colleague together and practicing the author knowing that he was or was not preobserving the stimulus. Thus it was predicted that the associations wrought by the practice sessions would occur in the visceral brain or limbic system, and thus very early in the ERP. A version of the experiment was published (Germine 2004), but did not include the detailed account of the conditions of the experiment and what it intended to prove, so this must be rectified.

It is beyond the scope of this book to represent the experiment in full technical terms, but the conditions and assumptions are important, as they must be met to replicate or reproduce the results. The difference between the preobserved and not preobserved conditions was statistically significant beyond any shadow of a doubt, at about one in ten with twenty-two zeros chance that there was no difference between the observer's brain-wave response in the two conditions. It was as if the observing brain of the author were anticipating the condition, causing the brain-wave patterns on the ERP to be perfectly out of phase.

Here we are questioning whether the existence of God and the One Mind model of quantum reality can be supported experimentally. However, we must base our judgment on Bayesian statistics. Briefly stated, the applicable variables in Bayesian terms are as follows: (1) Prior probability that God exists. (2) Probability of the God exists given the data. (3) Probability of the data given that God exists. (4) Probability of the data given that God does not exist. (5) Overall probability of the data is extremely low, so this factor alone increases the prior probability, meaning that the probability that God exists increases given the data. The new science is established in degrees. Bayesian analysis, although useful in terms of scientific hypotheses, is limited because the variables are difficult to estimate, other than factor five, which is the same as it would be in the usual Fisher-type statistical analysis. The purpose here is to show that the existence of God is amenable to scientific scrutiny.

Idealism was once held in high esteem. The lay definition is generally that one has a code of conduct and lives by that code, in a humanistic fashion. In physical terms, it means that reality is information, as Wheeler had said. In human terms, information is experience, and is comprised of meanings, forms, symbols, numbers, systems of thought, reason, and emotion. Perhaps I am biased, but I find materialists lacking in abstraction, intuition, and genuinely lacking in true understanding. The reasons for this have been discussed previously.

I recall once, as I was preparing for my board exams, meeting an extremely intelligent female psychiatrist who was also a devout Hindu. She wore the traditional clothing, and had the red dot in the middle of her forehead. She had no accent. As a Hindu, she was educated in the *Bhagavad Gita*. I innocently asked her what she thought about the meaning of the verses, paraphrased from the *Bhagavad Gita*: He is and He is not; He is everywhere and nowhere; He is within all and He is outside all. She was familiar with these verses, however, without a thought, she said that she never understood what these verses meant. I thought of this as a kind of test for abstractions of deep paradoxes, commensurate with her level of intelligence. She seemed much more interested in material things than spiritual things, and this, or course, was her prerogative. I know of no similar verses in the sacred books of the near-Eastern or Western worlds.

There are many levels or degrees of abstraction, and idealism, philosophically, reaches the higher levels. One of the hallmarks of schizophrenia is being concrete, being unable to form abstractions. A simple mathematical abstraction of numbers is that if a equals b, and b equals c, then a equals c (a = b; b = c therefore a = c). However, as Silvano Arieti (1974) reported, a schizophrenic women thought she was the Virgin Mary, because she was a virgin, Mary was a virgin, therefore she was a virgin. This showed that she didn't understand a simple abstraction, or the logic of simple abstraction. Materialists can be very logical and very intelligent, but if they endorse any spirituality at all, it is very superficial. It was perhaps because of the problem of abstraction that Jesus spoke in parables, yet the parables themselves may be difficult to understand fully.

Materialists also very often engage in doublethink. A well-known example is the mobster who is devoutly Christian, yet kills without remorse and exploits people with no compunctions. Doublethink is very prevalent in groupthink. Those outside one's group can be killed without remorse. We can bomb other countries with unmanned drone bomber jets, flying them by young men and women with joysticks and kill innocent people. Separating them from the jets, we can deny that we are actually waging war on another country. We would certainly think it so if it were being done to our country.

If we were to realize that we are all essentially One Mind, One Species, and One Consciousness, as it written "Ye are all Elohim," we would know that our so-called enemies are also Elohim, and that, what we do to them, we are actually doing to ourselves. This level of insight is not expected. Then perhaps we would search for this Beloved One within ourselves, rather than attaching our identities to our alter ego consciousness.

There is an Arabic story that has also been popularized by the Islamic mystics such as Rumi and Attar, the story of Layla and Majnun. Majnun was a Bedouin poet who professed his love for Layla, a women living in the same village as he. Layla's father would not allow their marriage, as it would disgrace the family, and Layla married another man. Majnun went into the surrounding desert, using many ruses such as disguising himself as a field animal by donning a skin, just to get a glimpse of Layla. He searched the sand, hoping to find Layla. He was known as a madman, and perhaps he was, but the story, in Sufi mysticism, symbolizes the total love for the Beloved, God. As Majnun searched for Layla, we must search for God, with total devotion, in our sciences, in nature, in philosophy, in our religions, in art, in music, in literature—everywhere and in everything. Like Majnun, if we *SEARCH GOD*, we will know will know the Beloved when we see Her, that She is real, and that She lives. God is male, female, male-female, genderless, singular, plural, depending on the context in the Bible and elsewhere. Ultimately, God is ineffable, and cannot be limited.

Chapter Twenty-Two

Forsake Usury

Books of prophecy, such as *Eli*, most often have rules or commandments that must be followed completely and without question. *Eli* has but one commandment, FORESAKE USURY, in capital letters to signify its importance, standing alone as the only words in chapter 5, verse 5. These are, by far, the two most important words in the *Book*. We have already spoken of usury and its evils in great detail. These simple two words are not negotiable or subject to any qualification. Usury, the lending of money at interest, is strictly forbidden.

Although the records of usury go back perhaps four thousand years, in the history of religion and spirituality it seems to appear first in the work of Zoroaster or Zarathustra, a Persian prophet who lived between 500 and 1200 BCE. People still practice Zoroastrianism in Iran and Pakistan, but there is little known of Zoroaster's life and times, and much of his work has been lost or destroyed. The passage presented here comes from the *Vendidad*:

> The Religion of God indeed, O Spitama Zoroaster! takes away from him who makes confession of it the bonds of his sin; it takes away the sin of breach of trust.; it takes away the sin of murdering one of the faithful; it takes away the sin of deeds for which there is no atonement; it takes away the worst sin

of usury; it takes away any sin that may be sinned. (*www.avesta.org/vendidad/vd3sbe.htm*)

Here is a record of confession for the forgiveness of sin long before the times of Jesus. *Eli* is not so generous, and calls for atonement of a new kind, which we will discuss later. The question is, why should usury be considered the "worst sin" in times as early as this, and why should it not be considered a sin at all today, but has become a way of life.

Chapter 5 of Eli reads,

1. **There is no greater crime than a crime against humanity.**
2. **There is no greater crime against humanity than usury.**
3. **The greatest violence, and the greatest threat to humanity, is the growth of money.**
4. **In the new faith, there is only one commandment. It is this commandment, and this commandment alone, that must be followed to end the times of suffering, which are soon to come.**
5. **FORSAKE USURY.**
6. **Those who have assets must withdraw them from the markets of loans. Do not accept notes of loan on speculation. Buy those things that provide food, water, clothing, shelter, and medical care for humankind.**
7. **The time will soon come when you will gain no profits from the markets of loans, and your wealth will be taken by the very few.**

Dante's analysis of usury in the Inferno, is brilliantly examined on a posting on the Internet, dated July 8, 2009, by a blogger who simple identifies himself as Brandon on *http://branemrys.blogspot.com/2009/07/dante-on-usury.html*. Brandon's synopsis of Dante's view of usury is very compelling:

> *Dante puts the usurers in the lowest sub-circle of the seventh circle of hell, with others whose sins are regarded as doing violence against nature and nature's*

God; many people have noted that usurers are placed deeper into hell than violent murderers, violent suicides, blasphemers, and sodomites. Dante regards usurers as perverting art, i.e., productive skill, by means of which we are supposed to produce and create and thereby imitate the goodness of God. Usury is the anti-art: it produces nothing substantial, being just a set of multiplication games with money, and therefore does not really contribute anything to "earning one's way and furthering humankind." It merely gives the illusion of doing so, and is therefore a sort of mockery of both human reason and divine providence—indeed, a sort of universal violence against neighbor, God, and one's own reason, an extraordinarily efficient form of violence by which you do the most damage with the least effort.

The Violent in Dante's hell suffer violent punishments; the punishment of the usurers is to sit while futilely and wearily trying to ward off with their hands the violent, whipping winds that sometimes shower them with burning sand and sometimes cover them with flaming fire.

Canto XI of Dante's Inferno gives us a very great insight into the evil nature of usury.

> *"Once more go back a little to the point,"*
> *I said, "where you state usury offends*
> *The divine goodness, and untie the knot."*
>
> *"Philosophy, to one who understands,*
> *Points out—and on more than one occasion—*
> *How nature gathers her entire course*
>
> *"From divine intellect and divine art.*
> *And if you pore over your Physics closely,*
> *"That, when possible, your art follows nature*
> *As a pupil does his master; in effect,*
> *Your art is like the grandchild of our God.*

> *"From art and nature, if you will recall*
> *The opening of Genesis, man is meant*
> *To earn his way and further humankind.*
>
> *"But still the usurer takes another way:*
> *He scorns nature and her follower, art,*
> *Because he puts his hope in something else."*

Nowadays, the common understanding of usury is the practice of charging excessive interest on loans, usually in violation of legal limits. This is an example of the ongoing corruption of language in our times in the interest of legitimizing the existing order of inequity. But the original meaning of usury was the exacting of any interest on a loan. How that kind of usury could, not so long ago, have been considered among the blackest of transgressions is a good indicator of how much our World has changed in last few centuries—and not for the better!

The nearly universal acceptance of usury as the norm is even more incredible when one considers that the most important ethical teachers of human history—Moses, Aristotle, Jesus, Mohammed, Aquinas—are unanimous in denouncing usury. If we look back into history, it teaches us that the result of usury is to concentrate wealth in fewer and fewer hands. Money increasingly ceases to be the means by which I exchange the fruits of my labor for the fruits of yours, and instead it becomes the coterie of bankers and financiers. When the widespread practice of usury first took hold in ancient Greece, the class of small independent farmers who had formed the backbone of Greek democracy vanished, their lands swallowed up by the oligarchs. Drawing upon this experience, the Greek philosopher Aristotle discerned that usury is an inherently unsustainable system that plunders mankind's collective wealth and engenders an intolerable hierarchal concentration of wealth and power at the top. Aristotle understood that money is a type of measurement, a unit of value, like a meter is a unit of distance and a pound is a unit of weight. In order for humans to live together as a community, such common units must be adopted, either by convention or by law, and they constitute a sort of social glue. But Aristotle also appreciated, as we moderns apparently do not, the imperative to distinguish between things that exist only in law and things that exist in fact.

We are now seeing what can happen, for example, when the law creates an artificial person, a.k.a. a corporation, and then accords that person all the rights and prerogatives of a natural person. Result? The priorities of society quickly shift toward the interests of the corporation, to the detriment of the people; the artificial person comes to dominate the natural person. And we fall into the same trap when we begin to treat money, which is an artificial measure of value, as if it were value itself. In reality, we can no more buy, sell, and rent money than we can buy, sell, and rent liters or miles. But if we insist of doing so nonetheless, then the unfortunate consequences are very much like what ensues when we endow a corporate entity with personhood: society's priorities increasing tilt toward the speculative interests of the money manipulators and away from the production of actual wealth. The nominal value of money comes to dominate the real value of goods and services.

And so, both the rise of corporatism and the growth of usury cause the social glue to become unstuck so that true community based on shared interests virtually ceases to exist. The free association of individuals is replaced by the compulsion of a corporate-dominated state, which increasingly becomes nothing more than an instrument of indoctrination and repression. Indeed the very state whose laws created the corporate creditors increasingly surrenders the people's sovereignty to those same private interests. In America, the usurers long ago usurped the very core of national sovereignty—the power to issue currency—and the last two presidents with the temerity to try to wrest that authority back both wound up with bullets in their heads (Lincoln and Kennedy).

Getting back to Aristotle, he also recognized that money, being an artificial creature of the law, is sterile, which is to say, it can neither produce any other thing nor reproduce itself. A cow can beget calves, a lathe can fashion furniture, a blast furnace can make steel, and thus there is a natural increase associated with real productive assets.

But alas, the lessons of Greek history that informed the views of Aristotle were soon forgotten by the Romans, whose patrician class increasingly turned from agriculture to usury as a source of wealth. Following a pattern that has been repeated over and over in history, the Roman Republic eroded along with its middle class, ushering in the autocracy of the Caesars. Augustus, the greatest of the Caesars, was sired by two generations of moneylenders. Once having allowed usury to decimate its productive economy, Rome devolved into a parasitic empire, dependent on imports to feed and clothe its population and on foreigners to fight its wars and do its manual labor. My readers doubtless recognize the parallels with modern America.

During the Middle Ages, the wisdom of Aristotle was revived by the Scholastics, who observed that usury not only undermines the function of money as a means of exchange, but seeks an increase that has no finite limits. The increases from real productive assets have natural limits. The propagation of cattle is limited by available fodder and pasturage, and the output of blast furnace is limited by the availability of iron ore and coal, as well as by the market for steel. Eventually a cow will become too old to breed, and the blast furnace will begin to crumble. But the multiplication of money by interest requires nothing but money itself, which never dies or becomes too old to breed.

Interest makes money self-augmenting—a recursive incremental loop without end. We can perhaps better understand this by considering the analogy of amplifying an electrical signal. If we feed the amplified signal at the output side—let's say from a speaker—back into the input side—let's say a microphone—we soon hear a piercing squeal as the amplification explodes beyond the acoustic range of our equipment. Compound interest works precisely the same way: interest is paid on the principal, then on the principal plus interest on the principal, then on the principal plus interest on the principal-plus-interest, and so on. There is the famous example devised by American lawyer John Whipple in 1836, which goes like this: If 5 English pennies had earned 5 percent compound interest from the year AD 1 to the present (Whipple's, that is), it would amount to 32,366,648,157 spheres of gold, each as large as the earth.

This helps explain why the practice of usury was once considered so heinous—and why it should still be shunned today. Not only does the credit system prey on society's most vulnerable elements—those who are poor, in ill health, or victims of misfortune—but it engenders a unsustainable bubble economy, which ultimately collapses, producing mass misery, loss of livelihoods, lands and homes, famine, want . . . and ultimately war. In a very true sense, the 180 million deaths from war and genocide during the twentieth century can be laid at the doorstep of usury. As the prophet Ezekiel recognized, the crime of usury lies at the source of every abomination that man commits against his fellow man. According to the prophet, murder, theft, rape and rapine are all subsumed in the abomination of usury (Ezekiel 18: 13, King James Translation):

> He who hath given forth upon usury, and hath taken increase: shall he then live? he shall not live: he hath done all these abominations; he shall surely die; his blood shall be upon him.

If I am a tailor and sew a coat, I will sell the coat for X dollars, and the value of the coat will be balanced by the value of the money paid for it so that the money and goods will freely circulate, and I can continue to make and sell more coats. But if I am a banker, what do I have to sell? I sell money itself, and I get paid in interest. But where does the interest come from? I have added no goods to the stream of commerce, my labor produces nothing that anyone can use or consume. So when I extract my interest from the borrower, I create an imbalance between the money in circulation and the value of goods offered for sale. The only way to restore that balance is to lend out the interest again. But that's only a temporary fix, because when the interest-on-interest comes due, there's an even bigger imbalance created. So the usurers must ceaselessly drag in new borrowers or push more credit on existing debtors to keep the system going. It operates exactly like a Ponzi scheme, with the payout at the top of the pyramid always depending on the influx of new suckers at the bottom.

But eventually, the burden on the debtors at the bottom of the pyramid reaches the trigger point of pervasive default. The flow of credit then gets abruptly cut off; there is not enough real money in the system to pay for the goods in circulation, and production itself comes screeching to a halt—the syndrome of periodic business crisis known variously as depression or recession. Mass anxiety, misery and want soon follow, not because society lacks the means to produce enough to satisfy human needs, but because society cannot keep pace with the insatiable appetite of the Dragon of Usury. The only solution after all social wealth has been sucked into the Dragon's hoard is to take a wrecking ball to what's been produced thus far and start the Ponzi scheme all over again. That wrecking ball is called war—a regularly recurring event in the boom-bust cycle of usury. And as the usurers achieve complete dominance of the world economy, as is happening now in our times, the ever-shorter intervals of peace disappear and war becomes an unending state of affairs.

Usury converts social wealth to private wealth. It promotes the idea that all wealth should be in private hands, and that social wealth is per se illegitimate—an imposition of the weak and idle upon the strong and productive. But let us consider for a moment the real origins of our society's wealth.

The productive capacity of any individual, no matter how talented, pales in comparison to that of a community of individuals. To whom does the surplus generated by our communal cooperation belong, if not to all of us? An individual has no continuity: he lives his life and dies. Unless that individual belongs to a community, his knowledge and skills die with him. Therefore, who is entitled to the benefits associated with the accumulated knowledge of our civilization, if not all of us? There is a social surplus that far exceeds the productive contributions of any individual or group of individuals, and no one man has any greater claim to it than any other. It belongs to the community as a whole, and to privatize it is to plunder our collective patrimony for the benefit of the very few.

Chapter Twenty-Three

The Future Of Usury

[Jesus said], "If you have money, do not lend it at interest, but give [it] to one from whom you will not get it back."
—Gospel of Thomas, Lambdin trans., p. 136

If you lend [to them] of whom you hope to receive, what thanks have ye?
—Gospel of Luke, King James Version (6:34)

Chapter 5 of *Eli* is pivotal to the whole discourse of this book. Perhaps it is difficult for the reader to accept the deeply immoral and evil nature of usury, since it is so engrained in our systems of beliefs and values. The idea of usury, lending money or resources at interest has, despite all to the contrary, is demonstrably evil, and it must not continue. Usury entails the false notion that money can grow, as if by magic. The money is, as we have seen, taken up by the very few. Our whole economy hinges on the idea that money can grow indefinitely, which is ludicrous, as we saw in the last chapter. Our governments are thinking that, the current financial crisis, which will soon become catastrophic, is just another cycle in the usury game of creating bubbles of prices on money and property that are far higher than the actual value of what we are receiving on loan.

The housing bubble was just one example, with many good and decent people losing the fruits of their labor as a result of borrowing money against a ridiculously inflated housing market. The housing bubble led to an avalanche of financial problems that were treated symptomatically by the US federal government going into huge financial debt. As we explained previously, this huge debt was incurred by loaning and giving money to our large financial institutions and corporations that were too big to fail, while many smaller business and individual interests were allowed to fail, and continue to fail. Our economic system is set up so that money invariably makes money for those on top, and money lent without interest is, in such an economy, a gift of welfare for the very few, allowing them to continue to extract money from the economy by charging interest on the money that they have received free of interest.

It is not likely that usury will be outlawed in the near future. Rather, those who believe as we do that usury is the worst form of social evil and needs to end will be prosecuted to ends that are difficult to see, but which might go so far as imprisonment and death, should this movement against usury create a real threat to our dying economy. What will occur, as per *Eli*, is that personal wealth will be lost, causing great suffering, and inevitably, the economy will collapse, not as it has done in former recessions and depressions, but cataclysmically and irrevocably. What will be left is a kind of post-apocalyptic shell of an economy, a structure that contains little or no wealth, it having been stolen in the feeding frenzies of usurers of high order, the very few who are among the most wealthy people in the world.

Michael Hudson, a Canadian economics professor, has written an analysis of the current economic situation at *http://www.informationclearinghouse.info/article28354.htm*. His article is entitled: "only the Crazies' Get the Bank Giveaway Right: Free money creation to bail out financial speculators, but not Social Security or Medicare."

The point of interest is his idea that cyclical business crises historically had the effect of wiping out debt—through widespread default, bankruptcies, foreclosures—so that the burden of enormous debt overhead was periodically relieved and prices of assets—e.g. securities and real estate—could fall back into line with actual value. But he points out the current trend of using the US Treasury to prop up bad debt so that the periodic adjustment never takes place, and the mountain of debt just keeps building higher and higher.

This is the economic explanation for the trend we found when you analyzed stock market prices and found them increasingly out of sync with underlying value in 1999. We correctly saw this trend of postponing the inevitable adjustment, and that the adjustment will be all the more cataclysmic the longer it is postponed.

The inevitable collapse of the this long-term debt-driven speculative balloon was delayed once by the 9/11 false flag and Iraq/Afghan petroleum wars, then again by the 2008 bailouts, but now the legacy of both of those moves has become a total drag on the economy. So the day of reckoning is getting close, and the very few seem to have used up all the tricks in their bag. Their only recourse is to squeeze whatever is left of the income and savings of the middle class, thereby creating a powder keg of social instability.

Such sins against humanity are the most grievous sins, not just because they effect large great numbers of people but, more importantly, because humanity or humankind is a single organism, not just a collection of people. As a single organism, I could perhaps lose a hand or an arm, but would continue to live, and might even be very happy doing so. However, there would also be consequences for humankind. If I were a laborer, perhaps I would lose my ability to do my job, and be thus prevented from giving to the greater good. Humankind is this greater good. An individual person might die but, according to one's beliefs, may go on to the greater glory of paradise after death. An individual might suffer from a disease, but the single organism we call humanity could continue to flourish and reduce such suffering in a variety of ways.

Usury is the opposite of charity, and thus of love. When the banks repossessed the farms and homes of those who were devastated by the dust bowl, so vividly portrayed by folk singer

Woody Guthrie and novelist John Steinbeck, they intended great malice, not only toward those individuals who were robbed and displaced, but also toward larger groups of individuals such as families and social systems. Protection of such social systems is the rubric of human ecology, such that the suffering of an individual or individual is a social crime that harms the ecological system of interdependent people.

Usury is the greatest crime that can be committed against humanity. Perhaps I owe interest on a home mortgage that I can afford to pay, and don't really suffer as a result of having to pay such interest. Many others are not so fortunate. However, the enormity of the crime of usury lies in the fact that it is the greatest of social crimes. It robs the poor, deprives people of their basic needs, and creates a class system whereby, as we have already explained, social wealth—the goods and resources of people—are stolen from the poor, and come to be owned by private individuals of great wealth. The economy of usury will collapse, totally, and this is the most important prophecy of *Eli*. However, to paraphrase Dickens, these are the shadows of things that might be, not of things that must be. However, this particular shadow of the future will fall upon us if we make no atonement collectively for the great sin of usury, by abolishing it, which seems doubtful.

As we know, a human being starts life as a single cell. The cell divides and is organized into interdependent tissues and organs. Once adulthood is achieved, this growth ends. Perhaps, if we did not know this, we would project that a foot of growth within a single year of adolescence would continue until, at age sixty, the person would be fifty feet tall. Our societies and governments are doing just that. They are banking, literally and figuratively, on indefinite growth the economy. It cannot happen, and it will not happen.

Usury is like a cancer on the body of humankind. Like cancer, the economy has been doubling in size, such that the Dow Jones Industrials Average has doubled every thirty years of so. Cancer starts out as a single cell, which, unlike normal tissues, continues to grow be cell division, into two, four, eight, sixteen, thirty-two cells, etc. When the tumor is several thousands of cells in size,

Chapter Twenty-Three The Future Of Usury

it becomes visible, and continues to develop by doubling, and then spreads to other organs in the body, eventually killing the host. The cancer of usury has grown with the growth of markets and or money, and it now threatens to kill the host, humankind, in much the same way that cancer does. Usury creates nothing, it produces nothing, quite the opposite, it drains the host, progressively as the tumor gets larger and spreads throughout the body. Perhaps we can cure the cancer with treatments such as surgery, radiation, and chemotherapy. The earlier we are able to do so, the better it is for the host. Surgery is generally the most likely way to cure the cancer, radiation and chemotherapy tend to just slow it down. We must cut out usury—make it illegal.

So this cancer, the growth of money due to usury, is the gravest danger that faces humankind. Its stigmata are war, disease, suffering, hunger, and death, to name a few. As we speak, and for the most part unknown to the American public, we are escalating war throughout the world. The wisest course is to excise the tumor of usury, the root cause of all these problems, but the world will not have it. The only alternative is survival, and this is the topic of the next section of chapter 5 of *Eli*. We, firstly, must stop feeding the cancer by ceasing to participate in all aspects of usury, including buying and selling goods and services on interest. The next step must be, for those who are sincerely committed to the future of humankind, to begin to take ownership of the means of survive, including the production of food, water, shelter, and medical services.

Humankind has entered the times of suffering, and it will get worse. This largely depends on us. If this book makes any impact in the near future, the author will become the enemy of the people, and likely judged insane and perhaps criminal. However, on the small chance that *Eli* is recognized in its own times, the earlier the better, we must create for ourselves economies that are relatively separate, isolated, and self-sufficient in preparation for the economic collapse soon to come.

Chapter Twenty-Four

The New Judgment And Atonement

> *A human being is a part of the whole, called by us, "Universe," a part limited in time and space. He experiences himself, his thoughts and feelings as something separated from the rest—a kind of optical delusion of his consciousness.*
>
> *This delusion is a kind of prison for us, restricting us to our personal desires and to affection for a few persons nearest to us. Our task must be to free ourselves from this prison by widening our circle of compassion to embrace all living creatures and the whole of nature in its beauty.*
>
> *Nobody is able to achieve this completely, but the striving for such achievement is in itself a part of the liberation and a foundation for inner security.*
>
> —Albert Einstein

Chapter 6 of Eli is about social justice. Humankind is a single organism, and the idea of separateness is, as Einstein said, a delusion. But it is a mass delusion, shared by the better part of humankind. The delusion of separateness is conditioned into us very early in life. The separation of humans, one from another, is very much like the phenomenon of dissociation, that we see most markedly in multiple personality or dissociative identity disorder, with each of us, in a sense, having undergone the trauma that was the Fall and having a sort of amnesia for what we had been through 95 percent or more of the existence of our species. So we are all like alter egos of the One Soul, God. This is the meaning of the story of the *Simurgh*, where the birds looked into the mirror of the *Simurgh* and saw that they were all *Simurgh*.

As we are one organism, we are all, collectively, responsible for the actions that harm another that we are either involved in, directly or indirectly, or have knowledge of and acquiesce to. One part of the organism does not wage war on another. One part does not eat and let the other starve. These things are all symptomatic of the delusion of separation.

The child is used as an example in *Eli* because the child is still innocent, it has not yet partaken of the greatest crime, usury, and is closer to that unity of humankind that existed before the Fall. But we are all children of God, and so the child spoken in *Eli* is every living human. In a sense, the child lives through a development that is very much like the development of humankind, ever more separate, ever more sinking into the delusion and the apathy of what we call the normal adult. In the *Gospel of Thomas* Jesus says, "Do not do the thing that you hate." In contrast, Henry David Thoreau said, "Most man lead lives of quiet desperation." Most of our so-called jobs are dedicated to turning the gears of the giant engine of usury that is consuming our species and our planet. Money is at the heart of usury, as it is the basis for loans and interest on loans. Our love of money is the same as our love of usury. Therefore, usury must be forsaken, along with the love of money, which rules our desperately separate lives. As it has been written, in the words of Jesus, you cannot serve two masters, God and money or Mammon. We have forsaken God because we serve Mammon. Now we must forsake Mammon; we must no longer serve this master.

We have become so separate and apathetic that we have lost all connection with our progeny. We have become greedy ancestors, creating a desolate future of many generations to come. However, as an organism, it is our collective sin, usury, that is robbing the coffers of the future. This is a very serious situation, where there is no love, there is no charity, there is only take, take, take, stealing bread from the tables for generations to come in the form of our own individual and collective progeny. It is as ghastly as it is frightening. Chapter 6 of *Eli* addresses these issues.

1. **Now hear of the new judgment.**
2. **You are judged many times more by what you do in groups then for what you do as individuals.**
3. **If one thousand of you participate in the murder of one child, then one thousand of you are a thousand times guilty.**
4. **You are judged many times more by what you give assent to others doing then what you do yourself.**
5. **If one million of you give assent to the one thousand who participate in the murder of a child, then one million of you are a million times guilty.**
6. **You are judged more by what you do passively then by what you do actively.**

We share collectively of the crimes against humankind that are committed so freely with our knowledge. There is no individual salvation for those who remain separate from the body of humankind. We have become players in crimes all over the world—war, disease, starvation—and we, such as we tolerate these situations with apathy, are all guilty of these crimes, personally in our deluded separation, and collectively in the Mind of God. We envy the usurers, we want to be like them, we want our children to be like them. We take away their ability to act and think and replace it with programmed garbage—television, video games, violence, anger, hatred, the culture of apathy and mindlessness. Our children no longer play like children; they enact video games.

When we reach the future from which we are stealing wealth we will find another future from which we must steal more wealth, endlessly. The people will be reduced to the status of slaves, in the skeleton of an economy that will became a house of straw. It will and it must collapse, like the current cookie-cutter houses, which are of high maintenance and are not built to last, with cardboard replacing plywood, often in flood zones. The usurers buy this land at little expense and then, through the influence of their money, have it rezoned into residential property, increasing its value several times over their investment and over the money they have paid to have the land rezoned. They then build out of cardboard, cookie-cutter houses, and sell them to unwitting consumers. Do you have any idea what a flood does to cardboard? We sink our money into our homes, yet the values go down. The usurers may sell for 400 percent of cost and for which we pay 1,200 percent or more of cost in our mortgages, and we will find that after we have paid this enormous burden of usury that these homes will have little value. We are left with perhaps 25 percent of the value when we have paid 1,200 percent by our own labor. Is this right? Is it ethical? It is robbery, pure and simple, yet we grant higher self-worth to these individuals, as self worth is now measured by money.

The horrors that will come, if we continue on this course, will only increase. The elderly will be cast aside and left to suffer and die. The people will be treated like slaves by the new bosses, branded like cattle with electronic bar codes or chips on identification cards. In the career of the author, he has seen that the good physician is not rewarded or valued, because he or she utilizes resources to benefit the patient. It is better for the physician to give poor service, take part of the money game, and let the patient suffer or die. Euthanasia is now routinely practiced for this very purpose. For those insured—yet another usurious form of robbery that our current health reform mandates is better for the patient to hate than to like or love his or her physician, and never come back—they will then utilize less services. Capitation then becomes, in a sense, decapitation. The money is coming from our taxes, going to insurance plans, and yielding the profits of usury, as the investors in the insurance plan, the very wealthy, continue to extract wealth in the form of usury as the value of their investments increases on the backs of the poor and needy. This is the real agenda behind health care reform. Health care is costing more and more and providing less and less. The sick and the elderly will ultimately be abandoned—far more profit is to be made on the young and healthy, providing well-care services. In the meantime, the sick and elderly are buried under copayments, and sold insurance, if they can afford it, to cover these copayments. However, as we know, no insurance plan will enter a market that does not produce profits—and, inevitably, these plans cost far more than they pay out. The elderly lose their homes and their savings for retirement, are cajoled into getting reverse mortgages, again paying interest to the usurers. We will see the horror of these trends worsen as the elderly population, the baby boomers of late 1940s to the early 1960s, are abandoned, humiliated, mistreated, and allowed to die, with the social security investments of a lifetime of income disappearing into the hands of malignant usury.

So it is imperative, it is urgent, to end usury. It's deceiving glory is paraded before us by the likes of Donald Trump, and we watch him in glee as he fires people who do not make money for him. This is sickening, it is perverse, and it is one of the ways that usury breeds apathy and widens the gulf between the people of this organism we call humankind. The organism gets sick, fragmented by the usurers and the media they control, which pushes us through mindless advertisement to buy things they don't need, or which are actually harmful, with money we don't have. The media has robbed us of independent thought—we are told what to think, how to vote, and how to live.

Usury is the greatest crime one can ever commit—but we are forced into by an economy that runs entirely on the basis of usury. This sickness in humankind is devouring people, killing people in wars, causing disease and starvation, ravaging the ecology and climate. The charge of chapter 6 of *Eli* is not to do these things, and the only way to stop is through our social systems, through the involvement of groups of people in taking responsibility for the atrocities they are committing. As individuals, we have just as much responsibility for these crimes as the people directly involved, through our apathy and denial.

The principal of social justice prescribed in *Eli* is expressed in Numbers. This passage of the Old Testament is too long to quote in full, but the general background is the scenario where a stranger among the congregation has violated the law as given to Moses, unbeknownst to the congregation, out of ignorance for that Law (Numbers 15:25, King James translation):

> And the priest shall make an atonement for all the congregation of the children on Isreal, and it shall be forgiven them . . .

There are a number of elements here that bear on the new justice of *Eli*, which is, in a way, not entirely new, as its basic principles are found here in Numbers. Firstly, ignorance is not an excuse. This is an even more widespread view of social justice than is explicit in *Eli*. Secondly, the sin of a stranger, much less a member of the congregation, falls on the entirety of congregation of the children of Israel. Thirdly, atonement is the act of delivering the congregation from sin, thus the sin, which is committed without the knowledge of the congregation, by a stranger, someone who is not a member of the congregation, falls on every member of the congregation. Fourthly, atonement, in this case an offering a sacrifice before God, absolves the soul of each individual member of the congregation, implying that the sin lies on all these souls, is the wrongdoing of all these souls, and must be absolved for the redemption and salvation of each individual soul. The sacrifice is (Numbers 15:24) "that all the congregation shall offer one young bullock for a burnt offering, for a sweet savour unto the LORD . . . ." along with other sacrifices. In this passage the English word LORD is a translation of the Hebrew Jehovah, the eternal, holder of the covenant. Later in Numbers (15:26) the resolution be atonement is described: "And it shall be forgiven all the congregation of the children of Israel."

We will tentatively use the word Elyon, Most High, to characterize the ultimate infinity of God in the hidden time, and suggest that the new science be called Elyonology and the congregation the church of Eli. Elyon is used in connected with Jehovah, Jehovah-Elyon, in Psalms (7:17; 47:2; 97:9). The passage of Psalm 47:2-3 is of particular note:

> 2. For the LORD most high [Jehovah-Elyon] *is* terrible; *he is* a great King over all the earth.
> 3. He shall subdue the people under us, and the nations under our feet.

What comes to mind here is the ancient Goddess Kali, the ferocious and fearful yet ever-caring mother, a goddess among some of the Hindu people, still worshiped in Calcutta and elsewhere. Along the same lines, in the *Bhagavad Gita*, Krishna manifests to Arjuna in many forms, including terrible or even monstrous form. Here is where the famous verse, uttered by Krishna, "behold, I am the creator and destroyer of worlds" comes from. J. Robert Oppenheimer (1904-1967), known as the "father of the atomic bomb," witnessed the first blast of July 16, 1945, in Trinity, New Mexico. He was quite familiar with the Vedanta, and when recounting the blast, he said it reminded him of the verse, recounted as "Now, I am become Death, the destroyer of worlds." Indeed, if we are to believe that God is the ultimate infinity, who brings into actuality the one universe from the infinite number of potential universes, God is indeed the creator and destroyer of worlds, literally.

In Genesis *Elyon* is mentioned in connection with Abram (later called Abraham). In this case, GOD is rendered from the Hebrew El (Genesis 14:19): "Blessed be Abram of the most high God [*El*], possessor of heaven and earth," and later, (Genesis 14:22) Abram says " . . . I have lift up my hand unto the LORD [Jehovah] the most high God [*El*], the possessor of heaven and earth . . ." *El Elyon* is also translated as the Most High God (Genesis 14:20; Psalms 9:2) expressing God's supremacy, sovereignty, and strength, somewhat like the English term "Almighty God." *El* [God] *Olam* [the hidden time] is translated everlasting God (Genesis 21:33; Psalm 90:1-3; Isaiah 26:4). This is reflected in Psalm 90 (subtitled a prayer of Moses the man of God), in verse 2 (King James Version):

> Before the mountains were brought forth, or ever
> hadst formed the earth and the world, even from
> everlasting to everlasting, thou art God [*El Olam*].

The author is not a Hebrew scholar, but it would appear that *El* is the more general term, and that all these names of God are connected express different aspects and qualities of God.

In the Christian tradition, atonement is not necessary, as the blood of Christ is the atonement for our sins. This, in the author's view, is one of those unfortunate concepts that was grafted onto the Christianity and that gives license, as we have quoted previously from Martin Luther, for the Christian to sin boldly. In *Eli* there is no such concept. We are to act correctly, and take responsibility, not only for our sins but for the sins of our kind. The sword of universal harmony exacts justice on all humankind, and as justice is paramount, those who transgress the will of God that the earth should become one people living in harmony transgress the will of God, and for this, there is divine justice, which is in the hidden time. It is thus that *El Olam* is the everlasting, and the hidden time the realm of souls that have departed from the plane of manifestation. The atonement of Judaism is thus favored over the forgiveness of Christianity and Zoroastrianism. We are not here advocating the methods of atonement practiced by the ancient Jews, but a different kind of atonement. In the new justice, the atonement is the atonement of the group in the hidden time, thereby affecting a reconciliation of those crimes we have committed against humanity and their future potential for manifesting in the potentials of the future.

Thus, for the abomination of creating atomic weapons to kill innocent people and possibly extinguish humans from the face of the earth, there must have an atonement, and that is total, worldwide, nuclear disarmament. By doing so, we will have done the Will of God, since the potential futures of human annihilation by these bombs require that such bombs continue to exist and the possibility of their deployment is still an enormous threat to the future of humankind, and only by disposing them entirely can we end the line of all possible universes that lead to such an outcome. The fact of such bombs is in no way mitigated by the vain imagination that we have been forgiven for the act of creating or using them. Such would be to upset the balance of the moral universe. There are a great many other actions of atonement of humankind in the hidden time, not least among them is our actions in controlling global warming, putting an end to war and starvation, and securing a future in fulfillment of the higher aspirations than God has for our species. The future conditioned by atheism is full or perils, and as are the futures of all those corrupted religions that promote false doctrines.

Atonement must be made for these failures by correcting them. The universe is not some magical theater where we go on to some imaginary heaven of ego-consciousness and its everlasting continuation. The ego atomizes when we leave the manifest world. To get to that reality that we call heaven in the hidden time, we need to take heed that we cannot bring our separate alter egos with us, but will once again become part of the One Soul, from which we have been born. As stated at the very beginning of this book in the quotation from the Rig Veda, the most ancient of all religious traditions existing on earth today, ego (alter ego) is the biggest enemy of humans. How is it, that some three or four thousand years later, that we have not yet learned this?

Heaven and hell are real—I have seen them both. Heaven is a timeless tranquility, joy, and harmony, where there is no conflict or suffering. Regarding where heaven is, it is found in the Greek *Logia*, which were fragments of the *Gospel or Thomas* that survived its systematic censorship from the Christian creed. Jesus said, "Cleave the wood, and I am there," meaning that heaven is on the inside of things. I have perceived it infused through all reality, like a hologram, complete in its minutest detail. In the *Gospel of Thomas* Jesus said, "The kingdom of heaven is among you, spread out over all the earth, but people do not see it." We only see it in the hidden time, the eternal now, and this is the time our ancestors lived in prior to the Fall. We are forced out of it with the act of world creation very early in life, by the adult world, which is in a complete state of amnesia for it. This is why we forget our earliest years of life.

Hell is the atomization of the ego. The ego seems to break up into pieces, and what once was the whole of everything we think we are, have been, and will be seems to fly off in pieces, or so it seems, scattered everywhere. It is the ego's loss of all the things that it has strived for, everything that it has called its property. It is horrific, beyond all imagination, even to recall.

The wise one has no property, for all the earth and the heavens belong to God. It separates us by distinguishing your property from my property. It is the playground of fools, because we have received our consolation on earth, and have no place in heaven, which place belongs, not to the ego, but to the soul. As in Luke (6: 31-24) "what thank have ye" if you only love those who love you, do good for those who do good for you, and lend to those that you expect return, much less return on usury, what thanks do have in heaven? These themes run through the Gospels, but are perhaps best exemplified in the parable of the pearls, of which there are two versions:

> Again, the kingdom of heaven is like unto a merchant man, seeking goodly pearls: Who, when he had found one pearl of great price, went and sold all that he had, and bought it.

> —Matthew 13: 45-46, King James Translation

> Jesus said, "The Father's kingdom is like a merchant who had a supply of merchandise and found a pearl. That merchant was prudent; he sold the merchandise and bought the single pearl for himself. So also with you, seek his treasure that is unfailing, that is enduring, where no moth comes to eat and no worm destroys."

> —Gospel of Thomas 76
> Nag Hammadi Library
> Patterson/Meyer Translation

The enduring pearl, that no moth comes to eat, and no worm destroys, is our place in heaven. The wise merchant sold all he had for a single pearl. The pearl is the Soul. The same theme is expressed in Mark (8:36): "For what shall it benefit a man, if he shall gain the whole world, and lose his own soul." At the end of this life, the soul is what survives. All that you have, be it the whole world, is not worth the price of this pearl. God has given it to us, it is our priceless pearl, and we must treasure it above all things.

Goethe wrote of this in the seventeenth century, where Faust sells his Soul to the devil. There are actually books and articles on the Internet that have been produced by the rising cult of Satanists that instruct one on how to do this, and stores that sell goods for the practice of what is called Satanic ritual abuse. Patients of mine have said that they have been abused in this manner, and have claimed that there are huge congregations of

Satanists engaged in ritual sacrifice, but actual evidence seems to be lacking. Their stories may or may not be true, but they are certainly chilling.

Much of what has been recounted to me regarding the dark, cult religions is based on the false prophet Aleister Crowley (1875-1947) who started a religious cult in the early 1920s that gained widespread support. Much of it was based on Egyptian mythology, and the egocentric philosophy of doing whatever you want to do. L. Ron Hubbard, founder of scientology, was apparently influenced by Crowley, and his group is also based on egocentrism. Both dabbled in the so-called occult world that also had made its way into the work of Madam Blavatsky, who founded the church of Theosophy. A world teacher was predicted, and groomed in the person of Jiddu Krishnamurti. Krishnamurti, however, split off from Theosophy after gaining a huge following, with his well-known "Truth is a pathless land" speech to his followers, who then dispersed. Krishnamurti founded his own movement, and had great influence on the Indian philosophical and spiritual figure, Vimala Thakar. Krishnamurti had a relationship and a series of dialogues with the great quantum physicist, David Bohm, who was exiled from the United States in the 1950s soon after writing his definitive text on quantum theory, which is used to this day. This was because his mentor was J. Robert Oppenheimer, a freethinker who had apparently explored communism, and Bohm refused to testify against him before the US Congress in the witch-hunt that is called the McCarthy Era.

This may seem very strange to us now, but we may soon see a witch hunt, against all those who have any sympathy for the terrorists, under the flag of the United States, who have begun to define terrorism in curious ways. For example, years ago it was not uncommon is America for people, in jest, to say, "I'll kill you." Now one can be arrested and incarcerated for saying this, as it is now considered a terrorist threat. Similarly, it is now criminal to make jokes of certain kinds. The rights of America are eroding at such a pace that we may soon see the suspension of habeas corpus, the fundamental right not to be incarcerated without due process of the law, such that people can be incarcerated in much the same way that we incarcerate our enemies who are held without due process or legal proceeding in court. Torture has become the privilege of the new war machine, and is permitted by our president, Mr. Obama, in violation of the Nuremberg Agreements, which establish international criminal actions. The forms of indictment at the Nuremberg Trials were the following:

1. Participation in a *common plan or conspiracy* for the accomplishment of a *crime against peace*
2. Planning, initiating and waging *wars of aggression* and other crimes against peace
3. *War crimes*
4. *Crimes against humanity*

Torture is, or course, a war crime, and Mr. Obama refuses to prosecute those in the military who have used torture in the course of investigations. Torture seems to have been involved in the successful effort to locate Osama bin Laden, but this information is highly classified. Films and pictures of torture have circulated widely, but Mr. Obama seems to have a Machiavellian belief that the ends justify the means.

Psychologically, such beliefs are evidence of psychopathy, and as leaders, such psychopathic tendencies can be dangerous. Mr. Obama has failed to keep a number of the promises that got him elected, including the closing of the American prison at Guantanamo Bay, where suspected terrorists continued to be held without due process. He had a series of slogans such as change we need but, under his administration America has changed for the worse, and Mr. Obama has made a number of slights of hand in the course of his administration, most particularly in his selling of health care reform for the American public, which is turning out to be a profit venture for the power elite, one more market conquered that was once sacrosanct. His support for the corrupt Karzai regime in Afghanistan, the invasion of which was a knee-jerk response meant to bring Osama bin Laden to justice, continues to escalate now that bin Laden is dead. In the meantime, he has transformed the war in Afghanistan from a counter-terrorist war to a counter-insurgency war against that is supposed to democratize the nation, all the while suborning the horrors in China.

The guile and trickery that has sold these wars to the American people is very well crafted, befitting of the growing psychopathy in America as it clamors and reels from what their enemies the terrorists have done. The face of usury and big petroleum is well hidden. People have become very fearful. America has changed in so many ways since 9/11 that its government is in danger of losing its constitutional right to govern. It derives its right to govern, according to the Constitution, as a privilege granted by its citizens. Government, according to the Constitution, is at the behest of the citizens, not vice versa as it has become. This is not sedition or treason, as we are not advocating the overthrow of the government. It is now time for American citizens to take that privilege back, before martial law is declared under the Patriot Act and we are incarcerated willy-nilly to control the unrest that is bound to occur if our government continues on its current course.

Our allegiance is to our nation and our people, not only in the US but the world over, and the course they are setting is aimed straight at the target of Chinese hegemony or predominance over our people and the very same state corporatism or fascism that rules China. Our government has already become corporate owners, as if the corporations belong to the people. It has defaulted so egregiously on the rights of Americans that we must ask ourselves exactly what we are trying to preserve, and how we can go about doing so.

Since all of us and our progeny have been placed under an enormous debt, the options are limited. We can replace our government and default on the debt, as it was not incurred by the citizens of the United States in a lawful manner, or we can let China step in an assume sovereignty. The situation, as this is being written, is at break point, and the future sovereignty of the American nation either will be preserved, or not. This need not have to be. The traitors among us are those who have sold our nation, and they are a clear and present danger. Some sacrifice will be required, but it is nothing compared to the alternatives.

With respect to freedom of religion, we will have none under our Chinese leaders. As for the Constitution, it will be thrown in the garbage by our adversary, and they will set the rules. Now that Osama bin Laden and Saddam Hussein have been brought to justice, perhaps we had best bring some of our own leaders to justice. Instead of projecting our problems on an imaginary enemy, the facts of 9/11 must be known to lift the spell that the great imposter has cast on us over the past ten years.

However, this is not intended to be a political call to arms, but an exposition of what the new justice means. Each and every one of us is responsible for the warfare we are waging, for the danger we are creating for our world, and for the atrocities that have been committed under the banner of our nation. Atonement involves a fairly radical change—it has gone much too far, and the times of suffering will soon escalate to domestic violence, as the thumb of oppression of over our people becomes too much to bear, and such unrest will cause further economic problems. The wheel of usury has been set spinning much too fast for this nation to maintain any measure of sovereignty as the process progresses. For this we can thank Reagan, Clinton, and Obama. Unfortunately, charisma is more often a hallmark of psychopathy than good intensions.

The act of world creation is the work of the ego, not the soul. The ego creates its own, delusional world around itself, as Einstein says in the opening quote of this chapter. It is a world in which we a separate alter egos, frightened by Moloch, as Ginsberg wrote in *Howl*, out of their natural ecstasy, the Paradise or Garden of the One Soul, the biblical Garden of Eden, and enter into the hell of Moloch, the consumer of children, demanding sacrifice. This is the Fall, it is the trauma of humankind and of every human being born into this world. The Fall will not last, it is a passage through hell, necessary before the ascension into heaven, for humankind. These are the times in which the furies of hell reach the inevitable end times or tribulation. We must be prepared.

The single commandment is all *Eli* asks us to keep. If, as a species, we are able to keep it, the times of suffering will quickly end. The engine cannot run without fuel. We are fighting wars to give more fuel to this merciless engine of usury, key among which is petroleum. Recently we have witnesses a series of nuclear catastrophes in Japan, which will poison the earth. My first career was as a geologist, and I reviewed environmental impact statements for land-use proposals. In order to build these reactors, the Japanese would have had to do borings into the earth to determine what sediments they were being built upon. From the sediments, they must have dated tsunami after tsunami, bringing sediments on to the very same land, and indicating that the reactors were being built in a tsunami zone. They could have been built on much higher ground—electricity is readily transmitted over long distances.

The disaster was caused by apathy and corruption. You will never hear this in the news media—they are part of the problem, not part of the solution. In the same way, the torrential rains, tornados, and flooding in the area of the Mississippi River Valley has ravaged many homes and devastated the lives of many good people. The waters in the Gulf of Mexico/tropical Atlantic have become warmer, generating more water vapor, and this air, laden with water, creates the torrential rains, along with flooding and tornados. This is very costly, emotionally and materially, to the American people and the American government, which must offer relief, and must borrow money at interest in order to do so. All this is a result of global warming, yet in watching the American news on television, there is not a whisper of such. A woman recently told the author that the rains were God's punishment for the American policy regarding the territory of Israel, which, she stated, will force them to give up some of their land. She had heard this on the media, and believed it. We are responsible for our environmental policy and for global warming. Magic doesn't work anymore. To the extent God is involved, we need to make atonement and cease or greatly diminish those activities that have led to global warming.

Very few people realize that we are in an interglacial period, and that the Northern Hemisphere has been repeatedly glaciated in the history of our species. We have been led to think that global warming will melt the glaciers, but this is not how it usually works. Glaciation is a product of the amount of snowfall, which accumulates at Northern latitudes without melting. As it accumulates, the weight on the underlying ice increases, causing the ice to flow away from the area of accumulation, which can only be to lower latitudes. The amount of snowfall depends on the temperature of the water that flows in currents to the northern latitudes from the tropical and sub-tropical latitudes. Warming of the water at these lower latitudes, thus produces snowfall at higher latitudes, as warmer water yields more water vapor. Climate is very sensitive and, to some degree, unpredictable.

All our models of global warming, crafted twenty or more years ago, are playing out on the worst-case scenario side of the predictions. We here nothing of it in the media, perhaps because our beloved China, as a result of whom the usurers are making those few extra dollars that they crave, is the producer of a large portion of the greenhouse gases that are fueling global warming, as are we. China has absolutely no regard for the environment. The tie you buy at Macys is made, in some measure, by the electricity that China is producing in its unregulated coal-fired power plants. Macys makes a few extra dollars and homes in America are flooded totally under water. Is there something wrong with this picture? Atonement, in this case, is to stop supporting China and its environmental policies, but those few extra dollars Macys makes on a tie add up, just a drop in the bucket of a huge amount of wealth America is pouring out of our nation and into the Chinese economy. Is this moral behavior for the people of America? The fact is, they don't care. Not caring no longer carries passes muster. You, I, every single one of us are responsible, as is written in the new judgment according to *Eli*.

This is only one of a number of end-time scenarios being created by malignant usury. Systems are quite complex, and the global financial system demands that we be obedient servants, subject to the barrage of garbage tabloid media in our new idolatry of television. Even the programming *American Idol*, etc., makes this quite explicit. God is merciful, but the great deceiver is not. As the song says, "You've got to serve somebody," (Dylan) and it is quite clear who we are now serving, with our fantasies of the end of the world and the accompanying irresponsibility toward the future.

These are the products of malignant usury. Unable to find markets in the current economy to plunder, they are creating markets at the expense of a huge and escalating federal and state debt. These are the markets of the war machine, the Federal bail outs, and of the personal debt owed to creditors, paid at high rates of interest by people who are barely making a living. Now, in order to allow people to buy these cookie-cutter homes, the government is subsidizing mortgages. This money is coming straight from the government debt and going directly to the banks—as it is they who are exacting the interest.

We must forsake usury, the sooner the better. It is our only choice. It is a war that we can't afford to lose, for our children's sake, if we care at all. Hopefully, the war will be peaceful, but it is more likely that our "government of the people, by the people," will turn its mighty power against its own people. Malignant usury will ultimately drain the markets of loans of all their real wealth, and the skeleton of the world economy will come to be filled with make-believe wealth, wealth burrowed from the future on interest, and we will be left with nothing—if it be allowed to continue. Every principle that this country (the United States) was built on is being, and will continue to be, eroded—freedom of speech is already gone; life, liberty, and the pursuit of happiness are on their way out. Democracy has become a sick joke as the Supreme Court has ruled that corporations can make limitless contributions to political candidates. The electorate is so misinformed by the media that they are no longer free agents in government "of the people, by the people." Unfortunately, such government has perished from this earth. We are living in a totalitarian state, where the criminal contract of usury, the growth of money, has come to dominate every area of government in accordance with operatives, engaged by the very few to assert dominion over the American people and over the world, who are, for the most part, unknown or invisible.

Chapter Twenty-Five

Justice And The Hidden Time

The final seventh chapter of Eli is perhaps the most difficult as it ties together the diverse content of the first six chapters. We have discussed a good deal of its contents, and we need not repeat this discussion, but only to highlight a few final points and conclude our discussion. Chapter 7 reads,

1. **Justice is paramount. The new judgment is the justice of the hidden time.**
2. **No crime is a means to an end. No crime can be rationalized.**
3. **The murder of a child has no justification, even if the bombs have missed their mark.**
4. **The starvation of a child has no justification, even if the crops have failed, or the population is too large.**
5. **Act correctly. Incorrect action cannot be justified by incorrect action. An incorrect action taken to cover an incorrect action is doubly incorrect.**
6. **Cleave to the common good. We are all responsible for bringing about the time of great suffering, for its continuing, and for its ending.**
7. **There is nothing hidden in the hidden time. Know that this, the hidden time, is your everlasting, and live.**

Justice is paramount. Our criminal government and its invisible actions and operatives have committed great crimes for which they must be accountable. There was website that I administered from my laptop from through in 1999 and 2000 that spelled it all out. It was confiscated by the police in 2001, weeks after 9/11, and I was jailed as a terrorist and forced to sign a statement that I was a terrorist as a condition of my freedom. I was never read my rights, and when I pointed this out, the officer just said sorry. I was subject to police violence at the time of my arrest, injuring my shoulder as my wrists were turned 180 degrees in a violent handcuffing. As I winched in pain, the officer told me that I better not be resisting arrest, or he would beat the s— out of me. I was told by police that I did not have the rights granted under the Bill of Rights, stripped naked and housed down, and given a very small jumpsuit, the crotch of which I had to tear to achieve some comfort. All the other detainees had two-piece garments. Police at the jail seemed have only two words in their vocabulary—"f— you." I was placed in a holding cell until two FBI agents arrived. I told them that I had family members who had died on the beach at Normandy in WWII and that I would not eat or drink fluids as long as I was detained until my death. The agents said they were there to defend my rights—a total lie. After two days without fluids, I began to become delirious, and thank God for my brother, Thomas Germinario, who is an attorney and flew out to get me released, I was sprung from jail. My brother was in a hotel and left his number for me to call upon release, but I was refused the number, and had to read it upside down and memorize it from over a desk to contact my brother.

I later learned from a colleague that many physicians had been incarcerated as they were perceived as representing a danger to the government's anthrax hoax. Such anthrax as to pose a danger has been documented as being produced by our government, while strains lacking such virulence to pose a danger were produced by other sources. The anthrax hoax was staged to draw attention away from the criminal acts of our government and its network of operatives on 9/11.

Regarding money, the Christian Bible in 1 Timothy 6:10, Douay Rheims translation, states, "For the desire of money is the root of all evils; which some coveting have erred from the faith, and have entangled themselves in many sorrows." What is there in money to be desired? It is the growth of money, which produces a parasitic wealth stolen by the lenders. The passage does not say money is evil, but that it is the root of all evils. And so it is, the root. And what is it that the root does? It forms a stem, a plant, leaves, fruits, seeds, etc. And would is it that makes these fruits of the root evil? It is the fact that usury is the fruit of money. Usury is not the root of evil, the root is the growth of the fruits of money, from which usury springs. Why else would anyone love or desire money—scraps of paper, of no real use but in trade. Trade and money are permitted in Islam, while usury is stricken and explicitly forbidden. Many Muslim banks function with no usury whatsoever. So Islam is the enemy of usury—it must be brought into the markets of loan to become a commodity for the wealthy. The attack on Iraq had nothing to do with 9/11, it was aimed at regime change and the creation of an American world.

The patriot act was created prior to 9/11. Our economy, on the brink of collapse, needed to have money created in order to continue, and the best way to do this was by warfare. The creation of money is the only function of warfare. Money is needed to finance the war—so more money must be created—burrowed, taken from the poor, etc. Then, the products of that money must be destroyed, so that more money has to be created. The vicious cycle of malignant usury requires warfare. It has nothing to do with freedom, democracy, human dignity, or any of the various guises of defense.

Our government and/or their operatives murdered more than three thousand people. Justice is paramount—these people must be identified and brought to justice, if not be our courts, by the world court. Their crimes dwarf the actions we had Saddam Hussein executed for, and the crimes of Muammar Gaddafi in Egypt, for which we seek to have him tried by the world court and removed from power to become incarcerated in the name of Justice.

Our president, at the time of this writing, Barack Obama, has allied himself with this very few, such as Oprah Winfrey. Oprah does not represent Black America. He has allied himself with the Reagan's and Clinton's economic policies to grow the economy by creating money to feed the dragon of malignant usury. There is a very large prison complex in Baghdad where terrorists, including children, are being held, and where torture is occurring. These are not prisoners of war, and are not adjudicated for any crimes, except that of our identification of the Al Qaeda group, an ill-defined group that we created, or with the Taliban, a lose affiliation of tribal peoples that we also created and armed to fight the Soviets. We now engage in a war against insurgency. *Webster* defines "insurgency" as "the quality or state of being insurgent; specifically: a condition of revolt against a government that is less than an organized revolution and that is not recognized as belligerency." The current president *Hamid Karzai* has been a known drug trafficker for many years, particularly in heroine, a profitable industry where "money makes money," and won election in 1999 in a process that was fraudulent in numerous ways. Is this democracy? What legitimacy can the Karzai administration claim that we should be protecting his presidency from insurgency in an endless war? Obama increased the number of troops in this decision to wage a war of counterinsurgency. The insurgents are presumed to be terrorists. Is the bombing of innocent civilians terrorism?

The collapse of our economy is inevitable—all the stop-gap solutions of giving money to the banks and corporations was a gift, in that this money, creating money that does not exist by usury, will not sustain the kind of growth of money that the usurers are after. Social programs are the victims of budget cuts. Wages are going down, food and gasoline prices have skyrocketed, housing values are down, and the ranks of the unemployed, underemployed, and indigent rises. The unemployment figures do not reflect people who have given up seeking employment, while employers are in a buyer's market with subjugated employees, reducing benefits, and are interested primarily in the creation of money.

Now we are looking at the loss of hard-earned union gains such as collective bargaining, and at essentially reducing the American worker to the level of slavery, serfdom, and peonage. The result will be widespread civil unrest, for which the federal government is prepared under the provisions of the patriot act, which allows our president to declare martial law and take military action against peaceful demonstrations, and denies legal rights including writ of habeas corpus, which is one of our most precious rights against being unlawfully retained. There will be armed forces in our streets, search without a warrant, false imprisonment, wiretapping and monitoring of electronic communication, and much more to come. This is not democracy. This is not justice. It is the police powers awarded to state corporatism, which has been fueled by our own elected officials and justified under the banner of the war on terrorism, all made possible by the events of 9/11 and the propaganda campaign that followed.

Justice is paramount, and must be preserved. The people murdered on 9/11 were not martyrs, they were victims. Those involved must be held responsible by the same code as applied in Nuremberg.

Justice for the usurers, the very few must await the enactment of laws against usury, which are unlikely to be promulgated unless, against all odds, the people of this nation are actually able to influence the political process now controlled by the power-elite. We will more likely see a shift to the right and a progression of the malignant process that began with inauguration of Ronald Reagan. We are now being fed lies by the media; they have taken over our minds, they tell us what to think, what to believe, how to vote, etc.

The justice in *Eli* is in the hidden time. Within the hidden time, the soul rules over the ego, which, through our own minds, has constructed separate worlds for each of us in which our egos are the rulers. The ego is fed by malignant usury—it is the product of usury—which values us not as God does, but for our personal power over our separate worlds and the judgment of a society that gages success by monetary gains. In the hidden time there is One Soul, and One World, the ego cannot live there it has its own, separate world of illusion. In human prehistory, we lived in the hidden time, as some of the Aboriginal people continue to do after a period of geographic isolation from the developing world. The Soul, our place in the hidden time or eternity, is unconscious; it knows nothing of the time our minds have created to order events. At first, the infant creates space and time through movement, which operates in the parametric field of space and time. The alter ego arises with the distinction of Self and world, its function is to negotiate the terms of our existence in each of our separate worlds. There is only One World. There is only One Soul. Humankind is a single organism.

Some of the hints of these truths come from the near death experience. We live by moments, beginning and ending, followed by the next moment. In death, the beginning of the moment is suspended—it never ends unless we are revived. Within this moment, there is internal time, a product of the process occurring in the system, which takes precedence over clock or cosmic time in the psyche. So within this attenuated moment of death, there is a Now that never ends. On this basis, people report seeing their life in complete detail, as it is the soul that ultimately holds the record. Sometimes people report seeing *all existent knowledge* in this moment. The soul holds it all, and it is the soul that is the source of mind, localized nowhere within the brain, but in heaven, the kingdom of God, the all-knowing. This is why Jesus said that to enter the kingdom of God we must become again as little children. The alter ego, the fallen angel, is born out of the One Soul and then imagines itself separate and god over its own world. There is no place for the alter ego in the hidden time, because its own world does not exist, except in hell. So there is a letting go of the alter ego, which must occur, much like the mind of a child, for whom the alter ego has not yet taken dominion and declared itself ruler over its own, separate world. The Soul, in turn, is not within the alter ego's dimensions of space and time and, in principle, has access to all that is known or can be known. This is the source of phenomenon of the savant. Some element of autism prevents the growth of the alter ego, as self, other, and world are not clearly distinguished, opening the door to the greater fund of knowledge. The individual Soul is born and grows within the love and nurturance of the mother-infant or caregiver-infant relationship, which is being rapidly eroded. They grow and develop according to conditions that are provided by family and culture, and they have a record of their own. The individual souls are pluralities with a Unity, which is the One

Mind, the Mind of God. Those who pass into heaven are souls that preserve such memory within the limitless memories of the One Mind, in the hidden time, as in the moment of death.

The Lamentations of Jeremiah (Authorized King James Bible) speak to the memory of the soul:

> 3:17: And thou hast removed my soul far off from peace: I forget my prosperity.
> 3:18: And I said, My strength and my hope is perished from the Lord.
> 3:19: Remembering mine affliction, the wormwood and the gall.
> 3:20: **My soul hath them still in remembrance, and is humbled in me**.
> 3:21: This I recall to my mind, therefore I have hope.
> 3:22: It is of the Lord's mercies that we are not consumed, because has compassion fail not.
> 3:23: They are new every morning, great is thy faithfulness.
> 3:24: The Lord is my portion, saith my soul; therefore will I hope in him.
> 3:25: The Lord is good unto them the wait for him, for the soul that seeketh him.
> 3: 26: It is good that a man should both hope and quietly wait for the salvation of the Lord.

Lamentations consists of five Elegies on the destruction of Jerusalem. Chapter 3 is sixty-six verses (3 × 22) composed of triads of verses commencing with the same letter, such that the twenty-two triads go through the twenty-two letters of the Hebrew alphabet consecutively commencing with Aleph. According to the Companion Bible, with its detailed concordance and many appendices, it is the central book of the five scrolls, Canticles, Ruth, Lamentations, Ecclesiastes, and Esther. Lord is translated from Jehovah. Mind has the same meaning as heart. Soul is translated from the Hebrew *nephesh*.

Conclusion

The ego-persona imagines itself separate, creator of its own world, and the god of that world. This illusion is fostered by usury, as we have discussed, which demands our conduct as separate entities, and blocks the light of the soul, coming from the hidden time and not located in any one place, but rather present everywhere, lighting the entire universe instantaneous, as part of the ineffable light of God.

The entire universe is simultaneously perceived, in a spiritual sense, by the reflection of this light. The simultaneous nature of the universe or kingdom within in us is the source of all mind and consciousness. Since time does not move in the hidden time, it has no velocity to measure. So in the hidden time, the star that is one hundred light-years away does not exist as it does in our perception, as it shined one hundred years ago, but as it is Now. The ineffable light cannot be described other than that it is an inner light, in the internal world of mind and consciousness, of which God is the only source. The separate alter ego absorbs the light, it does not reflect it, as the soul does in the hidden time. The alter ego exists in darkness, it has nothing of the eternal light, and so perishes. The soul has a remembrance, which is eternal, and which is forever in the One Mind, the Mind of God only to the extent that it has manifested the eternal light, which is dependent on our vision of the light, which is the wealth within the poverty of what is otherwise darkness. The light is of God is the absolute infinite, it is never diminished or exhausted.

The professors, the theologians, the scientists, the wealthy, the highly educated will, in the short term, reject this book.

It is a book of great complexity, that may perhaps been comprehended fully only by an elite group. Although this may seem paradoxical, that elite group is the disenfranchised of Black America. It is incumbent on the true leaders of Black America to bring this book to its people. This is because they are the victims, not the bearers of the Plague, and are closer to their ancestral roots. It is here, in the short term, that the Church of Eli will take root, as it realizes that the white man's religion has been used as a means of oppression and injustice inflicted upon their people. At this time the author will pass the administration of the Church of Eli over to them.

If humankind continues in usury, it will end in darkness, which will be the extinction of our universe. This must not happen, and we do not believe it will happen. Necessity will claim its due, as a world ruled by usury, our current world in its current course cannot be sustained. But humankind needs some guidance, and the heavens will not be silent. The unified consciousness, realized through the knowledge of the new religion and the new science, in perfect agreement, is in need of nourishment in order that the suffering and darkness into which we are rapidly descending will give way to a new dawn.

As the alter ego and its separate world and false hopes of a material immortality comes to be viewed as the maker of this dark night of the human soul, which can only end with the death of usury.

With the death of usury, the collective mind of humanity or Species Mind will rise toward the heaven of the Universal Mind. The false notions of separateness will give way to a World Commonwealth, ending the oppressive world order that the People of the Lie are leading us deeper and deeper into. The light of the hidden time will shine upon our Soul, and the redemption of Humankind will occur as our spiritual blindness occasional by the Fall will cease to be, ending our long sojourn that began with the exile form Eden and the Fall of the angels of God. This new light will bring peace, joy, prosperity, and love to all our kind for all the generations to come. The Long Night will end, in the prophetic words of Martin Luther King, we will be able to say: "Free at last, free at last, thank God Almighty we're free at last." I have seen it, and I know it is so.

Glossary

This glossary is intended to explain those terms and concepts that require such, and
not those terms in the book that do not required further explanation, and to elaborate on certain
concepts in order to deepen the understanding of the reader.

acausal: Having no cause. Used as an attribute of God.
acceleration: Increase in speed or velocity.
absolute: Highest possible, as in absolute infinity.
actual entity: The smallest quantum of experience. Also applied to God and perhaps Self.
actual occasion: Same as actual entity, but stressing the time experienced.
actuality: Refers to something that can be known or perceived.
ad hoc: A hypothesis based on a prior assumption.
agency: Having the quality of an agent. Implying an entity will free will.
albatross: Around the neck, signifies obstruction or frustration of effort.
algorithm: A formula for solving a problem.
alienated labor: Labor that has no relation to meaningful purpose of product.
alter: A separate identity.
alter ego: An identity of ego separated from the true ego.
anathema: Something forbidden.
annata: The Buddhist doctrine of no self or ego.
antisocial: Having little of no guilt or remorse.

Apostles Creed: A Catholic prior created by the church in the fourth, century outlining a belief system that espouses such things as the Trinity, deity of Christ, God/man myth, and other dogmas as well as truths.

apotheosis: Elevation to the status of God.

arboreal: Of the forest.

archetype: In psychology, an object or process inherent to the mind and generalized to a variety of mental constructs or forms.

Atman: The Self in Hinduism that is equated with God or Brahman.

atonement: A practice used in rectifying a sin before God. Collectively applied to group action.

austerity: Reflecting the loss of goods or services for want of money.

automata: A being or thing with machinelike qualities.

avatar: A god/man.

bailouts: Moneys given to prevent a corporation or institution from financial bankruptcy.

behavioral: (1) An experiment, idea, or therapy aimed at measuring or changing behaviors; (2) a system of psychology that stresses behaviors that are conditioned; (3) view of the mind as a "black box" defined only by response to stimulus.

behavioral modernity: The period in human evolution when fully developed language and symbols exist in the mind.

becoming: The perpetual state or flow of the actual arising from the potential.

being: (1) A living entity, (2) the product of becoming, (3) the pause of becoming in an entity.

benefits: Services, products, or moneys contracted from premiums or entitlements.

benign: (1) Harmless, (2) a noncancerous tumor or process.

big bang: The event theorized to have given birth to the universe by a sudden expansion.

biosphere: The sphere-like layer of life on the surface of the earth.

bottleneck: Episode of near extinction.

Brahman: Universal God of the Hindus.

brain, functional organization: The development and organization of the brain by the functional activity of a nonsubstantial mind.

brain, simultaneous integration: The process in the brain whereby a potentially infinite feedback loop is created during a period of time that has no before or after.

brain, spansules: Empty spaces in the brain that assume some function in future evolution.

bubble economy: An economy where prices are inflated with respect to value, ultimately "bursting" as the prices approach true value.

buyout: The practice of buying a company or corporation for the purpose of inflating money made over value, thereby producing profits from sale.

canary: A term used in organized crime for someone who violates the code of silence.

cancer: (1) A malignant tumor, (2) any process that invades and consumes the organism or society.

cannibalize: Extract value from.

canon: Books accepted into Bible.

capital: Assets of value.

cardinality: Degree of infinity.

capitation: The practice of selling services "by the head."

Cartesian: (1) A coordinate system of space, (2) dualism of mind and matter "stuff."

causality: Relationship of cause and effect. (1) efficient: cause of a future effect; (2) final: cause that is a goal in the future, or cause in future effecting the past; 3) formal: cause by plan or in relation to form.

cell migration: Directed movement of cells in embryo and developing animal. Can be assigned to genetic plan, by reiteration of past in evolution, or the ongoing function, as in the mind.

channeling: The so-called receiving of transmitted information from disincarnate entities, as performed in séances and by psychics. Does not include prophecy.

chaos: A quality of systems that are far from equilibrium, entailing unpredictability, amplification of small causes into large effects in the future, self-organization, and fractal structure. Edge of chaos describes systems poised between chaos and a predicable order, leading to self-organizing systems with exquisite dependence in initial conditions.

chordates: Phylum chordata, animals with spinal cords, includes all vertebrates and all animals with a central nervous system.

chromosome, Y: Sex chromosome coffering male gender and passed only through the male genetic ancestors. Determines patriarchal line of ancestors.

classical approximation: Form of causation where quantum influences are negligible. Useful in engineering.

clean up: Here specifically applies to process that occurred when vices were diminished in New York City.

coevolution: Evolution of two or more features that require each other to function.

concrescense: A term of art in process theory that involves the integration of influences into a single actuality or actual entity.

conditionality: Conditions of actuality.

consciousness: Awareness that implies knowing by some entity.

consequent nature: Term of art in process theology. Nature of God that is influenced by the world, or a consequence of interaction with the world.

conservation: In physics, matter and energy cannot be created or destroyed. Can be violated within uncertainty of measurement in quantum physics.

consolation: In religion, sins or gains on earth are losses in heaven, eternity, and the hidden time. Like a consolation prize, where paradise is lost in the hidden time. The consolation prize is damnation and eternal suffering in hell, in Judeo-Christian-Moslem traditions, where there is a balance that is used for the judgment at the mercy of God. In the east, consolation is reincarnation into suffering and/or a lower life-form in Hinduism and Buddhism, according to the wheel of karma.

conspiracy theories: Conspiracies exist and are written into jurisprudence. Conspiracy theories connote speculative theories not based on evidence.

continual rebirth: In process theory, entities or occasions become in a certain duration in time, and after having become into being, pass on to immortality. Rebirth involves the influence and repetition of the entities entire history, and interrelationship with God and all other entities, forms, and ideas—which completes the becoming with the concrescence, and a new entity is reborn, which then again passes into the immortal past. This is the theory of discontinuous existence modeled after quantum actuality by Whitehead. Certain sectors of Buddhism believe that this continuous death and rebirth is reincarnation.

continuum: Term of art in process theory. The continuum or extensive continuum is an abstract space that subsumes all relations. Here interpreted as the hidden time.

control parameters: A term newly defined here. In chaotic or dynamical systems, referral into the past actuates a final cause by influencing control parameters in the past in a reiterative process.

corporate raiders: Groups that gain ownership in a corporation and then extract profits to the detriment of that corporation.

credit, flow of: Under usury, wealth is extracted from credit or debt, which must flow or continue to be available in order that the usurious economy continue.

credit default swaps: Trade of defaulted debtors used to extract wealth from the remaining assets of the defaulted debtors.

credit leverage: Credit or debt is used as a lever to extract nominal value without increasing true value, generally through the trade of debt.

debt, subprime: Credit given at high interest rates to those who are likely to default; then wealth is extracted from the debtors. An instrument of credit default swaps.

decohere: In quantum physics, the cloud of possible states decoheres in the environment such as to become a superposition of states of the environment, which do not interfere with one another as do the possible states. The quantum Zeno's paradox of Stapp involves the continuous and repeated observation of a state in order to actualize a given quantum state against decoherence. Here we place the One Mind or God in this role of saying "be," and it is. Quantum decoherence is a major problem in quantum mind theory, fundamentally falsifying theories based on coherence of atomic or molecular processes. Stapp's theory involves consciousness preexisting itself, so it is likewise untenable, as it must then involve disincarnate entities. Multiplying entities violates parsimony so that the One Mind Model is a unique solution, but which requires God and is therefore rejected.

default, pervasive: Default is the process in usury whereby the debtor is unable to pay. Insolvency occurs when a corporation or group no longer have assets to cover their debts, primarily because nominal or paper value can no longer be extracted. This produces a chain reaction of insolvency in the international financial sector, leading to pervasive default, and international economic collapse.

denial: In psychology information that is dissonant with cognition or causes negative emotions is denied or repressed. This emotional energy, often in the form of anger or hatred, is projected externally.

depolarization: The neural cell membrane has a net negative charge on the inside due to the active sodium/potassium pumps. This hyperpolarization is maintained by energy from the cellular mechanisms. Action of receptors at the synapses, primarily in the dendritic network, can hyperpolarize or depolarize the cell membrane, such that the net negative charge inside the membrane can depolarize. Depolarization leads to opening of calcium channels, influx of calcium into the neuron, and firing of the neuron, sending depolarization signals through the axons, and activating portions of the brain and spinal cord.

derivative: In finance, secondary nominal value derived from benchmarks such as futures, options, swaps, or commodities, with value depending on the behavior of the benchmarks.

derivative occasion: In a society of actual occasions, the dominant occasion, such as soul, ego, or alter ego, in the psychological sense, gives rise to derivative occasions through the feeling or prehension of other occasions, including previous derivatives. Dissociation forms from derivative occasions, when the dominant occasion is fragmented.

disorder: In physics, particularly in thermodynamics, disorder is entropy, and equilibrium is the state of maximum disorder.

dissociate: To separate an identity or an experience from its agency.

divine selection: The power of the one subject, God, to determine one actuality in experience amongst infinite potentials. The proposed mechanisms are discussed in our definition of decoherence.

Divine Self: The dominant occasion of the universe. All other occasions of experience are derivative.

DNA, mitochondrial: The mitochondria are the energy factories of the cell, and are found in the protoplasm outside of the cell nucleus. The sperm is a bare nucleus without mitochondria, so the mitochondria are passed only through the female line, determining matriarchal descent of its own DNA.

due process: A legal term signifying that crimes be subject to the due process of the law, as is outlined by the Constitution, Bill of Rights, amendments, and federal and state laws.

ego: (1) Valuation of oneself, (2) in psychology, the ego mediates between the unconscious and conscious minds, and protects its integrity and identity through various mechanisms of defense, which include rationalization, denial, projection, sublimation, reaction formation, and altruism.

ego, abstract: According to von Neumann, the observer in quantum physics, which collapses the wave function of multiple potentials into one actual reality.

ego, alter: A dissociated derivative occasion of the true ego. May be pathological, as with multiple personality, or normal in our culture.

ego, particular: Alter ego, normal in our culture.

ego, true: The ego as it exists as part of the soul. This is the natural condition of the ego.

ego armor: Also, character armor of Wilhelm Reich. It stultifies the psyche's discharge of energy as emotion. Called character armor by Wilhelm Reich.

emotional reciprocity: The internal relation between self and others or objects that is not mediated by the ordinary senses and flows between people. The flow of energy, which is Love.

empirical: Based on hypothesis and the experimental testing of prediction(s) entailed by the hypothesis, according to the scientific method.

energy, dissipation: The loss of energy to the environment that characterizes disequilibrium systems and chaotic, dynamical systems.

energy, hidden: The energy that exists in the hidden time.

entropy: Disorder, measured from zero to one, with one being the equilibrium state and zero being the state of perfect order. In thermodynamics, the number of microstates in a microstate divided the number of microstates in the most likely state, at equilibrium.

epistemology: A branch of metaphysical philosophy that deals with knowledge.

eternal: Outside of ordinary time, without beginning or end, or before and after.

eternal forms: All known forms in the dimensions of space or of the three dimensions of space plus the imaginary time, which is spacelike. In idealism, forms are eternal and are derived from ideal forms.

Eternal Now: Singular Now, as it was, is, and ever shall be.

evil: Absense of the good.

evil one: Symbol of the alter ego, which caused the Fall, and which obstructs the purpose of God's manifestation by arresting the Species Mind in infancy. Also Satan, Lucifer, devil, demon, etc.

exaption: See "preadaptation."

exhortation: In this book, spiritual inspiration.

ex nihilo: From nothing.

experience: Awareness of a thing or event. Experience always involves an agency that experiences.

experientialism: In philosophy, the view that experience is the only actuality. Scientifically, experience is the datum of actuality. An unmanifest possibility in the future is real, but not actual unless it is experienced.

false flag: Historically, an excuse to go to war, generally enacted as an attack of a nation on itself. False in the sense of interpretation.

falsified: In science, falsification is the object of the empirical method. Hypotheses are falsified to the extent that they make incorrect predictions. The convention in science is that progress is made by experimentation, which tests a null hypothesis, which is that the hypothesis is not true. By convention, if there is a probability of 5 percent or less that the null hypothesis is not true, the experiment validates (not proves) the hypothesis by rejecting the null hypothesis. However, experiment only proves association and not causation, so that a more complex statistical method or induction of reasoning to determine a causal relationship is needed, at which point the hypothesis graduates to the status of a theory.

fascism: Corporatism involving the state.

forever real: The potentialities of infinite universes do not pass. What is real is always real. What is not real is forever not real.

form, latent: Latent forms are forms that have the capacity to become actual according to formal cause. Final causation has to be assumed because it is the future actuality that manifests the latent form.

forms, transformation: Forms can be transformed by deformation as long as they are not cut or torn, according to topology, a branch of mathematics. Thus, the spinal cord, through topological transformation, can yield the form of the entire brain. The soul is assumed to have the topology of a sphere, the most symmetrical of forms. It can be twisted, deformed, or reduced to a non-existent mathematical point.

forsake: Let go of something that you value.

frame of reference: In relativity, time and place are relative to position and velocity with respect to any event. This is the frame of reference.

free fall: Falling as if there were no resistance, like an object falling through thin air.

future, shadow of: Since the future is not fully determined, any prediction of the future is conditional on probability. However, final causes in the Mind of God are actual eternally.

gluons: Along with quarks, they are the forms that comprise the nucleus of the atom.

Gnostic: (1) Describes the act of knowing directly, or gnosis, (2) religious group that holds that there is God, who is good, and the Demiurge, identified with nature, which is evil.

God, absolute: God as causal, eternal, and unchanging. This is the view of Eli.

God, providential: God as the determiner of final causes.

God, relational: God that is subject to change through relations with the world. In Whitehead and the Whiteheadean school of theology, God has an absolute and consequent nature. The latter changes based on contingencies in the world, such that God and the world are mutually transcendent.

government abdication: Here, specifically, the abdication of the American government to the financial sector.

growth, exponential: Economic growth such that the size of the markets doubles during some interval of time, and the impossible belief it will do so indefinitely.

habeas corpus: The fundamental right to have a hearing in court in order to be detained beyond a period of time, at which time cause must be established. Detainees who are US citizens now have the right to file a writ of habeas corpus in America, which must be honored by yielding such right to the detainee. This right will be removed under law when martial law is declared under the provisions of the Patriot Act. It is currently not accorded to suspected terrorists from other nations with whom we are at war.

hegemony: The rule of the state by a dominant group of individuals.

Hippocratic Oath: The oath of a medical doctor taken upon receiving the medical degree that requires physicians to provide services to relieve suffering and in an emergency where other help is not available, without doing harm, twenty four hours a day and seven days a week, with no holidays.

hologram: Term used for something in which the whole is in every part.

hypnosis, indirect induction: A form of hypnotherapy by inducing a trance through progressive relaxation and dissociation.

hypnosis, into future: The practice of creating a future actuality in hypnosis that manifests in the present.

I-persona: The alter ego that is now the norm in our society.

"I am that I am": The absolute God with no qualifications or conditions.

idea, divine: Idea in the mind of God forming an eternal actuality that can be accessed by the mind directly without thought in the right conditions.

immortality, material: The idea that the material body is immortal.

impossible: Here used to indicate the idea that in an infinite number of potential universes, the existence of any actual universe is impossible except in the absolute infinity of an actual entity, which can only be God.

individuation: In the psychology of Carl Jung and Jungian school, the continued growth of the individual mind into adulthood and old age.

ineffable: Unimaginable, not knowable by the human mind.

infallibility: The idea that some person, be it a prophet or otherwise, is incapable of error.

infantile condition: Used here to indicate the condition of the infant who has not developed an alter ego and makes no distinction between self and other, self and mother, self and object, or self and world. The condition of developmental arrest of the Species Mind brought on by the trauma of false distinctions in the infantile condition.

information theory: As used here, state-dependent knowledge as opposed to knowledge of discrete parts. State dependent knowledge is a function of the complexity or elements of the state and the disorder of the state. Ordered states are less probable and, therefore, have more state information. This idea is contrary to representational theories of mental information, which is called the movie screen approach here. State dependent information can be the basis for a state-dependent mind or computer. It is opposed to algorithmic computation.

information monism: The theory of Wheeler that information is the only reality. Information is here equated with experience. In either case, information monism in the setting of an omniscient or all-knowing God would make God the only reality.

ingression: Term of art in process philosophy. Connotes the inclusion of an eternal object in every occasion of experience as a formal cause.

insolvency: The loss of viability of a corporate or business entity as a result of its inability to hold prices at such level that they can be subject to gain on usury. Leads to default or inability to pay debt to market owners of the company, in stock or otherwise.

insufficiency of reason: An explanation within science that is not supported by a reasonable examination of evidence. Always true for *ad hoc* explanations.

integration, simultaneous: When the process of mentality occurs within an interval of time in which time is simultaneous within some duration, a feedback loop is enabled whereby the processes can be indefinitely reiterated until the desired integration is achieved. This is not a property of any imaginable computer, occurs with limitation of duration in the human brain, and is unlimited in the Species Mind and in the Mind of God. It confers enormous cybernetic properties as well as allowing minute control parameters to implement some final cause.

intelligent design: In evolution, the idea that some intelligent agent is required to achieve an evolutionary outcome. The theory suffers from inadequacy of reason as it can provide only formal causes and not final causes, so that the latent design can never manifest.

intermediary: A mediator between God and man.

internal: Inside of all things rather than external. God is internal to all, and this is his agency, as opposed to the popular, concrete notion that God is external and throws down darts like a pagan god. The true teachings of Jesus espouse this view.

internal relations: Relations that are not externally mediated. Principle of Mind.

internal universe: All the universe is everywhere present, especially within the soul, such that the soul holds the objects of its perceptions and memories within itself. This makes the past present and the object as existent both within and outside of the brain or mind. Thus, the same object as is perceived as external is also in the mind.

intuition: A form of gnosis or direct knowledge, residing in the unconscious as opposed to logic, which does not know directly and is conscious. There is evidence that the lower evolutionary portions of the brain are involved, and so animal intuition may equal or exceed human intuition.

Janus: A pagan god with two faces looking forward and backward, symbolic of the duality of self and alter ego, as well as other dualities in the human psyche.

knowledge, all existent: Sometimes reported in near-death experiences. Signifies the oneness of God's omniscience with the latent knowledge of the soul, or of a passing of the soul into God's omniscience.

koan: A question in Zen Buddhism that, if fully understood, confers enlightenment.

language, meta: The language of the unconscious and of the hidden time and in the dreaming that confers meanings and associations unavailable and not ordinarily understood in consciousness. The principle language of former religions that we have now forgotten but which we are to relearn in the hidden time of *Eli*.

language, scientific: In our context, the meta-language of all religions can be translated into a scientific language, which will free us from logic contradictions and mythologies that are not now acceptable to the scientist or to ordinary scientific reasoning.

leveraging: See "credit leveraging."

life, flash of events: The common report in near-death experiences that one's life repeats itself before one's eyes in detail, in serial order and sometimes reverse serial order. Interpreted here as the complete memory inherent in the unconscious soul of humans. It is unknown whether other animals have such experiences.

light, spiritual: That which allows us to share something of the light of God in a higher consciousness, conferring sight of the unknown.

limitations of God: God has limitless powers to make any potential universe actual, but cannot create that which is not existent in potential form. *Eli* thus embraces naturalism, not supernaturalism as in other religions.

liquidity: Available assets.

Machiavellian: Political and personal actions that are not judged according to any ethics, morals, of guilt, as in Machiavelli's *The Prince*. The ends justify the means. A quality inherent in our leaders, equivalent to psychopathy.

made men: People in organized crime who act in complete secrecy for fear of their lives and the lives of their family members.

magic: Something or event that defies natural law.

malignant usury: The desperate and complex fraud that will increasingly manifest in the death of usury, essentially robbing the economy of all wealth within the markets and leaving a skeleton economy behind for the "vultures" who will then appear. Malignant in that it grows wildly and kills the organism, if left unchecked.

manifest: Made actual.

manifestation of eternity: The manifesting of our world and future world through the eternity of the Mind of God and the Species Mind. See "integration, simultaneous."

manifestation, planes of: The plane on which we live is fully manifest. The unmanifest potentials of the future exist on higher spiritual planes, as in the Tree of Life of the Kaballah. There is a veil that separates these unmanifest planes from the manifest plane, which is the veil on the temple in the Christ narrative and in the tree of life in the Kaballah. In the Kaballah it is the veil that separates illusion from actuality in the Tree of Life, which is comprised of ten ten sephiroth, or manifestations of God. The veil of illusion is generally placed just beneath the Tephiroth in the transmission of the light from the ineffable Ein Soph, which is above the top of the Tree. Beneath the line is the world of illusion, and the wordly plane is defined by the lowermost sephiroth, Malkuth. The line in the diagram below shows this line. Eli experienced the lifting of this veil, literally, conferring access to the unmanifest and prophecy. Once lifted, the prophet holds remembrance conferring access to the planes above the veil.

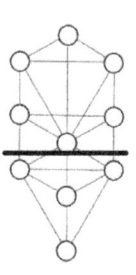

mankind's social body: Just as there is a social Species Mind, there is a social body of humankind that represents the dominion granted by God in Genesis.

materialist oligarchy: Group of prominent thinkers that enforce materialism on the people of the lie.

mechanistic: View of classical physics, still held by most of science, that everything is determined by a clockwork mechanism. A recent popular science book *The Blind Watchmaker* reflects this enduring dogma of classical science.

medical care, standards of: The former system of medical practice that outlined the standards of care and evaluation, including things like required laboratory tests, other procedures, evaluation by differential diagnosis, medical and pharmaceutical indications, necessary follow-up, requirements of physical and mental examination, indications for admission and discharge from hospitals, medical ethics, referral standards, and a host of other things. Now replaced by dictates of the usurers, resulting in "less for more" medical care, which is formalized as Health Care Reform. This situation has allowed many abuses of the system, at great cost to patient's lives and health, as well as skyrocketing spending, as well as exodus of true physicians and their replacement by technicians. In the process, a mockery has been made of the physician's oath, which is now just a hollow remnant of a lost profession, not unlike the skeleton of the economy which usury is now carving away.

metaphysics: Branch of philosophy dealing with the nature of reality.

microgenesis: Neurological process involving development of the mental state from the primitive to the recent functions of the brain, literally repeating evolution and development in a duration of simultaneity and actualizing objects of perception in the mind from the core of self. Based originally on the hierarchical organization of brain function by Hughlings Jackson, who had a great influence on Freud, and championed by neurologist Jason Brown as an ongoing school in the theory of mind. The repetition of history in the becoming of the mental state is extended to the beginning of time in "radical microgenesis."

mitosis: A concept developed within microgenesis implying that the core of self gives rise to derivatives that proceed through dreaming into consciousness or the object world.

money: We have discussed money in some detail in the text, as well is its properties. Unlike goods and commodities, money never dies. It is sterile and incapable of increase as in usury except in a nominal way, unsupported by increase in the true value. Because of these properties, the growth of money in usury cannot be sustained. Ordinarily, periodic crises erase the debt, allowing a resumption in the growth of debt or usury. In our case, we have a 1920s-like scenario, except that our government intervened with warfare, which destroys commodities, in essence creating a new market, and conquering other markets. In this case, as usury is very strictly forbidden in the Qur'an, conquering Islamic nations has the effect of creating new markets for usury. Another measure is for the government to absorb the imbalance by going into greater and greater debt, as it has down, and this has been the principle means for the government to feed the exponential growth, which must continue in usury based on pure mathematics. The government also creates new markets through its policies. Wages go down, entitlements are taken away, but still, without the actual erasing of debt, the vicious cycle only worsens, deepening the crisis. The exponential growth of money, at this point, has become unsustainable, ever more so. National economies collapse, creating a domino effect of ever-widening default on the international market of debts, and finally to complete international economic collapse. At this point, the engines of production, fueled by usury, is unable to sustain human needs, leading to a global crisis. Nuclear weapons then become a more and more viable option for erasing the debt. In the final analysis, a skeleton of the economy remains, to be picked upon by "vultures," which, at the time of this writing, has already occurred in Ireland. People flee, but eventually, there is nowhere to go. When economies collapse, their currency collapse.

mutations, neutral: Mutations that neither increase or decrease adaptation. They are fixed in the genome at a rate much greater than expected given the theory of evolution by natural selection.

neoteny: A reversal of evolution to a former state of development. When neoteny occurs for one particular structure or function and not others, it is called heterochrony. These phenomena are visibly displayed in brain injury. In humans, our loss of bodily fur is an example of neoteny back to a fetal stage of development and the evolutionary life of the most primitive chordates. As advances occur in other areas such as brain growth, the overall development is described as heterochrony.

Now: The period of becoming of the actual from potential through the agency of God. Now is like the light of actualization. Time moves through a stationary Now and is like a thread with beads added as the as it passes through the Eternal Now. After having passed now, the world line becomes permanent in its actuality of experience. There is no collapse of the wave function or forking off into parallel universes, as all universes remain forever potential and real, and actuality is fully based on experience, with world lines repeated themselves from the beginning of time to the now, as they are etched upon a permanent space-time manifold or abstract surface.

objectification: All of actuality is subjective or experiential and is so related to the mind. This subjectivity gives life to the world in a felt sense, making it a paradise. The alter ego, split from the soul, has no felt sense, and thus objectifies the world, causing the exile from paradise, traumatic for the infant and in the history of humankind. This trauma causes a developmental arrest of the psyche at the time of the trauma, as it cannot move forward by fully absorbing the trauma without a complete death of its world. The psyche heroically creates its own world to ward of its existential extinction, where subjectivity is not totally lost but is fragmented and attached to the alter ego. Paradise then falls into amnesia.

Occam's Razor: See "parsimony."

One Mind Model of quantum reality: A model currently evolved into a combination of a many worlds or infinity of parallel universes that remain forever the same while experience of the One Mind, which includes the plurality of individual minds, brings a single universe into the realm of experience. Physical reality can be divided, but all minds are derivative occasions of the One Mind, which is God.

ontological principle: According to Whitehead, the ontological principle is that all actual entities or occasions are the reason for their own becoming, through satisfaction of the subjective aim, which is supplies by God.

ontology: The metaphysics of becoming.

oxymoron: A word or phrase that contradicts itself.

parsimony: The principle in science that entities are not to be multiplied unless necessary.

partial existence: In quantum theory, entities up to the universe exist as multiple potentials or potential, which have a statistical probability and therefore exist only partially.

participation mystique: Term of anthropologist Levy-Bruhl. Indicates a mystical relationship of souls as feeling one another fully, characteristic of certain "primitive" people. Particularly applied to the mother-infant relationship. In *Eli*, a quality of relations in the hidden time, to which humans must return.

panentheism: The idea that God is within all that exists. Here applied it subsumes panexperientialism, since God is Knower of all experience.

panexperientialism: The theory of Whitehead that all that exists is experience, which also holds that all reality in composed of quanta of experience.

position and momentum (Heinsenberg's uncertainty principle): According to Heisenberg's uncertainty principle, the more one knows about position, the less can be known about momentum, and vice versa. Also applies to energy and time.

phantom: A human without a soul.

phase coherence: The lining up of the peaks and troughs of waves.

photon: A particle of light.

Ponzi scheme: A fraudulent scheme, originally where stocks were created with no actual value and were sold in pyramid type fashion such that each holder of the stock had to recruit additional holders indefinitely. The Ponzi scheme is generalized to include sale of imaginary assets that have nominal value but are lacking actual value. Currently, the sale of imaginary assets has become standard in the global economy, creating a global Ponzi scheme. Debt is the primary imaginary asset in this scheme. Such schemes inevitably default because the wealth created is imaginary and does not exist.

possible histories: The wave function of a particle or the universe is the sum over all possible histories. Thus, the history of an entity or the universe is repeated, theoretically, in imaginary time or the hidden time.

power, explanatory: The power of a hypothesis to explain phenomena as extensions of the hypothesis and not by *ad hoc* explanations.

pre-adaptation: In evolution, the false notion of an adaptation developed to serve and different function than it comes to serve in future evolution. Preadaptation theories are almost always *ad hoc*, and used to create imaginary explanations without evidence that fulfill the requirements of natural selection.

prehend/prehension: Feelings that are received by an actual entity in its becoming, based on internal relations. See "internal relations."

prehension, conceptual: The internal relations of concepts as preexisting ideas in the Mind of God.

premiums: The prices paid for insurance contracts.

prime mover: The classical concept of a mechanistic, deterministic universe set into motion by God, who then plays no further part. The fallacy of this idea should have died with the quantum revolution, but has continued to be used by authors of popular books seeking to disprove the existence of God.

prime number: A number that is not divisible into an integer other than itself and one. Excludes all even numbers except two.

probability, existence of God: Taking the existence of God as a hypothesis, there are various scientific ways to falsify God's existence, which are limited by God's ineffability. In general, the probability of God hinges on the fact that certain phenomena, such as the existence of our universe and near-death experiences, which cannot be otherwise explained.

psychopath: One who lacks remorse and acts in an immoral fashion, being self-centered, or narcissistic, and antisocial. In a collective sense, nearly the entire population of the earth suffers from collective psychopathy, thus the social justice prescribed by *Eli*.

psychopathic usury: Usury practiced with no remorse regarding its adverse effects, for the self-gain of an individual or group. Toxic products imported from China is used in this book as an example.

quantum: The fact that energy exists in discrete packets or quanta, and is not in a continuous quantity. The basis of quantum theory or physics. Whitehead applies this to quanta of experience, the irreducible experience of an actual occasion or entity.

quantum eigenfunction: A function that defines position and momentum of every particle within the limits of uncertainty. Can be viewed as a microstate in statistical mechanics, the quantum formulation of thermodynamics. As such, a group of microstates that are equivalent in terms of experience can be viewed as an experiential macrostate, not subject to further distinction in experience.

quantum field theory: A complex field, used here to define the world line and the permanence of the world line, since time is a parameter or measure and not a dimension in quantum field theory.

quantum mechanics: As opposed to quantum field theory, time is a dimension. Described mathematically originally by Heisenberg as a matrix theory, and shortly thereafter by Schrodinger as an equation. Formulated as a theory of "our knowledge" and saying nothing about the underlying reality or ontology, which is still an unsolved problem, solved by many alternative theories, including, here, the One Mind interpretation, originated by Euan Squires. Squires never fully developed the model and it has remained obscure. Here we describe a particular version of the One Mind Interpretation, which involves God.

quantum operator: A mathematical function applied to the wave function according to Schrödinger's equation that alters the probabilities of certain eigenfunction, and can also eliminate or create certain eigenfuction. See "eigenfunction."

quantum revolution: The revolution of scientific thought brought about by quantum physics, which falsifies determinism and classical mechanics within certain parameters, and can bring in the observer in certain interpretations.

quantum theory, bare bones: The known elements of quantum theory that say nothing about the underlying reality or even of its existence. A science without a "ground." Here God is used as a ground.

quasi-divine: The god-man myth.

reify: To make real or actual.

recursive: A procedure that can repeat itself indefinitely. Often used to describe the operating systems of computers, which are not truly recursive because the repetition is finite. Only God and the Soul, derivative of and subsumed by God, can be infinitely recursive.

reiterative: In a special case, the history of an entity or the universe involves the reiteration of its entire path. Critical to the theories of microgensis (see entry) and the Species Mind. Reiteration may or may not be recursive.

religion, all equal: *Eli* has preference for no particular religion, but rejects certain religious orthodoxies.

repeated observation: According to the quantum Zeno's paradox of Stapp, continuous and repeated observation protects the wave function or state of a system from decoherence, and brings about the actualization of the state. Ultimately, this theory requires disincarnate entities that are observers, violating parsimony. God is accorded this function here as the Universal Observer, or, in *Eli*, the One Subject.

savant: One who knows without learning. Here, connected to the realm of the hidden time or ideal realm, and to connection with an omniscient God through the individual soul.

segmentation: The spinal cord and cranial nerves are segmented or divided into segments subserving different areas of the body. This is inherited from the segmented worm in evolution.

self, core of: See "microgenesis." Term of Jason Brown, here taken to be the soul, thus yielding a neuropsychology of the soul.

self, separate: The mass delusion that the souls or selves of people are not connected and are not a part of a higher unity.

self organizing criticality: The state of the system at the edge of chaos and order that is the critical state of self-organization.

Selfhood: A term of William Blake used to describe what we call the alter ego. See "alter ego."

selfish neurons: A principle of neural Darwinism, which is that neurons are selfish and that there function is thus fully determined by natural selection. Selfish genes is a similar concept, but is falsified by the fact that all adaptations begin as pre-adaptations, thereby manifesting final causality. Final causality is not allowed in mainstream science, thus the new science of *Eli* is needed.

sigmoid curve: A curve with a gentle slope at the beginning and end and a sharp slope in the middle. Characteristic of growth curves, and of the economy, where the curve of nominal wealth is currently poised well above the leveling off at the end of the curve of actual value.

signature, quick: The current practice of physicians signing documents without reading them, including all of the work of technicians working under their medical licensure, computer readings of EKGs, and other documents. A means of decreasing utilization and maximizing profits.

simultaneity: In systems theory, a period of time where before and after cannot be applied, creating the possibility of recursive reiteration. In the brain, estimates of period of simultaneity range from 0.03 to 0.2 seconds. For God, simultaneity applies to all of time, such that reiterative recursion is boundless.

society of occasions: In Whiteheadean process theory, a group of actual occasions joined to one another in an enduring system. There is great confusion regarding the distinction between societies or actual occasions and actual occasions, such that, in the author's opinion, the distinction cannot be defined and may not exist.

soul, topology of: See "forms, transformation." The idea that individual souls can be described as Platonic forms and topologically transformed such as to produce variations within and between individuals who embody a soul (see forms, transformation).

Species Mind: The idea that the human species has a single mind that evolves over time and which recursively reiterates its entire past, leading to process in human mental capacity without natural selection or genetic mutation. This concept is opposed to ad hoc explanations of how the brain has evolved be natural selection and its capacities have increased rapidly.

Final causality is employed where the finality of evolution of the Species Mind is very far into the future and approaches the Mind of God as its final cause. The species mind was the same as Elohim in the oral tradition of Eli, as this is what Eli experienced in the call.

Thus, "ye and all Elohim" applies to the Species Mind. God's purpose is the manifestation of the Mind of God in the Species Mind, which exists eternally. As the Species Mind is in its infancy, arrested, in essence, by usury and its consequences, the abomination of usury must end.

teleology: Final causation.

uroboros: The symbol of the serpent eating its tail, a Jungian symbol of the primordial self.

World Commonwealth: The projected state of the world that will develop after the times of suffering.

world line: The trajectory of the actual universe in an abstract space representing the state of the universe. It is permanent in the past, and reiterated in the Eternal Now as the becoming of the actual in experience.

worldwide prohibition: Eventually, to include usury, but in these times, worldwide nuclear disarmament must occur to eliminate the potential for nuclear war, which could cause human extinction. As such, extinction would be the ultimate evil, in that it would prevent the full manifestation of the species mind, intervention is now urgent on the agenda of those who choose to accept the *Book of Eli*.

Zeno's Paradox: See "decohere." The quantum version of Stapp implies that continuous observation incrementally brings a quantum state of the brain to a state close to its goal, preventing decoherence of that state. Stapp posits that this causes a material "collapse" of the wave function of alternate states of the brain into a single state, which is thus a microstate, or an eigenstate, which is a single, irreducible quantum state. This requires a disincarnate entity for every individual observer. Here we posit that states are macrostates of sets of equivalent microstates in the experience of the observer, and that there is only one observer, God. God here is what Cantor called the "absolute infinite," which we have simplified here to a state of higher infinity of cardinality or numbers per set. This is not the exact formalism but suits our purpose. The higher order infinity of the Mind of God has full purview of the lower infinity of universes, allowing repeated observations much in the sense of Stapp, only here the potentialities are not collapsed into one state, which would violate relativity, and the wave is actually not materially collapsed but becomes the only universe that is experienced. Here there is unity of experience that applies to every actual entity, occasion, and society that includes the entirety of the universe. Adopting panexperientialism, there is nothing but experience, which is a plurality within the unity of the One Mind includes all of nature.

Index

A

abomination, 55, 67, 196, 210

aborigines, 23, 171

abortions, 54, 136

Abram, 20, 26-27, 72, 76, 144, 146, 209

Abramic tradition, 20-21, 24-25, 72, 144

absolute infinity, 91, 227, 229

abstract, 22, 107-9, 165, 177, 183, 187-88

acausal, 30, 229

accidents, purposeless, 174

accountability, 160, 221

action

  correct, 17, 157, 175, 178, 210

  incorrect, 17, 220

actual entity, 32, 90-91, 94, 115, 117

actuality, 32, 34, 85-86, 97, 100-101, 105-6, 114, 128-29, 137, 168, 209, 229, 232, 234, 236-38, 245

actual occasion, 94-95, 117

Adam, 8, 60, 140, 144, 170

Adams, John, 83

adaptation, 35, 161, 166-68, 178

addiction, 159

ad hoc, 165, 167, 171

adolescence, 143, 201

adult, 204, 211

adulthood, 201, 239

advanced technologies (9/11), 45

adversaries, six nuclear, 68

African Savannah, 167

agency, 88-89

agents, knowing, 88

age of darkness, 54

age of peace, 27, 84

age of prophecy, 40

age of science, 40

age of usury, 64

age regression, 121

ages, 11, 84, 141, 150, 195

agriculture, 23, 195

AIDS, 172

albatross, 43, 229

algorithms, 165

alien, 120-21

alienated labor, 136

Alighieri, Dante, 61, 64, 191-92

   Inferno, 61, 64, 191-92

Allah, 74, 106

all-knowing, 14, 140, 177, 180, 225

all knowledge, 116

Almighty, 37, 209

almighty state, 97

Al Qaeda, 223

alter ego, 23-24, 26-27, 39-40, 75, 91, 95-96, 122, 128-29, 135-38, 140, 143-46, 156-57, 225, 227-29, 234-36, 238-40

   dissociated, 26, 32, 95

fused, 91

inflated, 144

isolated, 135

troublesome, 135

American Insurance Group, 65

American people, 41, 61, 215, 217, 219

American worker, peonage, 223

amnesia, 120-23, 204, 211, 245

analysis, 38, 75-76, 187, 191, 199

anathema, 74, 83, 165, 229

anatta, 146

ancestors, common, 170

anesthesia, 131

angelic advocate, 57

anger, 139, 205, 234

animal kingdom, 23, 34, 39

animal phyla, 168

annihilation, 26, 210

anonymous author, 19, 37

anthrax, 221

Antichrist, 26

antidepressant, 185

antipsychotics, 124

antisocial, 122, 229, 247

Apostles Creed, 25, 230

apotheosis, 25, 75, 135, 143, 145, 230

appetite, 96, 197

Aquinas, Thomas, 193

arboreal lifestyle, 167

archeological, 147

archetypes, 26, 142, 182, 230

Arieti, Silvano, 188

Aristotle, 93, 182, 193-95

Arjuna, 21, 209

Armageddon, 66, 144

armed forces, in streets, 224

arrogation, 137

art, 140, 192, 209

  divine, 192

asbestos, 44-45, 56

Asia, 171

assets, 15, 58, 65, 191, 194-95, 200, 233-34, 241

  productive, 58, 194-95

  real productive, 194-95

assumption, 160, 165

  false, 171

asteroid, 154

atheism, 143, 146, 175, 210

Atman, 21, 31, 39, 140, 146, 230

Atmanspacher, Harald, 130

atom, 80, 85, 103-4, 237

atonement, 26-27, 190-91, 201, 203-4, 206, 208-10, 212, 214, 216-18, 230

  for future potentials, 181, 210

  new kind, 191

atrocities, 26, 49-51, 54, 135, 207, 216

attachment, 156

Attar, Farid, 148, 189, 291

Augustine, 98

Augustus, 195

austerity measures, 66

Australia, 23, 112, 171

authenticity, 77-78, 80

autistic disorders, 64

automata, 160, 230

avatar, 73-74, 81, 230

B

babies, 54, 79-80, 123

baby boomers, 207

Bach, J. S., 119

Baghdad, 223

Baha'u'llah, 71

bailouts, 200, 230

banking, 41, 201

banks, 22, 41-43, 47, 58, 158, 200, 219, 223

  Muslim, 222

baptism, 25, 79

Barnabus, 25-26, 77

Barry, 136, 291

"beads on the thread," 11, 34, 111

behavior, 64, 104, 136, 139, 145, 218, 234

behavioral experiments, 183

behavioral modernity, 171, 230

behavioral therapy, 64

beliefs, system of, 137

Beloved, the, 39, 189

benefits, 61-62, 197, 223

benign, 141, 230

Beverley Hills, 46

Bhagavad Gita, 21, 24, 71, 99, 112, 187-88, 209

Bible, 25, 40, 75, 78, 99, 189, 222, 226, 231

  New Testament, 75-76

Bill of Rights, 82, 221, 235

biography, 73, 81-82

biosphere, 168, 230

bird, 161, 163

birth, 21, 124, 146, 156, 166, 177

birthright, 79, 116

Black America, 22, 51, 223, 228

Black Moslem, 51

Blake, William, 100, 135, 146, 249

blind material, 178

blood, 26, 43, 51, 158, 177, 196, 209

book, popular, 76

Book of Eli (movie), 19, 27

bottlenecks, 29, 172-73, 230

  evolutionary, 67, 173

Brahman, 140, 146, 230

brain, 22-23, 32, 34-35, 85-86, 88-89, 107-8, 116-17, 130-32, 134-36, 161-64, 166-67, 171, 180-84, 186-87, 230-31, 250-51

  brainstem, 131

  cerebral convolutions, 164

  cerebral cortex, 131

  developing, 164

  diencephalon, 163

  electrical oscillations, 131

  emotional, 186

functional organization, 164

gamma oscillations, 130-31, 134

hemispheres, 163

human, 161, 164, 166-67, 240

material disconnected, 160

mesencephalon, 163

as movie screen, 107

polarity, 130

simultaneity, 113, 129-32, 134, 155, 174, 181

simultaneous integration, 131

spandrels, 166

telencephalon, 163-64

thalamus, 131

brainwash (China), 54

brake linings (sepiolite asbestos), 56

Brazil, 41

Brooks, 166

Brown, Jason W., 32-35, 115-17, 131

bubble (hypnotic), 123, 163, 198

bubble economy, 196, 231

Buddha, 146

Buddhism, 74, 98, 106, 143, 232-33

burning bush, 72

Burrow, Trigant, 138, 292

Bush, George W., 61

butterfly effect, 87, 181

buyout, 58-59, 231

C

cadmium, 56

Caesars, 195

calamity, 75

Calcutta, 209

Cambrian explosion, 168-69

canary, 47, 231

cancer, 56, 201-2, 231

canon, 77, 231

Cantor, Georg, 104, 117, 251

capital, 151, 153, 190, 231

capitation, 61-63, 206, 231

cardboard houses, 205-6

Cartesian type, 108

cataclysm, 54

catastrophe, 66, 152, 155

causality, 30, 85, 87-88, 104-5, 155, 160, 164, 166, 168, 171, 174, 178, 181-82, 231

efficient, 181

257

formal, 182

causeless, 91

cells, padded, 64

Center for Process Studies, 9, 92

channeling, 71, 231

chaos, 87, 231

  edge of, 181, 249

charisma, 216

charity, 86, 200, 205

cheating fruition, 96, 138

childbirth, 166

children, 8, 13, 16-17, 26, 54-55, 64, 79-80, 157, 160-61, 164-65, 175-76, 178, 204-5, 208, 219-20, 225

  devouring, 157

  fornication by clergy, 26

  little, 80, 225

  ritual sacrifice, 26

children abuse, 64

chimpanzee, 172

China, 41, 53-57, 68-69, 214-15, 218, 247

  being oppressive, 53

  brutality of, 53, 55

  nuclear attack plans, 68-69

  religious practices, 53

  toxic substances of, 56

Chinese imports, 55-56

Chinese products, 55-56

chordates, 169, 232

Christ, 25-26, 71, 75, 82, 107, 157, 209, 230, 242

  charismatic, 75

  sayings of, 71

Christianity, 19, 24-26, 73-74, 78, 80-81, 152, 209-10

  mass murder of, 74

Christians, right-wing, 75

chromosome, Y, 170

CIA, 47, 51, 60

circular reasoning, 165

city of God. *See* kingdom of God

civilization, 21, 38, 67, 197

civil unrest, 43, 224

Clairmont School of Theology, 9, 92

clandestine operations, 48

classical approximation, 87, 232

Cleave the wood, 79-80, 211

Cobb, John, 43, 80, 91-92, 95

code of silence, 47, 231

cognition, 139, 145, 234

Cohen, Leonard, 8, 141

collective action, 27

collective desperation, 145

collective disease, 135

collective memory, 27

collective responsibility, 27

Coming Age, 86

commandment, 15, 37, 190-91, 216

common good, 17, 220

communism, 60, 213

community, 128, 138, 193-94, 197

Companion Bible, 226

compassion, 21, 40, 84, 203, 226

competition, 35

complexity, 88, 182, 239

computer, 88, 117, 119, 159

conceit, 38

concepts, 31, 89, 95, 100, 103-4, 110, 209

concrescence, 90-91, 94, 233

Conference of the Birds, the, 148

confession, 190-91

conscience, 57, 86, 142

conscious experience, 98-99, 109

consciousness, 21-22, 33-34, 39, 98-99, 102-9, 119, 128-29, 131-32, 134-37, 140, 142, 156, 163-64, 179, 188-89, 227-28

conspiracy theories, 50, 152

Constitution, 50, 215, 235

consumer goods, 43

contact, direct (interpersonal), 138

contradiction, 74-75, 78, 81, 147

control parameters, 88-89, 94, 233, 240

copayments, 206

Copernicus, 95

Coptic language, 80

corporate megalith, 97

corporate raiders, 59

corruption, 85, 193, 217

costs, 61-63, 91, 155, 206

counterpoint, 119-20

crash, 50, 151

creator, 35, 72, 108-9, 127-28, 146, 160, 173, 209, 227

credit, 58-59, 63-65, 196, 233

   default swaps, 64-65

crisis, worldwide economic, 38

cross, 25-26, 105, 107

Crowley, Aleister, 213

259

crusades, 74

Cuba, 60

culture, 39, 52, 57, 79, 84, 147, 159-60, 171-72, 175, 205, 225, 235

cultures

  maladaptive, 129

  materialistic, 86, 136, 156, 175-76

currency, power to issue, 194

cycle, 87, 90-91, 113-14, 127, 151-52, 155-56, 184, 197-98, 222

D

Dalai Lama, 96

damnation, 139, 232

darkness, 39-40, 53-54, 86, 95-96, 227-28

dark night of the human soul, 228

Darwin, Charles, 162

Darwinism, 38, 96, 164, 168

data, 132, 170, 187

Dawkins, 86

day of reckoning, 200

day schools, 64

deadly venom, 57

dead matter, 39, 107

death, 13, 21, 25, 44, 48, 57, 65, 75, 84, 135-36, 152, 155-57, 176-77, 199-200, 225-26, 228

debt, 41-43, 53, 58, 64-65, 67, 155, 199-200, 215, 218-19, 233-34, 239, 243-44, 246

  high-risk, 64

  national, 41, 53, 65

  subprime, 64

decapitation, 61, 206

decay, 152, 155, 175

decohere, 86, 233, 251

default, pervasive, 196

deity, 146, 230

deluge, 27

delusion, 42, 86, 124, 137, 144, 203-4

demonic infant, 26

denial, 22, 139, 207, 234-35

depolarizations, 184, 234

derivative, 32-34, 134-35, 137, 179

derivative occasion, 137

derivatives, 32-33, 64, 135, 234, 243

desolation, 96, 157

despair, 96

desperation, 75, 138, 145, 204

detail, complete, 156, 225

deterministic, 30, 175

devaluing, 42-43, 135

development, 23, 26-27, 35, 38-40, 61, 92, 129-30, 137-38, 143-44, 164, 170-71, 173, 175-77, 204, 243-44

devotion, 189

Dhammapada, 98, 107

dichotomy, false, 35, 91

Dickens, Charles, 201

dimensions, 11-12, 33, 89, 93, 98, 105, 111, 114-15, 128, 150, 154-55, 174, 248

  of awareness, 128

  fifth, 105

  of space, 105, 107, 225, 236

Directed/Adaptive Planning Capability, 68

directionless (natural selection), 127

discernment, 145

discontinuous, 32, 91, 94

discord, 143

disease, 75, 86, 135-38, 152, 172, 177, 200, 202, 205, 207

disruption, 38, 53, 143, 166

dissociative identity disorder, 121, 123, 204

dissonance, 119-20

disturbed milieu, 96

divine selection, 127, 234

Divine Self, 74-75, 235

divinity, 74, 117, 146

divorce, 136

doctrine, 21, 24-26, 74-78, 80-81, 87, 97, 102, 104, 107, 137, 143-44, 146

dogma, 21, 25, 38, 106-7, 162

dominant occasion, 32-33, 94-95, 116, 122, 124, 129, 132, 134-35, 137, 234-35

Dow Jones Industrials Average (DJIA), 65, 151

dream, 52, 112-13, 132, 158

dreamtime, 23, 52, 75, 93, 112, 116, 133, 156, 171

Drew, David, 167

drives, 142

drug abuse, 136

drug trade, 48

Druids, 113

dualism, 32, 100, 108, 181, 231

dubious battle, 144

due process, 43, 213-14

duration, 71, 91, 94, 111-12, 115, 130, 132, 184, 186, 232, 239-40, 243

Dylan, Bob, 218

dynamical system, 117, 130, 180-81

E

earth, 21-22, 27-29, 40, 80, 87, 95-96, 101, 107, 113-14, 127, 129-30, 141, 144-45, 154, 208-11, 216-17

earthquakes, 12, 150, 154

East, 44, 74

Eastern world, 24, 31, 188

ecology, human, 201

economic collapse, 65, 151, 202

economic crisis, 38, 69

economic distress, 138

economy

   skeleton of, 205

   steady state, 43

ecstasy, 79, 157, 216

Edinger, Edward, 143, 182, 291

education, 31, 64, 97, 153, 165

ego, 23-27, 32-34, 39-40, 73-75, 79, 91-92, 95-96, 108-9, 128-29, 134-38, 140, 142-46, 210-11, 224-25, 227-29, 234-35

   materialistic, 24

particular, 75

true, 23, 229, 235

ego armor, 137, 235

egocentrism, 95, 135, 213

ego consciousness, 33-34, 39, 128-29, 135-37, 156, 189

ego-consciousness, shell of, 134

Egypt, 75, 81, 222

   mythology of, 147, 213

Einstein, Albert, 76-77, 203, 216

elderly, 206-7

electricity, 131, 158, 184, 195, 217-18

electroencephalogram (EEG), 183

Elegies, 226

elements, 31, 72, 78, 87, 91, 117, 120-21, 143, 182, 196, 208

Eli, 19-23, 31-40, 54-55, 67-73, 75-77, 79-85, 89-93, 97-103, 109-13, 135-39, 145-47, 149-55, 201-5, 207-11, 215-21, 249-51

   call of, 70

   church of, 208

   identity of, 73, 82

   mission of, 138

   oral tradition of, 19, 37

   revealed book, 37

elite, 47, 50, 58, 61, 66, 214, 224

Elohim, 72, 110, 113, 146-47, 149, 156, 160, 188, 250

El Olam, 29, 111, 209-10

Elyon, 208-9

Elyonology, 208

embryo, 164-65, 231

Emergency Response Options (ERO), 68

emotion, 160, 187, 235

emotional connection, 137

emotional reciprocity, 139, 145, 235

Emperors New Mind, 103, 292

empirical data, 132

endless recapitulation, 127

end of all cycles, 155

end times, 145, 216

energy, 39, 44, 81, 89, 97-98, 100-101, 104, 106, 108, 155, 180, 232, 234-35, 246-47

  vacuum, 89

  zero point, 89

engineering, 44

enlightenment, 71, 76, 240

Enneads, 31, 292

entitlement programs, 41-42

entity, 32, 41, 72, 90-91, 94, 115, 117, 175, 194

entropy, 128, 234-35, 291

environmental, 66, 152, 166, 217-18

epiphany, 96

eras

  Cenozoic, 173

  Mesozoic, 173

  Paleozoic, 173

  Psychozoic, 173

ERO (Emergency Response Options), 68

errors, prone to, 71

essence, 8, 90, 109, 115, 138

established, 13-14, 89, 93, 106, 108, 114, 122, 156, 170, 176, 180, 183, 186-87

Eternal, 24, 29, 31-33, 36, 79, 81-82, 93, 95, 99-101, 105, 107, 110-11, 113-14, 132-33, 141-42, 227

eternal bliss, 141

eternal forms, 95

eternal material body, 107

Eternal Now, 99-101, 110, 113-14, 128, 130, 132-33, 174, 179

eternal object, 32, 93

263

eternity, 11, 21, 40, 84, 93, 106, 109-11, 113-16, 132-33, 156-57, 179, 225, 232, 242

ethos, 136

euthanasia, 136, 206

evangelical, 25, 75, 145

eve, 60, 144, 170

event-related potential (ERP), 183

everlasting, 17, 111-14, 132, 209-10, 220

evil, 20, 26-27, 54, 84, 91, 144-45, 157, 190, 192, 198-99, 222, 236-37

evolution, 22-23, 27, 35, 39, 67, 91-92, 106, 115, 117, 127-28, 131-32, 136, 160-73, 178-79, 231-32, 246

  end of, 136

  of humanity, ongoing, 39

  positive force, 39, 173

evolutionary diversity, 166

evolutionary process, 35, 182

Evolutionary science, 161, 164

Evolutionists, 161

exaption, 162, 168

excursions, 123. *See also* hidden time

exhortation, 21, 114, 146, 154, 236

existence, 8, 14, 24, 32, 34-35, 38, 68, 74, 77, 81, 94, 98-100, 102, 160-61, 175, 187

ex nihilo, 98, 101

exodus, 99-100, 243

experientialism, 36, 38, 85, 138, 236

experiment, 45, 103, 173, 183, 185-86, 230, 236

experimental model, 142

experimental prediction (one mind model), 142

explosives, 44-45

extensive continuum, 33-35, 92, 94

eye, the, 86, 167

Ezekiel, 196

F

fable, 82

fact, 31, 34, 38, 40, 43-44, 51-52, 57, 99-100, 102-3, 109, 112-13, 138-39, 145-47, 150-51, 162, 178-79

failed species, 138

fairy tales, 161

faith, 11-15, 19, 25-26, 39, 70, 72, 76, 79, 84, 87, 90, 104, 110, 138, 174-76, 180

Fall, the, 144-45, 216

false flag, 44, 60-61, 200

famine, 152, 155, 177, 196

fascism, 53, 215, 237

father, 11, 25, 46, 72-73, 79, 81-82, 141, 189, 209, 212

Faust, 212

FBI, 221

Federal Reserve, 41, 46-48, 51, 59, 65, 68, 153, 199, 218, 224

Federation of American Scientists, 68

feedback loop, 181

feeding money, 153

feel, 33, 73, 125, 128, 174, 185

feeling, 32-34, 39, 70-71, 116, 123, 135, 138, 145, 183

felt sense, 39, 137-38

female, 36, 54, 78, 147, 166, 170, 187, 189

fetus, 162, 165

   ectoderm, 162

   endoderm, 162

   mesoderm, 162

   neural tube, 162-64

   primitive gut, 162

field, 23, 30, 33-34, 36, 38-39, 76, 89-90, 92, 94, 100, 123, 144, 189, 225

Filth, 157

final answers, 160

final causality, 30, 35, 85, 88, 105, 116-17, 121, 134, 160, 162, 164-66, 168-69, 171-72, 174, 181-82

finality, 38, 85, 94, 250

financial institutions, 153, 155, 199

financiers, parasitic, 59

fire, 20, 79, 157, 182, 192

fish, 123, 163

flag, 44, 60-61, 200, 213

flesh, 78-79, 106

flowing movement, 114

focus, 12, 53, 107, 125, 150, 154

food, 13, 15, 43, 54, 176, 183, 191, 202, 223

foolish, 42

fools, 211

forecast, 150

foreign goods, cheaper, 59

forever, 29, 98, 111, 165, 227

forever real, 98

forms

   latent, 169

   transformations of, 93

forsake usury, 37, 219

265

frame of reference, 30

France, 87

fraud, 61, 64

freedom, 53, 83, 91, 215, 219, 221-22

freedom of speech, 219

free-fall, 44

free will, 54, 109, 229

Freud, Sigmund, 142

fruit, 20, 222

function, 34, 39, 66, 86, 90, 93, 95, 104-5, 107, 128-29, 132, 142-43, 166, 222, 231-32, 246-47, 249

fundamentalists, 44, 82

future, 42, 87-89, 91-92, 98-99, 105, 111-12, 114-16, 120-21, 152, 155, 168, 172-73, 180-81, 201-2, 204-5, 210

  possible, 27, 168

  shadow of, 201

future potentialities, 181

G

Gaddafi, Muammar, 222

Galileo, 21, 87, 95

gambling, 48

gangsters, 47

garbage, 54, 205, 215, 218

  programmed, 205

Garden of the One Soul, 122, 216

gasoline, 43, 223

gateway, dreamtime, 23, 52, 75, 93, 112, 116, 133, 156, 171

Gautama, 71, 98, 107, 146

Genesis, 72, 129, 147, 193, 209, 242

genetic, 115, 136, 164-65, 169-72

genetic diversity, 136, 172

genius, 82, 158, 182

genome, 171, 244

Germine, Mark, 24, 121, 186

Gibson, Mel, 25

Ginsberg, Allan, 79, 158

Giuliani, Rudy, 46

Giuliani's clean up, 49

glaciation, 217

glaciers, 217

Global catastrophe, 152

global warming, 154-55, 210, 217-18

gluons, 85, 237

Gnostic, 81, 237

goal, 61, 142, 173, 231, 251

God, 20-21, 23-27, 32-36, 38-40, 70-81, 86-91, 96-102, 105-14, 127-30, 140-48, 174-77, 179-83, 208-12, 224-30, 237-42, 244-51

  absolute, 35, 238

  androgynous, 147

  beloved, 40, 189

  creation, 175

  creativity of, 91, 94, 128

  fiat of, 129

  living, 40

  love of, 21

  male and female, 78, 147

  providential, 76

  relational, 31, 91, 95, 138

  singular and plural, 98, 107, 115, 117, 128, 140, 147, 178, 185, 189

  will of, 38, 109, 210

  and world, 91

God and nature, 35, 91

God Delusion, 86

God in God, 109-10, 140, 146

God of Abraham, 20, 26-27, 72, 76, 144, 146

God of Israel, 114

Goethe, 212

gold, 42-43, 71, 195

Gonzalez, Billy, 119

good and evil, 91, 144, 157

Gospel, 25-26, 40, 75, 77-78, 80-82, 106, 110, 112, 127, 139, 198, 204, 211-12

Gospel of Barnabus, 25-26, 77

Gospel of Thomas, 75, 77-78, 80-82, 106, 110, 112, 127, 198, 204, 211-12

Gould, Steven J., 167

government abdication, 66, 238

government money, 64

government officials, 46

grace, 81

Great Being, 140

great deceiver, 26, 218

Great Depression, 151

Great Lie, 12-14, 129, 174, 176-78, 180

Great Mother, 182

Greco-Roman mythology, 25, 78

greedy, 160, 204

Greek philosophy, 78

Greeks, ancient, 31

Griffin, David Ray, 52, 92

gross domestic product (GDP), 41

ground, infinite, 88, 90, 181

ground of reality, 95

growth, exponential, 69, 151, 244

grow the economy, 42, 223

growth of money, 15, 96, 191, 202, 219, 222-23

Guantanamo Bay, 214

Gulf of Tonkin, 60

guru, 84

H

habeas corpus, 43, 213, 224, 238

Hantkenina, 137

harmony, 77, 141, 210-11

Hartshorne, Charles, 80

Harvard University, 47

hatred, 205

Hawking, Stephen, 93

heal, 177

health, 61, 63, 66, 134, 136-37, 196, 206, 214, 243

health care, 63, 206, 214

Health Care Bill, 63

heart, 11-13, 39, 54, 70-72, 129, 174, 176-77, 204, 226

heat, 97

heaven, 80, 84, 93, 101, 109, 112-13, 127, 129-30, 132, 140-41, 143-44, 209-12, 216, 225-26, 228, 232

   as imaginary magical theater, 210

   infused through all things, 211

Hebrew, 20, 25-26, 37, 72, 77, 99, 111, 113, 146, 208-9, 226

Hebrew Bible, 99

Hebrew Gospels, burning of, 77

hegemony, 60, 215

heinous, 26, 75, 195

Heisenberg, Werner, 102

hell, 84, 156-57, 183, 191-92, 211, 216, 225, 232

   ego atomizes, 211

   machinery of, 157

   reign in, 144

Hercules, 74

heroic, 143

Hidden Energy, 39

hidden time, 11-12, 17, 23, 27-29, 33-36, 40, 90-94, 98-100, 105-7, 110-24, 128-35, 155-57, 208-11, 220, 224-28, 232-233, 235, 241, 246 cyclical, 93

simultaneity of, 113

Higher Criticism, 75-77, 80

Hindu, 21, 140, 146, 187, 209

Hinduism, 74, 140, 230, 232

Hippocratic Oath, 61-62, 238

historical, 77, 80, 82, 140, 144, 152

historicity, 80, 82

HIV, 172

hologram, 112, 211, 238

holographic mode, 135

Holy Spirit, 40, 79, 139

homeless, 155

homicide, 47, 136

Homo erectus, 170

Homo sapiens, 29, 136, 170, 172-73

Homo sapiens sapiens, 29, 136, 170, 172

honesty, 42

Hong Kong, 41, 65

hope, 38, 83, 154-55, 193, 198, 226

horrors, in China, 214

hospitals, 49, 63, 243

houses

cookie-cutter, 205-6

in flood zones, 205

housing market, 153, 199

Howl, 79, 138, 157, 216

Hubbard, L. Ron, 213

Hudson, Michael, 199

human contracts, 136

human extinction, nuclear, 67-68, 135

humanity, 15, 39, 86, 138, 152, 182-83, 191, 200-201, 210, 214, 228

single organism, 200

humankind, 13-15, 21, 26-27, 38, 40, 86, 129, 135-36, 139, 176-77, 191-93, 200-205, 207, 210, 216, 228

body of, 139

human organism, indivisible, 34

human relations, 137

humans, 22-24, 29, 34, 40, 67, 71, 79, 84, 107, 109, 135-36, 154-55, 160-61, 166-67, 172, 182, 244, 246

human soul, 32, 54, 135, 228

hungry ghost, 129, 135-36

Huxley, Aldous, 74

hyperpolarizations, 184, 234

hypnosis, 119, 121, 123, 125, 238

   Erichsonian, 120

   indirect induction, 120, 125

hypnotherapy, 121-23, 238

I

I am that I am, 99-100

id, 142

idea, 20-22, 32, 35, 44-45, 59, 71, 84-88, 91-93, 98, 100-101, 109, 145, 160, 164-65, 182, 197-99

   divine, 109

Ideal Forms, 32-33

idealism, 31-32, 36, 38, 85, 102-3, 108-9, 175, 177-78, 187-88, 236

identity, 24, 74, 121, 123, 140, 181, 204

idolatry, 96, 100

idols, 96

IFS defaults, 42-43

ignorance, not an excuse, 97, 207-8

illegal cocaine trade, 47

illegal wagers, 65

illness, 122, 124, 143

illusion, 79, 115, 128, 143, 192, 224, 227, 242

illusory ego, 21

illusory money, 58

image, 26, 50, 109, 112, 138, 147

imaginary time, 30-31, 33-35, 40, 87, 89-90, 92-93, 114, 134, 137, 236, 246

imagination, 107, 156, 210-11

Immaculate Conception, 25

immortality, material, 228

impossible, 88-89, 96, 102, 105, 107, 117, 160, 178

impossible accident, 160

imposter, great, 144, 216

incarcerate, 43, 213

incarnate, 73

incurable, 135

India, 31, 71, 170

indiscriminate, 68

individuation, 90, 142, 239, 291

industrial desperation, 138

ineffable, 132, 189, 227

inequity, 65, 75, 193

inexplicable, 110, 169

infallibility, 71, 239

infancy, 23, 92, 135, 236, 250

infantile condition, 143

infants, 23, 27, 54-55, 79, 92, 137-38, 166, 177, 225, 239, 245

infect, 138

infects humanity, 86

inference, 99

Inferno (Alighieri), 61, 191-92

infinite cycles, 127

infinitely complex, 117

infinite Now, 113

infinite possibility, 100

infinite range, 88

infinity, 88, 104-5, 117, 128-29, 231, 245

   cardinality of, 118, 231, 251

inflation, 143

information monism, 178, 239

information theory, 178

injustice, 57, 228

inner, 11-12, 39, 51, 78, 111, 148, 150, 154-55, 174, 203, 227

inner dialogue, 39

Insanity, 138, 291

inside, 32, 80, 90, 107, 124-25, 139, 162-64, 211

insight, 81, 188, 192

insolvency, 65, 234, 239

instinct, 82

institutions of knowledge, 90

instrumental music, 119

insufficiency of reason, 108

integrity, 42, 45

intellect, 108, 142, 192

intelligent design, 35, 162

interest, 21-22, 37, 41-42, 56-59, 63, 82-83, 170, 190, 193-96, 198-99, 201-2, 204, 207, 217, 219

interglacial, 217

intermediary, 72, 240

internal, 33-35, 43, 92, 94-95, 107-8, 130, 132, 135, 179, 225, 227

internal enemy, 43

internal existence, 34

internal objects, 95

internal relations, 33, 92, 95, 235, 240, 247

International Financial Sector (IFS), 22, 41-42, 65, 97, 234

Internet, 25, 37, 46-47, 50-52, 54, 103, 121, 191, 212

interpretation, 19, 75, 92, 97, 185

intuition, 24, 128, 187, 240

investment, 41, 58, 65, 206

271

invisible, 60, 112, 219, 221

I-persona, 138, 238

Iran, 68, 190

Iraq, 151, 200, 222

Isaac, 72, 76

Islam, 73, 77, 84, 109, 222

  as enemy of usury, 222

Israel, 99, 114, 208, 217

I will be, 99-100

J

Jacob, 72, 76

Japan, 41, 216

Jesus, 20, 24-27, 40, 71-75, 77-80, 82-83, 91, 106, 108, 139, 143, 188, 191, 193, 204, 211-12

  personality of, 74

  reformer, 83

Jews, 57, 67, 210

jobs, 56, 204

John, 73, 77, 80, 82-83, 92, 95, 110, 195, 201

Johnian, 78

joysticks, 188

Judaism, 19-20, 78, 84, 152, 210

Judeo-Christian, 76, 144

judgment, 16-17, 27, 47, 49-50, 57, 81, 84, 111, 139, 157-58, 187, 204-5, 218, 220, 224, 232

Jung, Carl, 142, 182, 239

Jupiter, 83

justice, 17, 55, 68, 84, 203, 207-8, 210, 214, 216, 220-22, 224

K

Kafkaesque, 49

Kali, 208

kangaroo, 171

Karzai, Hamid, 223

Kaufmann, Stuart, 166

Kelvin, Lord, 166

Kennedy, John F., 194

king, 20, 147-48, 196, 198, 207-9, 212, 226

King, Martin Luther, 228

kingdom, 41, 78-80, 108, 227

kingdom of God, 11, 111-12, 148, 225

King James Bible, 226

kinship, 138

Knower, 32, 80, 130, 173, 179, 246

knowing, theory of, 85

knowledge, 24, 45-47, 49, 72, 80-81, 90, 116, 140, 144, 149, 157, 181, 197, 204-5, 225, 239-40

koan, 106, 240

Krishna, 21, 24, 209

Krishnamurti, Jiddu, 39, 173, 213

Kristenson, 68

L

Lamentations of Jeremiah, 226

landscape, 171

language, 11, 23-24, 34-35, 37, 39-40, 72, 75, 80, 84-86, 88, 104, 110, 138, 166, 170-71, 241

  corruption of, 193

  development of, 23, 170

  of the heart, 72

  of science, 24, 35, 84-85, 138

  symbolic, 39

  verbal, 23

  vocalization of, 171

  vocal tract, 171

Laplace, Pierre, 87

Last Judgment, 57

laws, 30, 44-45, 98, 166, 168, 178, 193-94, 207, 213, 224, 235, 238

  martial, 215, 224, 238

laws of physics, 44-45

layers, 62, 119, 162-63, 230

Layla, 189

lead, 53, 56, 58, 68, 87, 155, 163, 204, 210

legal asbestos substitute, 56

Letters of Luke, 78

leveraging, 58, 241

Leviticus, 79, 157

Levy-Bruhl, 138

Libet, Benjamin, 132, 292

lie, 12-14, 58, 86, 129, 174-78, 180, 221, 228

life after death, 84, 111

light, 30, 39, 54, 77, 81, 85-86, 89, 96-97, 105-6, 108, 114, 129, 168, 227-28, 241-42

light of consciousness, 105-6

limbic system, 186

Lincoln, Abraham, 194

liquidity, 65, 241

loans, 15, 41, 56, 63, 191, 193, 198, 204, 222

interest on, 204

Logia of Thomas, 80

logical, 75, 88, 188

logos, 78

loneliness, 143

love, 21, 39-40, 84, 86, 138-39, 141, 145, 158, 160, 175, 179, 183, 189, 200, 204-6, 211

love of money, 40, 204

Lucifer, 75, 144, 236

Luke, 77-78, 112, 198, 211

lunar eclipse, 70

Luther, Martin, 139

M

Machiavellian, Obama, 214, 241

machinery, 43, 157-58, 166

Macys, 55, 218

made men, 47

madman, 189

magic, 143, 198, 217

Maine, 60

mainstream, 21, 85, 138, 165, 181

male, 54, 78, 147, 170, 189

malice, 201

malignant, 129, 141, 152, 207, 218-19, 222-24, 241

Mallarme, 79

mammals

  marsupial, 171

  placental, 171

Mammon, 204

Manhattan, 9/11, 46, 51

manifestation, 30, 36, 101, 106-7, 109, 132, 156, 173, 210, 242, 250-51

  plane of, 132

manufacturing base, 60

market, expanding, 60

market share, 59

mark of the beast, 42

marvel, 106, 108

Mary, 20, 25, 72, 78, 188

Mary Magdalene, 78

mass delusion, 137, 144, 203, 249

mass misery, 196

material, 22, 24, 32, 74, 79, 85, 98, 100, 107-9, 160, 164, 175, 178, 228

materialism, rejection of, 21

materialist, oligarchy, 159, 242

material substance, 22, 32, 85

mathematical, 33-34, 103, 180, 188

mathematical idea, 103

mathematic point, 30. *See also* hidden time

matriarchy, 147

Mayan calendar, 145

McCarthy Era, 213

meaning, 19, 27, 34, 37-38, 57, 61, 79-80, 90-91, 98-99, 106-8, 111-13, 129-30, 156-57, 177, 182-83, 187

meaningful relationships, 160

measurement, 184

mechanism, 157, 164, 166

mechanistic, 88, 164, 175, 242, 247

medical license, 62

medical staff, 48

medicine, 62-63

meditation, 148

melodic theme, 119

melt, 44-45, 217

mental, 32, 35, 64, 88, 90-91, 115, 123, 128, 157, 181-82

mental disorders, 64

mentalism, 108-9

mentality, 88, 90, 103, 108, 117, 144, 181-82, 239

Mesothelioma, 56

Messiah, 25, 27, 84

meta-language, 75, 241

meta-meanings, 108

metaphor, 149

metaphysics, 93, 95, 100, 134, 181, 243, 245

microgenesis, 34, 115, 117, 131, 165, 243, 249

   radical, 131

Middle Ages, 195

Middle East, 44

Midrash, 57

military, 43, 60, 214, 224

   fist of, 60

Milton, 141, 144

mind, 22-24, 26-27, 32-36, 39-40, 88-96, 98-103, 106-8, 115-18, 127-32, 137-45, 164-66, 177, 185-88, 224-28, 230-31, 245

   human, 32, 128, 173, 177, 239

   individual, 23, 33, 88, 108, 239, 245

   intangible, 164

   manifestation of, 173

Mind of God, 23, 33, 40, 76, 100-101, 107, 112, 118, 127, 129, 141-43, 165, 177, 179, 182, 226-27, 250-51

Minerva, 83

miracle, 45, 106-7

miracle of miracles, 106-7

mirror, 148-49, 204

misogyny, 78

Mississippi, flooding, 217

Mitchell, Edgar, 96

mitosis, metaphysical, 32-33, 35, 116, 124, 135, 137, 162

mob, 46-47, 51

mob bosses, 47

Mohammed, 193

Moloch, 79, 157-58, 166, 216

  fire to, 79

  hell of, 216

moment, 32, 93, 98, 100, 110-12, 115, 117, 130, 132, 134, 156-57, 197, 225-26

momentum, 86, 97, 246-47

money, 22, 37, 40-43, 50-51, 57-58, 62-65, 129, 139, 153, 190-96, 198-99, 204, 206-7, 222-23

money from money, 168

moneylenders, 195

money manipulators, 194

monkey, 164

morality, 74

moral turpitude, 177-78

moral universe, balance of, 210

Morocco, 51-52

mortgage, 41-42, 201, 206-7, 219

mortgages, reverse, 207

Moses, 72, 99, 146, 193, 207, 209

Moslem, 51, 76

mother, 8, 54, 72, 124, 138, 166, 177, 182, 208, 225, 239

multiple personality disorder, 24, 121

mushroomed, 96

mutations, neutral, 170

mutually transcendent, 91

mystery, 89, 114, 128, 148-49

mysticism, 147, 189

myth, 74, 102, 136

N

Nag Hammadi Library, 75, 81, 212

nameless, 71

narcissism, 129

National Command Authority, 68

national sovereignty, 194

natural ecstasy, 79, 216

naturalism, 107, 241

natural law, 127, 168

natural selection, 23, 35, 86, 105, 115, 118, 127-28, 136, 160-62, 164-66, 168-70, 178, 244, 247, 249-50

nature, 31-32, 34-36, 38-39, 70-71, 73-74, 85, 87-89, 91-92, 98-100, 109-10, 112-15, 127-29, 131-32, 136-37, 146-47, 191-93

  beauty of, 77

  perverting, 92

  worship of, 36

Neanderthals, 173

negation, 146

neighbor, 192

neoteny, 27, 244

nephesh, 226

nerves, 162-63

nerve system, crossed, 163

nervous system, 162-63, 182, 232

  autonomic, 162

  central, 163, 182

Neumann, Erich, 142-44, 182

neurons, 160, 163, 234, 249

  lower motor, 163

neuropsychology, 32, 36, 115, 249

New Age cult, 96

new dawn, 228

new earth, 141

new faith, 11, 15, 19, 70, 72, 76, 79, 84, 87, 90, 191

new heavens, 141

New Jerusalem, 141, 155, 176

new judgment, 16-17, 27, 50, 204-5, 218, 220

new justice, 55, 208, 210, 216

new religion, language of, 35

Newton, Isaac, 87, 102-4

New York City, 46-47, 49, 232

9/11, 26-27, 43-44, 49-52, 68, 135, 152, 155, 200, 215-16, 221-22, 224

9/11 demoltion of, 26

9/11 foreknowledge of, 50-51

9/11 mineral wool, 44-45

9/11 remnants of asbestos, 45

Nobodaddy in the sky, 100

noise, 89

nonsense, 88, 96-97, 107, 168

Normandy, 221

North Korea, 68

Now, 11, 33-34, 63, 67, 84, 91, 93, 99-101, 110, 113-16, 121, 128, 130, 132-33, 156, 174

Now Past, 33

Now Present, 33

Nows, recursive, 34

nuclear, 27, 29, 53, 67-69, 155, 210, 216

nuclear disarmament, 27, 210

nuclear preplanned options, 68

nuclear war, 27, 29, 67-68, 155, 251

nuclear weapons, 67-68

Nuremberg Trials, 214

O

Obama, Barack, 42, 223

objectification, 27, 135, 245

objective attitude, 23, 91

objective limit, 162

objectivity, 23, 27, 135, 179

object of perception, 33

objects, living, 135

object world, 34

    dead, 135

obscure, 21, 45, 50, 78, 110, 248

observable, 30, 39

observation, repeated, 127, 233, 249, 251

observer, 30, 85-86, 108-9, 114, 132, 179, 185-87

Occam's Razor, 177

occasions, 32-33, 46, 52, 93-94, 116, 128, 134-35, 137, 165, 192, 232, 234-35, 239, 245, 251

occult, 213

oddball paradigm, 184

Olam, 29, 209-10

Old Testament, 29, 111, 207

olfactory, 123

olm, 111

ominous, 48

omniscience, 80, 112

The One, 142

"one child" policy, 54

one hand clapping, 106

One Mind, 33, 39, 98, 100, 106-7, 142, 177, 185, 187-88, 225-27

One Mind model, 142, 187

One Self, 140

One Soul, 34, 122, 137, 204, 211, 216, 224-25

One Spirit, 98

one subject, 13-14, 27, 32, 89, 98, 106, 109, 115, 176, 180

ontological principle, 94, 245

ontology, 85-86, 97, 245, 248

Operation Northwoods, 60

operative, 48, 59, 152, 161

Oppenheimer, J. Robert, 209, 213

opposable thumb, 167

opposites, 91, 143

optical delusion, 203

oracles, 71

organic unity, 33

organized crime, 45-47, 50

oriental, 74

Origin of the Species, 169

orthodoxy, 81

  materialist, 175

outdated, 71, 87

outside all, 100, 112, 188

over inflated, 144

overutilization, 63

ownership, 202, 233

oxymoron, 75, 168, 245

P

P3, 131, 184-85

P 300, 184-85

pagan, 74, 240

pain, 138, 163, 221

  worldwide, 138

Pakistan, 190

panentheism, 32, 76, 80, 94, 246

panexperientialism, 32, 76, 128, 246, 251

pantheism, 32

paper trail, 45-47, 49

parable, 212

paradigm, 87, 178, 184

paradise, 144, 183, 200, 216, 232, 245

paradox, 128-29, 149, 156

paradoxes, deep, 188

paradoxically lame, 96

parasites, 64

parasitic organism, 139

parenting, 159

parsimony, 101, 177, 233, 245

partial existence, 102

participation mystique, 138, 245

particle-wave duality, 104

Passions of Christ, 25

pathology, serious, 135

patients, 48, 61-63, 123, 135, 206, 212, 243

patriarchs, 147

patriarchy, 147

patrician class, 194

patrimony, collective, 197

patriot, 215, 222, 224

Patriot Act, 215, 222, 224, 238

Patton Hospital, 9, 45

Paul, 25-27, 77-78, 82

Pauline, 77-78

Paulism, 78

peace, 27, 84, 92, 141, 148, 152, 197, 214, 226, 228

people, 22, 40-42, 44-45, 47-48, 53, 55, 63-64, 74-75, 124-26, 136-37, 159-60, 185-86, 199-202, 205-11, 215-19, 222-25

People of the Lie, 86, 228

perceptual, 143

Perennial Philosophy, 74, 292

perfect, 228

perish, 94, 115

pernicious doctrine, 24, 144

persecution, 141

Persian Sufi, 148

person

artificial, 194

natural, 194

personality, 24, 73-75, 121-23, 204

executive, 122

personal name, 39, 73

petroleum wars, 44, 52-53, 200

phantom, 135, 246

pharmaceutical companies, 63

philosophy, 31, 36, 74, 76, 78, 90, 92, 95, 102, 104, 115, 138, 175, 182, 189, 192

photon, 85-86, 89, 97, 246

physician, 47, 56, 61-64, 135, 206, 221, 238

physician assistants, 62

physician-entrepreneur, 63

physician of the human soul, 135

physics, 30, 34, 40, 44-45, 76, 85, 87, 90, 93, 95, 97, 102-4, 114-15, 165, 177-78, 182

Pilate, 77

placebo, 185

planet, 23, 39, 68, 107, 159, 204

Plato, 32, 93, 103, 182

Platonic realm, 103

Plotinus, 31-33, 36, 292

plunder, 27, 61, 66, 84, 145, 197, 218

plurality, 40, 109, 146-49, 181, 185, 225, 245, 251

police, 48, 50, 56, 221, 224

police state, 50

political connections, 46

Ponzi scheme, 58, 63-65, 69, 196-97, 246

pope, 96

position, 48-49, 87, 108

possibilities, 27, 85, 88, 93, 97, 103-5, 108, 112, 116-17, 121, 127

possible histories, 93

potential, eternally, 99

potentialities, 97-98, 103, 105, 115, 181, 237, 251

potentials, cloud of, 105

poverty, 63, 106, 108, 155, 158, 227

power, 14, 21, 39, 43, 45, 47, 49-50, 53, 108-9, 117, 127, 147, 193-94, 218-19, 224, 246

  computational, 117

  explanatory, 174

power elite, 47, 50, 214

preadaptations, 161-62, 166-68, 171, 178, 236

predators, 171

predatory elite, 61, 66

predictions, 20

prehension, 32, 91, 115-16

prehensions, conceptual, 91

premiums, 63

presence of the past, 121

prices, 43, 59, 198, 200, 212, 231, 239, 247

prime mover, 87, 247

prime numbers, 156, 247

primitive, 34, 79, 83, 89-90, 107, 131, 136-37, 162-63, 169, 182, 243

primitive personalities, 137

Principia Mathematica, 94

principle, 22, 24, 35-36, 38, 64, 75, 87, 89, 94, 108-9, 127, 130, 133-34, 142, 172, 179

prison, incomprehensible, 158

probability, 97, 104-5, 116, 127, 187, 236-37, 247-48

  prior, 187

process, 31-32, 34-36, 87-95, 97-99, 103-5, 114-17, 120-24, 128-32, 134, 137-38, 154-55, 162-63,

165-67, 181-83, 223-25, 230-32

Process and Reality, 31, 88, 90, 97, 182

process theory, 36, 90, 92, 232-33

profit, 43, 55, 58, 62, 96, 206, 214

profits, lust for, 62

program, 119, 162

prohibition, 57, 68, 71, 165

projections, 27, 235

prophet, 20, 22, 25, 70, 84, 138, 152, 190, 196, 213

    Cantor, Georg, 117

    King, Martin Luther, 228

prosperity, 27, 141, 152, 226, 228

Proverbs, 146

Psalms, 120, 208

pseudoscience, 96

pseudospirituality, 96

psyche, 23, 39, 142, 145, 162, 173, 225, 245

psychiatrist, 9, 49, 119, 123, 165, 182, 187

psychology, 145, 159-60, 230, 235, 239

psychopathic usury, 57

psychopaths, 47, 69, 247

Ptolemy, 95

public morality, 74

public treasury, 65

punishment, 64, 192

purpose, 27, 38, 40, 50, 71, 76, 108, 127, 129, 160-61, 164, 168, 171, 174, 177-78, 187

    meaningful, 129

Q

quantum, 30, 76, 85-90, 94-95, 97, 102-4, 108, 117, 127, 142, 177-78, 181, 185, 187, 213, 247

quantum eigenfunction, 86, 247-48

quantum field, 94

quantum field theory, 94

quantum mechanics, 102-3, 108, 248

quantum revolution, 85, 247-48

quantum theory, 76, 85, 87, 97, 103, 181, 185, 213, 245, 247-48

quarks, 85, 237

quasi-divine, 74

Qur'an, 25, 73, 80, 106, 109, 129

R

race, 172

racial genetic homogeneity, 172

Radha, 146

rational, 142, 178, 181

rationalist, 76

reaction time, 185

Reagan, Ronald, 42, 224

Reagan Revolution, 59

real estate, 41, 200

reality, 12-13, 24, 31-33, 70-71, 85-86, 88-90, 97-101, 103-4, 106-9, 114, 116, 142, 174-79, 182-83, 187, 211

  classical, 85

  quantum, 108, 142, 187, 245

recession, 197

recording studio, 51, 119

redemption, 145, 208, 228

Red Menace, 60

Reformation, 107

Reich, Wilhelm, 137, 235

reiterate, 30, 40

reiteration, 35, 231, 248

reiterative path, 164

relationship, provider-client, 62

relativity, 30, 103, 114, 116, 237, 251

religion, 19-20, 24, 35-36, 38-40, 53, 72, 74-75, 86-88, 95-96, 98, 104, 141, 145, 189-90, 241

  true, 145

remedy, 122, 135

remembrance, 226-27

remission, 123

remorse, 188, 229, 247

representation, 39, 85

repression, 194

research, 13, 56, 90, 176, 178

responsibility, 27, 68, 175, 177-78, 207, 210

resurrection, 57, 81

reveal, 148

revealed text, 20, 55

revelation, 37-38, 42, 77

Rice, Condoleeza, 51

right to govern, 43, 215

Rig Veda, 19, 24, 211

roles, 87, 129

Rolls-Royce, 46

Rome, 195

Rumi, 96, 138, 189

Rumsfeld, 50

Russell, Bertrand, 94

Russia, 41, 68

S

Sachs, Oliver, 156

sacred, 20-21, 38, 40, 55, 70-72, 99, 141, 188

sacred mysteries, 141

sacrifice, 26, 113, 208, 213, 215-16

saint, 81

sanctity, 35, 74

Satan, 25, 75, 140-41, 144, 236

  fall of, 140

Satanic ritual abuse, 212

Satanists, 212-13

satisfaction, 142

Saudi Arabia, 44

schism, 35, 144

schizophrenic, 48, 188

scholar, 52, 209

scholarship, 13, 76-77, 90, 176, 178

Scholastics, 195

school of Thomas, 78

schools, 13, 55, 64, 77-78, 176, 178, 243

sciatica, 163

science

  done backward, 167

  history of, 165, 175

  idealist, 175

  inadequacy of current, 87

  materialistic, 22

  process of, 93

  proper, 183

science and religion, 24, 72, 77, 86, 95-96, 98

science and spirituality, 86, 102, 104

scientific, 20, 32, 39, 86, 93, 98-99, 102, 104, 107, 110, 113, 130-31, 138-39, 160-62, 167, 187

scientific materialism, 102, 139

scientific method, 167, 235

scripture, 71, 139

search, 34, 90, 189, 224

secret, 46-47, 50, 148, 161

secret government, 46

sects, 44, 83

sedition, 50, 215

seeing, 43, 103, 124, 146, 157, 173, 194, 225

segmentation, 163, 249

selection pressure, 169

self, 21-24, 26-27, 31-34, 73-75, 81-82, 94-95, 116-17, 123-24, 134-38, 140, 142-46, 156, 166-67, 229-30, 239-40, 249

  core of, 32, 117

  new, 123, 134

  separate, 73

self atrophies, 135

Selfhood, 135, 146, 249

self-hypnosis, 126

self-image, 138

selfish neurons, 160, 249

self-knowledge, 81

self-organizing criticality, 166, 181

sensations, 146

sepiolite asbestos, 56

serfdom, 136, 224

serpent, 57

set, 42, 45, 57, 85-87, 144, 156, 177, 184, 192, 199, 215-16

shadow, 23, 25-26, 43, 47, 49-50, 114, 187, 201, 237

shadow boss, 49

shadow government, 43, 47, 50

Shakespeare, William, 164

shaman, 84

She is, 170, 189

sigmoid curve, 151

signals, 134, 152, 163, 181

signs, 151

silver, 42-43

Simurgh, 110, 148, 204

sin, 40, 75, 139, 143-44, 190-91, 201, 204, 208, 210

sinners, 57

sleep, 132-33, 155, 174

snake, 57

So be it, 113, 129

social Darwinism, 95

social justice, 68, 203, 207-8

social programs, 153, 223

Social Security, 42, 155, 199

society of occasions, 93-94, 116, 134-35, 137

solar system, 87, 95

Solitude, 157

songs, 119-21

son of god, 24, 72-73, 77, 81, 84, 144

soul, 21-22, 31-34, 39, 94-96, 110, 122, 137-38, 156-58, 160, 175, 208, 210-12, 224-28, 240, 245-46, 248-50

  immortality of the, 76

  individual, 40, 146, 208, 225, 249-50

  living, 110, 135

  separate, 31, 140

Soul, Essential, 31-32

soulless jailhouse, 158

sources, 42, 45, 75

Soviet empire, 60

space-time, 30, 89, 92-94, 115, 117, 179

Spanish-American War, 60

speciation, rate of, 172

species, 22-24, 26-29, 33, 35, 39, 67, 79, 87, 91-92, 115, 135-36, 143-45, 147, 167-73, 204, 216-17

Species Mind, 22-24, 26-27, 29, 35, 79, 91-92, 95, 115, 128, 135, 143-45, 147, 171, 173, 239-40, 250-51

Species mind, divided, 79

spending, 153

sperm, 170, 235

Spinoza, 76-77

spirit, 24, 39, 78-79, 85-86, 90, 93, 98, 102, 106-8, 127, 138-39, 141, 144, 160, 175, 177

spiritual awakening, 155

spiritual connection, 135

spiritual creation, 137

spiritual creatures, 84

spiritual darkness, 53, 86

spiritual growth, 86, 96

spiritual light, 105-6

spiritual living, 178

spiritual realm, 84

spiritual world, 23

sponge, 162

states, brain, 86, 88, 131-32, 181

steel beams, 44-45

stigma, 57

stimulus, 131-32, 163, 183-86, 230

stomach, 186

strata, 163

subjective aim, 90, 134, 181

subjective antedating, 132

subjective realm, 93

sublime, 71

subspecies, 29, 136, 170-72

suffering, 14-15, 17, 22, 28, 38, 40, 45, 67, 75, 121, 145-46, 152, 155-56, 176, 199-202, 216

Sufi, 148, 189

suicide, 28, 135-36, 192, 291

sum of all histories, 165

sun, 87, 95, 107, 113, 148

superego, 142

superstition, 87, 150, 160

Supreme Court, 219

Supreme Intelligence, 117, 128

supreme law, 160

supreme principle, 160

survival, 44, 67, 166, 170, 178, 202

Suso, 109

sword, 13, 176-77, 210

symbols, 34, 39-40, 183, 187, 230, 236, 250

syndicate, 47-50

synopsis, 32, 191

synthesis, 29-30, 32, 34, 36, 95

T

tachyons, 30

taxpayer, 41, 65

teach, 11, 70, 72, 157, 164, 175

technocracy, 159-60

technology, 45, 96, 173, 176, 181

teleology, 168, 250

television, 47, 50, 52, 54, 96, 159, 205, 217-18

Templeton Foundation, 95

termination, 123

Tetragrammatron, 99-100

Thakar, Vimala, 213

theology, 35-36, 72, 76, 80, 82, 90-92, 95, 134, 138, 237

theory, 30-31, 36, 85-87, 89-90, 92-94, 97-98, 102-3, 127-28, 130-32, 160, 162, 164-66, 168-69, 178, 239-40, 248-49

theory of mind, 34, 90, 127, 138, 145

Theosophy, 213

therapeutic response, 185

therapy, 64, 123, 138, 230

thermodynamics, 166, 234, 236, 247

Thomas, 75, 77-82, 106, 110, 112, 127, 198, 204, 211-12, 221

Thoreau, Henry David, 204

thought, 22, 29-30, 34, 39, 83, 88, 97, 123, 128, 143, 156, 166, 170-72, 179, 183, 187-88

thrust into objectivity, 23, 27, 135

Thurau, 103-4, 292

time, 11-13, 25-31, 33-36, 38-44, 46-52, 57-61, 89-94, 97-101, 105-7, 109-24, 128-37, 154-58, 174-77, 184-86, 208-11, 223-28

time and permanence, 89

time machine, 89

times of suffering, 15, 38, 45, 121, 145, 152, 176, 191, 202, 216

Tobo supereruption, 29

tone, absence of, 184

tones, 72, 184-85

too big to fail, 65, 199

topology, 88, 157, 163, 237, 250

topology of the soul, 88, 157

Torah, 55

torture, 214, 223

tradition, 19-21, 24-25, 32, 37, 57, 63, 71-72, 92, 110, 143-44, 209

trance, 120, 122-23, 125, 238

transformations, 88

translation, 20, 37, 71, 75, 77-78, 80, 98-99, 107, 147, 196, 207-8, 212, 222

traumatically dissociated, 91

trial, 48

tribulation, 40, 145, 151, 176, 216

Trinity, 74, 209, 230

New Mexico, 209

Trump, Donald, 207

truth, 11-12, 14, 71, 73, 84, 87, 89, 103, 109, 113, 130, 134, 141, 143, 159-60, 164-65

tsunami, 217

2020, 155

twenty-first century, 61

Twin Towers, 44-45, 49

two into one, 78

U

Ugliness, 157

uncertainty, 76, 155

unconscious, 33, 79-80, 91, 99, 108, 116-17, 119, 122, 124, 128, 131, 133, 135, 137, 140, 142-43

unconscious lust, 157

understanding, 12, 20-21, 23, 27, 32, 38, 45, 87, 92, 96, 103, 136, 150, 182, 187, 193

the undivided, 79

unforgivable sin, 40, 139

union, 59, 223

United Kingdom, 41

unity, 33, 38-40, 75, 78, 95, 109, 147-49, 204, 225, 251

Universal Consciousness, 39

Universal Mind, 39, 88, 141, 228

universe, 14, 29, 33-35, 93-95, 97-98, 104-8, 112, 114-18, 128-29, 141-42, 173, 177-81, 209-10, 227-28, 245-48, 251

  moral, 210

unpredictable, 87, 89, 155, 168, 181, 218

unreal, 98, 100

unsustainable growth, 43

uroboros, 143, 250

US dollar, 59, 66

usury, 21-22, 37-38, 40-44, 52-58, 60-68, 95-96, 129, 139, 190-202, 204, 206-7, 215-16, 218-19, 222-24, 227-28, 243-44

utilization, 61-62, 64

V

values, 86, 129, 136, 142, 175, 198, 206, 223-24

Vedanta, 23, 31, 209

Vendidad, 190

vengeance, 141

very few, 15, 22, 42, 50, 58, 61, 153, 191, 197-200, 217, 219, 223-24

vicious cycle, 222

video games, 159, 205

Vietnam War, 60

violence, 15, 57, 178, 191-92, 205, 216, 221

virgin, 71, 82, 188

visceral, 186

visible directly, 156

visionary, 87

volition, 102, 109

von Franz, 182

von Neumann, 108

vote, 207, 224

vultures, 66, 241, 244

W

wages, 42, 223, 244

war economy, 153

warfare, 26, 29, 43, 50, 53, 60, 69, 75, 135-36, 216, 222, 243 war on terrorism, 152, 224

Watts, Allan, 39

wave nature, 128

wealth, 15, 22, 37, 42-43, 45, 56, 58, 61, 108, 193-95, 197, 199, 201, 205-6, 218-19, 233

wealth and power, 193

weight of an atom, 80

welfare, 21, 138, 199

West, 74

Western, 21, 71, 74, 147, 188

Whitehead, Alfred North, 31-33, 52, 79-80, 88, 90-93, 95, 97, 114, 116, 134, 142, 182-83, 233, 237, 245-47, 250, 293

wicked, 141

Wiley, 166

wings, 160-61, 181

wisdom, 11, 20-21, 24-26, 36, 73, 80, 84, 195

witch hunt, 213

within all, 94, 100, 112, 188

women, 47, 50, 54, 78, 121, 123, 188-89

the Word, 71, 75, 78

working people, 42, 66

works, 72, 81, 134, 141, 155, 161-62, 164, 195, 217

world, 21-24, 33-36, 43-45, 65-67, 79, 90-92, 105-6, 112, 117-18, 135-37, 141-45, 150-52, 211-13, 215-16, 224-25, 227-28

world civilization, 38, 67

World Commonwealth, 228, 251

world creation, 143, 211, 216

World Health Organization, 136

world line, 33-34, 105, 245, 248

worm, 162-63, 169, 212

worthless, 42, 64

wrong turn, 91

Y

Ye are all Elohim, 149, 188

Z

Zen Buddhism, 106, 240

Zeno's paradoxes, 127

References

Arieti S (1974) *Interpretation of Schizophrenia*. Second Edition. New York: Basic Books.

Attar, FUD (1961) *The Conference of the Birds*. Nott, C. S., and Garcin de Tassy, Trans. London: Routledge and Kegan Paul.

Auyang SY (1995) *How is Quantum Field Theory Possible?* New York: Oxford University Press.

Barry, B (1989) Suicide: The Ultimate Escape. *Death Studies* (13:2) 185–190.

BMI (2001) *Trail of Tears Trilogy*. http://www.myspace.com/trailoftearstrilogy/music/playlists/trail-of-tears-trilogy-s-playlist-1206772

Brookes DR, Wiley EO (1986) *Evolution as Entropy: Toward a Unified Theory of Biology*. Chicago: University of Chicago Press.

Brown JW (1991) *Self and Process: Brain States and the Conscious Present*. New York: Springer-Verlag.

Brown JW (1996) *Time, Will, and Mental Process*. New York: Plenum.

Brown JW (2011) *Neuropsychological Foundations of Conscious Experience*. Belgium: *Les Editions Chromatica*.

Bullinger EW (1922/1995) *The Companion Bible: Notes and appendices*. Grand Rapids, Michigan; Kregal Publishers.

Burrow T (1932) *The Structure of Insanity*. London: Kegan Paul, Trench & Trubner.

Edinger, EF (1972) *Ego and Archetype: Individuation and the Religious Function of the Psyche*. Boston: Shambala.

Galt AS (1995) Trigant Burrow and the laboratory of the "I." *The Humanist Psychologist* (23) 19–39

Germine M (2004) Process psychotherapy in a case of multiple personality. *Acta Neuropsychologica* (1) 428–435.

Ginsberg A (2006) *Collected Poems: 1947–1997*. New York: HarperCollins.

Hawking S (1988) *A Brief History of Time*. New York: Bantam Books.

Huxley A (1970) *The Perennial Philosophy*. New York: Harper Colophon.

Kauffman SA (2000) *Investigations*. Oxford: Oxford University Press.

Kauffman SA (2009) Toward a post-reductionist science: The open universe. *Physics Archives*. arXiv:0907.2492 [physics.hist-ph].

Kauffman SA (2003) *The Origins of Order: Self-Organization and Selection in Evolution*. New York: Oxford University Press.

Kimura M (1968) Evolutionary rate at the molecular level. *Nature* (217) 634-626.

Libet B, Elwood EW, Wright W Jr., Feinstein B, Pearl DK (1979) Subjective referral of the time for a conscious sensory experience. *Brain* (102) 193–224.

Marajaja SBRSDG (accessed 6/25/11) *The Loving Search for the Lost Servant*. http://www.scsmathglobal.com/media/CSM_PDF/lovingsearch.pdf

May R (1989) *Love and Will*. New York: Random House.

Milton J (1667/2005) *Paradise Lost*. U.K.: Oxford.

Morris S (2003) "On the First Day, God Said . . ." *American Scientist* (91:4)

Neumann E (1954) *The Origins and History of Consciousness*. Princeton: Princeton Princeton University Press.

Penrose R (1989) *The Emperors New Mind*. New York: Penguin Books.

Plotinus (2010) *The Six Enneads*. Translated by S. MacKenna and B. S. Page, eBooks@Adelaide.

Stapp H P (2007) *Mindful Universe: Quantum Mechanics and the Participating Observer*. Berlin: Springer-Verlag.

Thurau W (2011) The Missed Opportunity of Physics in the Twentieth Century, accessed 3/5/11, *ezinearticles.com/?The-Missed-Opportunity-of-Physics-in-the-Twentieth-Century&id=5970103*

Wheeler JA (1998) *Geons, Black Holes, and Quantum Foam: A Life in Physics.* New York. W.W. Norton and Company.

Whitehead AN (1927) *Religion in the Making: Lowell Lectures 1926.* New York: Macmillan.

Whitehead AN (1929/1978) *Process and Reality: Corrected Edition.* Ed. DR Griffin and DW Sherburne. New York: The Free Press.

Printed in Great Britain
by Amazon